MW01258479

ALSO BY KEVIN YOUNG

POETRY

Stones

Brown

Blue Laws: Selected & Uncollected Poems 1995–2015

Book of Hours

Ardency

Dear Darkness

For the Confederate Dead

To Repel Ghosts: the remix

Black Maria

Jelly Roll: a blues

To Repel Ghosts: the double album

Most Way Home

NONFICTION

Bunk: The Rise of Hoaxes, Humbug, Plagiarists, Phonies, Post-Facts, and Fake News

The Grey Album: On the Blackness of Blackness

AS EDITOR

A Century of Poetry in The New Yorker, *1925–2025*

African American Poetry: 250 Years of Struggle & Song

The Hungry Ear: Poems of Food & Drink

The Collected Poems of Lucille Clifton 1965–2010 (with Michael S. Glaser)

Best American Poetry 2011

The Art of Losing: Poems of Grief & Healing

Jazz Poems

John Berryman: Selected Poems

Blues Poems

Giant Steps: The New Generation of African American Writers

Night Watch

Night Watch;

poems.

KEVIN YOUNG.

ALFRED A. KNOPF • NEW YORK • 2025

A BORZOI BOOK
FIRST HARDCOVER EDITION
PUBLISHED BY ALFRED A. KNOPF 2025

Published by Alfred A. Knopf, a division of Penguin Random House LLC, 1745 Broadway, New York, NY 10019.

Library of Congress Cataloging-in-Publication Data
Names: Young, Kevin, [date] author.
Title: Night watch: poems / Kevin Young.
Description: First edition. | New York: Alfred A. Knopf, 2025. |
"This is a Borzoi book"—Title page verso.
Identifiers: LCCN 2024055711 (print) | LCCN 2024055712 (ebook) |
ISBN 9780593319628 (hardcover) | ISBN 9781524711979 (trade paperback) |
ISBN 9780593319635 (ebook)
Classification: LCC PS3575.O798 N54 2025 (print) |
LCC PS3575.O798 (ebook) | DDC 811/.54—dc23/eng/20241216
LC record available at https://lccn.loc.gov/2024055711
LC ebook record available at https://lccn.loc.gov/2024055712

penguinrandomhouse.com | aaknopf.com

Printed in Canada
2 4 6 8 10 9 7 5 3 1

The authorized representative in the EU for product safety and compliance is Penguin Random House Ireland, Morrison Chambers, 32 Nassau Street, Dublin D02 YH68, Ireland, https://eu-contact.penguin.ie.

for Tuddie
1946–2023

Mama Annie
1923–2024

& Auntie Gail
1950–2025

How will I know you in the underworld?
How will we find each other?

—EAVAN BOLAND

Contents

Night Watch

Cormorant

Nobody's angel—
        even your crown, unkempt,
looks like an egret

in an oilslick, inelegant
        pelican, diving
down to feed—burnt

goose, orphaned stork,
        you skim close
to the water, *nigger-*

bird we called you, laughing—
        I've seen you perched
on a stump in a swamp, drying

your waxless wings
        raised like a crucifix
unpraised. Black swan, you flood

back to me among
        the memory of my father
driving home, his hands a map

pointing out shacks where Negroes
        once lived, now
only timber, & anger, still there

for him forever. Besmirched
        crow-cousin, dirty seraph,
today you are enough—

you'll do—if only
        I could see you again, hungry,
waiting, at the edge of the bayou.

All Souls

Harvest moon.
My howling heart—

mouth a mask.
What say you?

The sun
knows nothing.

Only night—

my voice raised in it
tall as wheat.

The maize
of your breath.

The body
betrays us—

so we run.
Still the moon

bearing babies
above us, waxes

unlike the leaves.
Burn on,

saith the trees.

*

Save yourself.

*

October, almost—

Ghost moon.
Haunted heart.

No, I won't.

The rain slows, shows
the earthworms

they were wrong—
far harder to breathe

here, above earth,

than below
where the storms

shelter their own.

*

The heart can't
help it—

forgets. Beats
like a bird

against the wind,
or the pane.

Slim to none.

Only its shadow scares
it away.

Strange, how hard
it is to donate—

so we wait.
Lend me your eyes.

Hatchet moon.
Late heat.

*

Execution moon.
Hanging there

helpless. Try this
on for size.

The weatherman
never goes outside.

Grief a garment
that shrinks each

wash. Scarecrow stuffed full
of hay, newspapers

hawking yesterday.

*

Waste away.
Why not.

Like a stone.
Like a limb.

Like a lamb.
Like a rind.

Take your time.

Like a shore.
Like a sea

or its shell, itself
an ear

hearing the sea.
Like honey.

Make me.

*

Suffer the salmon.
The dolphin

& the meek.
The whale

who finds the shore
& our poor prayers.

The horse, though broke,
who can't quit

running. Why wait.
Half of nothing

is still nothing.
What keeps

you here, baying?
Even inside-dogs circle

tamping down grass
no one but them

can see.
Suffer

& shelter me.

*

How it hammers,
the heart.

Go head on
without me.

For the journey,
jettison nothing.

Let autumn do that—

how it sheds
clothes like a runaway

heading steady north.

*

So cold, you cry
when the wind

meets your eyes

Here autumn's only
winter in disguise

Sun carved
bright on the stoop

Say you're mine.

*

Plague me
O Lord.

Wound me
like the worm moon

cut in two.

Hurricane
& tornado me

Let loose
your levees

& the thunder—

the sky stained
with bright.

Prove it.

*

Monk moon.

Alone in a sky
studying itself.

God's many
guises—

dervishes, darkened
ballparks.

Artificial hearts.

*

Leave me be.

In the city along
the freeway a coyote

crawls from under
the guardrail—

crouches on hindquarters,
kneels even, like a man

tired as I am.

*

Let there
be night—

*

Out my window
a soldier in dress blues

beneath the faint
midday moon

lays a wreath
on a well-kept grave

& with what
arm he has left

salutes.

The Two-Headed Nightingale

one.

WHITEVILLE

We was born
    blue
conjoined
    but breathing—

both of us
    at once

body & soul
    entwined
twinned

    we sang
our cries
    for comfort

for air
    & for our mother whose
water we once swam

    like a man
thrown overboard
    clutching driftwood

our faces
    smooth
that we shared

    Even a stone
has a soul

We was torn
from mother's bosom
soon

after we were born
soon
as we could sing

Two yolks
in one egg

Nightingale
they called us
made us one
not twin

Our harmonies
our disguise

As the sun
is stolen
by the night—

we were
taken in daylight
from our Mother

Our Father

Our souls
broken
body stolen

from her who
once we were
one with—

We hollered
in unison
for milk

for more
Our arms
a clock's—

the seconds
never did
hold enough

The agony of being
    alive

of a body
    & soul both
entwined—

If ever
    one day she died
before I
    would I perish too?

Is there a moment
    between death

of the body
    & the beyond?

It is this gap
    we live in

who have never
    known alone

When you slept
    I slept
When you dreamt
    I did too

When Sunday
    was sent
we sang

When we could
    we filled
the woods with
    dark notes

Each of us
    an echo.

two.

AFRICAN UNITED TWINS

When we sing
we are one voice
We rise

mornings
with great
difficulty—

Promise
is our front feet

My hands
in this photograph
holding each other

We are the other's
mourner

We are the mother
    of Christ holding
his body
    disbelieving

the stone
    rolled back
from the heart
    of the mount

the hole
    now left
behind—spirited away—

Will we, Mary,
    Mother of Everything,
one day in heaven be

    cleaved?
Will we know

    what it is to roam
without—
    It is her arms

that hold me tight
    chained
to my side

We're a contraction
    like *can't*
or *shan't*

I know
    no one's alone

Though we
    might pray to be—

Us a nation divided
    doubled.

Sometime before
    the War
we were stole

It was New Orleans—

The loud harbor
    Congo Square
Like the sea we were stole

    like a gnarled
cut-down tree—

yoked
    driven north

It was years before
    I were brought home

Taken
    torn
we was always being
    born

from each other
    We are the other's
mother

From one
    another
we ate

    what
the other did

As one we sang,
    we spake—

She was the body
    I the soul
Without one
    Perishes the whole

We each
    latched
yoked
    so knew

when they said
    we were sold

that whoever claimed
    they owned me

was chained
    to us too

We was born
 blue
beneath a Carolina sky

Where we will die

 A horizon
inside us

We are like
 the Carolinas, blue,

& our country—
 cleaved in two.

three.

ODDFELLOWS HALL

What
    are we

our masters ask
    Never *who?*

How much?
    Never

How many.

We are one
    of the wonders

Another 8th—
    a note—

What if
    what if
we were sunder—

    would we
be nine?
    or none?

Married
    to each other
so long, such

    a cleaving
would kill us—

One death
    Undoes both

An octopus—

    the doctors
self-appointed
    & -taught
think us—

A circus—

Our eight limbs
    they always
want town to town

    to peer under—
to peek—

The ocean
    is deep

For them
    we are specimen—

A woman
    only in word

The Carolina
    Twin—

The milk
    of a man
Wine
    of a woman.

2 Headed Nightingale
sings duets exquisitely
one trunk one vertebral column

A Marvellous Being
a Female
at 34 years of age—Mother living —

Each have sensitive of lower parts
but only sensitive
of each upper part

I conversed with this
these person-s
and found Her quick

and of pleasant manners

Both at times
have identical dreams

It is our mind
    doctors without schooling fail
to mention

They grant themselves
    degrees
like freedom

Each of our hands
    a language

8 limbed
    2 headed
We own
    many tongues.

four.

LEVEES

All over
    Europe we sung
Saw the Devil
    drawn

like us—
    many-limbed
dark

    We devour nothing

The Doctor's Despair,
    The Dual Unity—

Are raised up
    by applause
& what the crowds
    recite along

Two heads four arms
    four feet
All in one perfect body meet

My maker knows what
    he has done

The audience's hands
    delighted

made one.

It is the after
    both of me
is after

No grave
    wide enough
to hold us—
    or deep—

I who held
    each other
alive
    entwined—

Us
    is what

we wrest
    from the dust.

Still we sang—

But only
    each other—
no longer

did we tour
    this land
or another

Us—I—
    prophets
proffering tongues—

We recite to each
    other's backs—
hum hymns

to the neighbor children
    & even
to the Siamese Twins

whose land adjoins ours

in the Carolinas
    where I was born
where I hope one day

to go
    how the snowflake goes—
unique but

never alone.

Fire came for us
    at last
at home

We escaped right
    before the roof
became the floor

& watched it burn.
    All is
ash.

That night—
    perched in the cold—
the white

plague caught
    Millie by the throat—
our chair

made of antlers
    survived—
our books all

scraps, singed,
    pasted back
like us
    together.

What the daffodils decide
    early
to do—

    bloom—
our body
    decides too—

The crooked dogwood—

    The pear tree
a crabapple
    is grafted onto—

both bear
    their fruit—

The bitter
    not-quite apples

The pear tree entwined
    around itself—

This the ivy found—

Tomorrow we'll be
    buried together
wedded
    & dead—

Past the deepest weeds—

    I shall go first
then follow—

The blossoms blizzard
    all around.

Tomorrow a cold spell,
    unexpected, will
frost the crowded ground.

Darkling

one

THE DARK WOOD.

It is bitter almost as death itself is bitter.
But to rehearse the good it also brought me
I will speak about the other things I saw there.

—DANTE, *Inferno,* Canto I,
trans. Seamus Heaney

1. *The Dark Wood*

In my living
    room, the skull
of the coyote

discusses with me
    our pending appointment
with bone—the canine teeth

of time. The middle
    of my life. His grin
is not found

in the smaller antlers
    of the antelope
once found by my father

that also flowers
    from the wall. Down
in the square, trees

bare as bones, their crown
    of leaves shorn. The hounds
of the constables hollering—

the lure of light & kerosene burning
    in lanterns. Guns. My feet
deep in the mud

of what is called Wood
    or Gardens the government
built just for us. Your mama's

leopard clutch
    rustling with peppermints.
A one-eyed cat.

A wolf in silhouette—
    that whistle. The coyote
in the quiet.

    The hour of our hunger
is his, only longer.

II. *The Descent*

What will
    become of us?
The blue light

& the arrows aiming
    us on: No Exit.
No Trespasses

No Breath.
    Are you willing
& able to assist?

the Captain asks.
    Dry docked
& airlocked, the cruel capsule

we barely glimpse
    earth from.
Ladies & gentlemen,

we cannot move till everyone
    is seated.
We hold each

other awaiting
    the splash of landing—
prepare for impact—

our vessel's crash
    & flush
sounding down in the blue.

The lake of my heart.
    The light departing.
All around us, new

in the briar of after—
    a lone goose, or loon,
low overhead. The white

ring around their necks.
    What was next:
arms raised to reach

the banking birds—
    hands up don't
shoot—or as if we might

ourselves take flight.

III. *City of Woe (Vestibule)*

Babylon was busy.
    Frisked & let through
we stepped into

Death's waiting room.
    The magazines old
as your mama's—

Time or *Life*
    with the address
ripped off. For safety.

Ebony. The Doctor will
    see you now—will
bill you, will

kneel on your chest
    to stop the bullet
or breath. *Jet. Black Stars.*

Sweet Spirit. Each body only
    what will not be.
Each room an emergency

none yet can see.

IV. *Limbo (Circle One)*

Skeleton-still.
    We stood. Those
before us who once

Almost believed, arrayed
    like statues, trophies
of the child killed

We couldn't bear
    to dust
or box away.

The dark threshold
    to the lost teen's
bedroom, jersey

Now empty, baseball team
    down a man—
out with an injury.

Wild pitch. Passed ball.
    Technical knock-out.
Technical foul.

Flagrant two. The flagration
    of the car turned over
he lay dead beside

A good while.
    Dark dye
seeping into the street.

No pop flies. No catch—
    player to be
named later—

No sheet we'll provide—
    Just the blue-tail fly
doornailed, hungry,

Fit to die.

v. *Noli Me Tangere (Circle Two)*

The dead want us
    to want them, lovers
of what isn't there—

or is that us—
    leaning close, infidels
of the world's invisible

unliving long train.
    The dead, wedded
to this world, vow

beneath a veil.
    In the mirror
we meet the dead

each morning—
    shaving, say,
we rake our faces

of yesterday—
    or darken our eyes
in order to leave

out the house. When we smile
    the dead nod back—
when we laugh the dead don't

seem to mind. Tonight
    the lost rise
with the moon above

the mountain, a stone
    rolled back
from the tomb—the body

stolen of its soul—
    the blind world
or whirlwind—

In daylight, see it
    list in the sky
sometimes, the moon—

ghostly eye, great
    reflected rock,
bare mirror

    where we
cannot breathe.

VI. *Underworld (Circle Three)*

We are born
  with all our grief
already in us, like teeth,

& time works it out
  of us—our mouths—pain
for a spell & then there

grief sits, a lifetime, shiny,
  lucky. Pomegranate. Made
before I was unmade—

If not, the gaps
  where once milkteeth sat,
replaced by these holes

  we hope to eat with—
each supper a reckoning.

VII. *Black Spring (Circle Four)*

I hate the heart—
    how it ain't
ever done, finds

its way forward
    though the head
may not want. We may

have to say Let go
    to those we love,
it's alright to leave—

not permitted to stay—

that very night, absolved,
    stigmataed with tubes,
they up

& do. The world apparently
    is hard to fight
free from, rocketing

away from gravity
    & the cherry trees
blooming early

before I was even ready
    to believe again
in beauty.

VIII. *Wake of Souls (Circle Five: The Styx)*

The dead don't know
    what to do
with themselves.

Aren't enough,
    our arms—
See them crowd

the river's edge
    eager, or afraid
to cross

this marsh of souls.
    The boat late,
of course, its skeleton

crew of one.
    Infected light.
Sunless tide.

So many. They yearn
    for what
they fear—

Our prayers cheer
    or jeer them along—
the oars enter

    the water
with a moan.

IX. *The Orchard (Circle Six)*

Wounded, the dead wait
    & do not heal—
instead, it's we the living

relearning to walk
    & to wake—
the smudge of lips

or blood. Breath.
    We're helpless, cannot
help but help

ourselves—& hope.
    The lizard who knows
loss means escape

    grows his tail back
within a week.

My father-
    in-law who lost
his spleen at twenty

has since grown back
    not one, but many.

The dog, three-headed, docked,
    chases where once
his tail wagged

    & was—each of us
this orchard of scars.

x. *Necropolis*

The entrance to the darkness
    is day.
A bright way.

*

Each day the whole
    foods store like a church:
organic this

& that, the timed machine
    of mist anointing
the kale dark & hale.

Long list of herbs for her
    to crush like the doctor
with his 6-month

    prognosis. She'll show him.
Bald head in a hat.

*

Night starts at noon—

the shadow enters slow
    like a child
into the shallows.

*

They took him in
    after he'd complained
for a time—

First thought he was
    just acting, you know
boys, but when the cough

started thought
    we better go. Soon
as the doctor saw him

started for surgery—
    scary. He was about
to go under when the x-ray

saw cancer everywhere
    inside him like eggs
in a fish. That much.

Kidneys failing like words.

*

Each day we die
    a little, the one-armed man
knew well.

*

The heaven that is hers
    lets in no one.
For her Paradise

always unfinished.
    Awaits what
she cannot name.

Says to the darkness
    Why not? Or,
Why bother?

Heaven isn't overrun,
    needs new tenants.
To let. Yet

won't go it
    alone, so decides
to take both herself

& her son
    into oblivion.
Loads the gun.

The heaven she wants,
    the earth in her
hands, eats

up everyone.

*

Nothing
moving.

*

Shell attracts shell
    she said, showing him
how to retrieve the smallest

pieces from the bowl. Her last
    little tricks taught him
so he wouldn't forget or wish

he had asked. Her head
    bald as an egg.
The yolk sometimes red.

He nodded. When next she woke
    in the hospital, both her kids,
the oldest,

the sullen husband,
    had shaved
their hair to match hers.

She grew angry, feared
    they were mocking her—
not meeting.

Shell attracts shell,
    the boy said then
& she couldn't help

but laugh.

*

Slipping sleep.

*

Is there faith
    without belief?
Yes, it's known

as life in these parts.
    A steep stair.
Where we hail from

the storm sends its hail
    all a sudden, out
of nowhere & it rains

like nobody's business
    which is shuttered
with our windows.

Everything must go—
    even the stuffed swallows
& the sad, sewn giraffes

in the museum where nature
    believes history—
the hyenas made

of fur & wire
    watch & grin
at whatever's missing.

XI. *City of Dis (Circle Six: The Heretics)*

The dead won't leave
    us be. See
them crowd

the photograph at the edges,
    the negative,
unblinking in the glare

of the flash—
    their moment is over
& thus forever—

a still, a fraction
    of the will. What
keeps them never letting

us alone—companion,
    onion skin,
dark dog whose eyes

    the camera sees behind,
blooms white.

XII. *The Depths (Circle Seven)*

The dead, newborn,
    need learn
a new tongue—

must learn to live
    with a body & not
inside one—

the innards' symphony.
    River of blood.
Enough, the infants cry.

Too much,
    say the dead,
who prefer to live

without pain
    or its opposite—
grace—the dead

all share the same
    fate—memory—
the figurehead of a ship,

salt-worn, grimaced, arms
    akimbo, fording
the faceless sea.

XIII. *The Grove of Suicides*

Why do they do
    themselves in,
why? Yet all I

can think to ask
    is how. Enormous
thorn. Bleeding leaf.

Silence
    other end of the line.
O wounded soul,

speak.

XIV. *Beyond (Circle Eight)*

What if the body
    is what
we bring

with us
    beyond?
It is the soul

stays here, sullen,
    inconsolable,
not so much

wandering as waiting
    to be found,
reunited, dirtied,

in the end—
    it is enough,
then, to see

the soul let loose only
    in those moments
of ecstasy, not when

we leave
    our body, but
when our body

arrives finally & our soul
    sups, fed
like the dead—

hands hungry
    as stray gloves.
Fingers may fill them

but still they need
    the noun
of the soul—

the soul's smell,
    its plangent
personhood. The more

they eat
    the more they need.
The body

always becoming—
    who verbs its way
over & under

while the soul rocks
    in the old folks'
home—the soul who

    shivers, grown
suddenly cold.

XV. *Ninth Circle*

The season stolen—
    the cold comes
without a word.

I wish you would—

I save all the smallest
    things, which, one day,
I'll braid into a bloom

    that tries to live
beyond these bare rooms.

*

How the soul
    slanders the body—
calls it

a vessel
    or temple, either
way empty, unful-

filled—
    How the body
buries the soul—

rends & does
    not mend it, broken
like a spirit

    or the soul's shiny
bones, which grow.

*

The dead grow more
    distant each day
like their fingernails,

or the future.
    Nights, nearer—
squint & you

can see them. The dead
    visit in the taint
between sleep

& waking, between being
    a body & being
aware of one, the shades

    shutting out
no more light.

*

Pity the body—
    how it outlasts
even its clothes—

no, how its clothes
    outshine it—
Better to live

beyond everyone
    else you know, left mourning
oneself? I saw the sun

decide to rise—
    though I thought
it would rather not—

    wanting to sleep
longer, forever & a day.

*

Who knows what the cold
    is called by those
who cannot feel it—

the dying—anymore—
    The Antarctic
explorer, soldier, rations

running out, declares
    I am just going outside
and may be some time

knowing full
    well he'll be found
never—or much

later, his words
    ice—all of ours—
what no thought can thaw—

coating, like ash, our lids
    & lashes.

XVI. *River of Lamentation*

Do the dead know.

Where they are.

Who.

They're through.

With us, above.

Or below.

Our feet sunk.

In shadow.

The body.

We barely know.

Or own.

They speak like the leaves.

Rustling.

Holding onto the tree.

Winter starlings.

A bee trapped in honey.

Their very tongues.

Undone.

XVII. *The Hotel of Hell (Circle Nine, Round 3)*

The exhalation
    of all evil.
Me & the Devil

walking side by side—
    his feet terra cotta.
His hair a cold fire.

Dogs despise him.
    Infants cry
at the sight.

His thin skin blood orange.
    His treble tongues
like a red tail or necktie

jutting just past
    his wide waist.
His eyes a squint,

breath a bellows.
    House a white
washed shack

his mouth a crack.
    His friends all
well paid. Gold-plate.

A swine's pearls. A cold
    fire. His exes
turned into pillars

of snow. Black milk
    of nightfall.

*

Each eve he eats
    his friends face first.
I wondered

was that worse? to see just
    where we're going
or to be devoured

by the feet, bottoms
    up, watching
how far we'd come.

The crossroads where
    I take my leave
from him—

an eggshell walking west.
    A knife with legs,
ears pierced with arrows

& the sea a shallows.
    Short-fingered, fickle
as a cock, a cuckold, a fraud—

a goat with a tire
    round its neck.
On the wall a dirty bed.

*

A cold fire. I climbed down
    his slouched
unsuitable back,

the tower he made
    of himself, night
manager for this Hotel

of Hell. The manger.
    He turned
away all—

no matter if the lady
    were full with child,
radiant, starred, hailing

from the middle
    of the world—
or the Lord.

Him scared
    of stairs
& saints.

*

Down I scaled, reader,
    escalatoring
till I passed

the point—the equator—
    the loin—
where the Devil's

legs & everything else
    was now
upside down. Above, again,

I found myself alive in a city
    without angels
that Easter Monday, alone

in a land that might be ours—
    street covered in scat, all tar—
the graffitied gravestones—

& looked up, peering
    past the haze
through which I thought

    I almost caught
the stars.

two

WEREWOLF HILL.

So much undone to be undone.

—KAMAU BRATHWAITE

I. *The Stair*

The heart, it hoards—
how I know this—

The small, strangled
shining room Keats lost
his life in—and to—

beyond the window sunlight
arranging itself
on the Spanish Steps

while the poet watches.
Sweet azure
of the east—

Outside, snapshots
of the tourists

& teenagers tired
of what they don't
know yet. What will

become of us? Ash.
Unasking. The death
mask made of Keats

no longer breathing—
look at it
not look at us.

Beyond the window
    the stairs stretch heavenward
stranded, without

one ounce of shade.

II. *Cardinals*

Today I do not know
    what the trees will do—
barely believe tomorrow

they will bloom
    whites & blues, the dogwood
winking at you.

Reed about
    my waist. Tomorrow
something will give way—

green will crowd
    the winter out—
but today all brown, the sky

& ground devour
    each other, swallow
us down. What lives

in the buffeting
    must bend.
The cedar out-

lasting winter—
    how it leans, sheds
limbs like a soldier.

III. *Ledge*

No use telling
    the dead what
you've learned since

they've learnt it too—

how to go on
    without you, the mercy
of morning, or moving,

    the light that persists
even if.

*

Beauty is as beauty
    does, my mother says,
who is beautiful & speaks

loud so she can be understood
    unlike poets who can't
talk to save their lives

so they write.

*

It's like a language,
    loss—
can be

    learnt only
by living—there—

*

What anchors us
    to this thirst
& earth, its threats

& thinnesses—
    its ways of waning
& making the most of—

of worse & much
    worse—if not
this light lifting

up over the ridge

IV. *Necropolis (Garden of Stone)*

Today cleaning I found
    shots of my trip to Cuba
legally, back when

that was still
    possible. The blurred
lights of Havana

from above, the heat
    that greeted you at night
at the airport. A thousand

taxi drivers in the dark. The hot rods
    we rode in were from an America
now rotting in barns, or restored

in a rich man's garage.
    Later, we'd ride one
to the Necropolis—

miles & miles of the dead,
    of monuments & small
homemade shrines—aren't

they all—a bird's green
    wing, doll
of a child. Not a toy,

you understand. Tourists
    wanting to take pictures
of even the girl-doll

in her fading dress
    as if the dead need nothing
except our memories. Palm trees

swaying among the stones
    & just beyond, near
the fence, the smolder

& smoke & scent—
    not unpleasant—of coffins
now empty, or emptied,

being burnt.

v. *Cenotaphs*

FOR MICHAEL

Summer covers everything, yet not
Even the heat can hold you now

FOR FICRE

There's a moon without
You in it

There's a sun
& I cannot see it

FOR KENNETH

We can't keep not
Meeting like this

FOR TUDDIE

Even the sun
Knows you're gone

FOR YOU

May we grow
Old till

Our heads bloom
White & curly

As the dogwood
Come April

VI. *Tulips*

What the dead want—
    shelter—opposable
thumbs—to quit being

compared to taxes,
    as if they can be
evaded. Each April

sadly,
    sadly wiser,
& alone

they push up
    like tulips from the earth,
perennial as pain.

Trouble me again.

VII. *Trinity*

Like August the foxes
    surprise us, our fields
full of them—or one—

who darts like the day
    across the shoulder
of the road. The world.

What isn't
    there to want?

Gone, I still saw her
    small & thinking
not of me

but leaving.

*

In November the deer
    quit the fields, cross
the road like Sooners

seeking food. We never
    saw them coming, our cars—
where they went

after, no one knows.
    Or does
but does not say.

I do not want
    a thing.

But to sleep long
    & wake early,
the bucks & does silent

    who might still
be seen.

*

Underfoot, the graves grow
    like the echo
the loons make across

the static, icy lake.
    For each other,
for no one

    in particular,
they moan.

VIII. *Ditch*

Day he died,
    Samuel Beckett's father, doctor
said, was doing better—

Doctor scarcely out the door
    when dear Dad collapsed,
sweet pea all over his face.

At the promise, Beckett
    had donned the brightest
clothes he could find, later

watched last words
    fall from Dad's
pained mouth: *Fight,*

fight, fight. And, *What*
    a morning.
Three days after,

Beckett wrote
    his friend, *I cannot*
write about him—

the letter proof
    to the contrary. *I can only*
walk the fields and climb

the ditches after him,
    his father buried
between the mountains

& the sea. *God*
    love thee—Sam.

IX. *Potential Epitaphs*

1.

Your turn.

2.

What more
do you want from me

3.

Based on my infant
son's favorite phrase:

All done.

x. *Elephant Funeral*

Stoking the body
    like coals, dying,
of the calf who stumbled down

& stayed, the elephants
    rumble & yell
almost, in a pitch

we now know
    we cannot hear.

Or bear, I bet—
    this mute
trumpet, their cries, reach

only each other
    & their pity,
their piety, many

miles away. Dead as language,
    stony body
the elephants parade

past & circle—they nudge
    & lift again
again the struck young

with their trunks.
    Their ears semaphores.
Giant shadows.

Later in the red
    mud they'll wallow—
the tamped-down grass

a pale echo.

XI. *Blake*

And then there's poor Blake—

his face flushed
    like a baby's
mouth suffering thrush—

bent over the bed
    of type, the etching press—
every word

backwards & made
    of acid
or lead.

How fragile each
    letter is, if dropped
it will slant.

Blake paints
    a Tyger who's scarier
because it looks

nothing like a tiger.
    He's not seen, only read
about one, unlike God—

its asymmetry
    resembles the moon
above us, burning—

shines lopsided
    as every line, the pages
the words bite.

XII. *Crows*

They hop like the humble.
    Like sinners hotfooted
in hell.

Like old men
    they grumble.
They do not sing,

just cry. Theirs
    is the only eye—
plead with it,

or try.

XIII. *Thrush*

On the heath Hardy
    lost, angry
at the sky

for not raining—
    Hardy empty
at the pub.

In the woods
    Hardy hears
not a bird, exactly—

but lower, & further
    away, like God—
whom Hardy knows

never hears—its song
    a distant axe against
the trees. His wife

days dead, Hardy's
    hands deep
in a pocket, still ringed,

outlive all belief.

XIV. *Vigil*

Here, in the terminal,
    almost too much
watching them

holding each other, the soldier
    flown home & his
wife or promised not wanting

to let go. She squeezes his face
    browned by desert
while their friends gather, hang

back, hover, snap
    a shot or two.
Everyone grins

like jack-o'-lanterns. A half hug
    for the men, an arm
still between them

& few words. At last
    she is done
waiting, this bewildering

vigil—by phone,
    by soap & talk
show—keeping her hands busy

& the clock's.
    Fingers latched
with his, she begins

walking slow—counting
    to herself, waiting for him
to have to return

like spring, its stings, again.

xv. *St. Mary's*

Dried out like a flower,
    Berryman spends his hours
in bed revising, addressing

poems to the Lord
    in this his latest stint
in recovery—swallowing the steps

finally, he's drinking less,
    a cactus. Kate
his last wife worries,

tears open
    wishes with her finger:
Get well soon. The living thing

of his writing he nurses
    like a wound.
His beard Whitman's,

the Death-Bed Edition—
    even his bones he names Mister
as if a skeleton in science class—

talks to, & the plants.
    Berryman plays the blues
brought here from home—

the LP's grooves scratch
    an itch he can't
quite reach. Out there,

in the cold, the bridge
    he will find & fling
himself from, beckoning.

His glasses, soon broken,
    he'll first fold closed
carefully, pocketing

their dark wings.

XVI. *Last Suppers*

Just as living's lost
    on those alive

so death's something
    the dead haven't
perfected—yet—

would give
    their eyeteeth to understand—
& do. Subsumed,

toothless,
    they roam—gum,
hungry, their world

& ours—

*

The grave where
God lives

*

The dead are writing
    a diary
of the living—

just as we keep
    each day
a diary called dying—

every entry
an exit.

*

Pulled apart
by God

by the world
where you aren't

*

Holes in my hands.

Buckets,
what I cannot hold.

You, water,
worlds away—

*

I'd wager the dead
think of us
again as much

as we of them—
what else have they
to do? God's grace

a given. Or the ground's.
And the unforgiven?
Taken care of

by us, who curse, busy
    hugging groceries
up the steep stairs

thinking only of our last
    meal, or next,

out of breath—

XVII. *Milkteeth*

My son issues cries
    all through the line

to see your house, Anne
    Frank, the house now
named for you, factory

of fear, of jam your father,
    on paper, could no longer own.
Indoors, in the near-dark,

my wife nurses our son
    silent. He meets sleep
in her arms while a tape

repeats of the woman
    who hid you, unlikely
angel, employee.

Who also kept
    the loose leaves
of your diaries. The hydrangea

in the courtyard behind
    the house so beautiful
it seems unreal—

your words cover
    the walls, postcards
& stars you pasted

to keep yourself company—
    Rudy Vallee & boys
blond as those who'd later

betray you.
    I have no one, you told
a friend across the final fence.

My son wakes now
    that my wife weeps
& I picture you

alone. Words,
    I have none.

Only my son's
    wordless stories, his song
half hunger, or pain,

    milk teeth coming in
& yours did anyone save?

XVIII. *Shine*

The stars here shine
   brighter & there
are lights somewhere

saying my name—
   I know all this
Lord must go. That even

the dark is not there
   tomorrow—morning
comes too early

for me, who can sleep
   when the world's emptying?
The desert cold, the wild

of what goes.

three

RESURRECTION CITY.

I have nothing new to ask of you,
Future, heaven of the poor.

—W. S. MERWIN

1. *Resurrection*

I was dead awhile
    when I woke.
Rested,

almost. This world
    bests us
all, I know—

how best to live
    the living ask
& the dead do too—

in whispers, the answer,
    in the dark
where our talk

sounds louder. Bright
    bothered death.
How I wish

to take your hand
    & tell you—
to hold again

you like breath.

II. *Faith*

How do the small birds
    in the street know
how not to die—

that whatever
    they gather,
hunger for, is never

enough to keep them
    in the road
when our wheels bear down

upon them? They feast on
    what I cannot see
then fly away

& sing.

III. *Vita Nuova*

Will my hands never
come clean?

They've tried the river
& prayer, have severed
themselves in the town square—

More weight,
I beg. Each stone
piled on my chest

the belief in something
unseen gathering—
Spring in the bare

branches of the tree.

*

I want to name
my daughter Winter.
I want to be in love

with what comes, not
wish for whatever lies
over the next hill.

I want to be bothered
by God again.
I like the science

of silence, how it
never is. There's always
the wind, that lilac

I planted in the heatwave
    & later managed
to save. Keeping alive is brave.

*

    I been slippered
by the Lord.

I've been struck
    by thunder.
All hail.

I have lingered outside
    the Stop & Go, doing
just that. Fill, if you please,

my hat with coins—
    each stamped a year
you can't get back.

*

My body came
to bury me—

All the papers
were in order

I followed it
out into the street

& held me
in my arms.

Such a din—

I set forth
after it

down into the soil
like a sea parted

just for me

*

One day the song
    will cease—what
a relief. Music unmade

    like a bed.
I lie—
    I love this

life, its airports
    filled with souls
sailing anywhere

    not here. This world
with its mysteries—

    We land
the day before we began.

IV. *Diptych (Portraits of Light)*

NIGHT WATCH

You can fall in love

in a museum, but only
    with the art
or its silence—or the stranger

you don't mean to follow
    suffering past the Old Masters
& the unnamed

servants. Rembrandt's face
    half in shadow—
you can fall for what

isn't there already, or
    with the 13th century—the swan
raising up, roosters hung

upside down to die on a cross—

Even the tourists gathered
    round the docent, the same
jokes & half-truths,

loom beautiful—
    the children crying hurried
out of sight. Forget

The Night Watch, the crowds,
    instead follow the quiet
to the portraits of light

entering a room. These walls,
    few windows, hold
the world—what the world

couldn't say till someone
    saw it first—and now
it's everywhere. The braids

of that woman's hair.

SELF-PORTRAIT WITH FELT HAT

One should never be in love

when in a museum—
    better to be alone, if not
utterly, then practically—

tired of feet, & routine,
    forge ahead beyond
the bounds of audio-tours

& family, isolate, avoid
    this couple oblivious
to it all, the captions & arrows,

kissing like no tomorrow
    beside Van Gogh's sunflowers—
bruised, chartreuse, brilliant

& wilting for years, yet never
    managing to. Skip
holding hands & Gauguin's

portrait of Van Gogh
    painting what he saw. The crows
gather like clouds, black—

or the crowds—that the couple
    doesn't care about—
numb to all else. Best

    believe in the world
more than yourself.

v. *Drum*

 In the dark
I return home

after the storm.
 What transforms
has been blown.

With their blue lights
 crews chop
& clear all night.

Before dawn
 things turn on—
the birds, more rain,

the lawn. Too late
 for me & my defense-
less shins

already banged
 in the black
like a drum.

Or a dream.
 Twilight still
dark, a tomb.

 In it, we dress
like a wound.

VI. *Knock Wood*

Not the past
    but the future the dead fill—
their will

will not
    be moved—
the opposite of the pollen

that the trees send
    in the hopes
they'll live again—

yellow ash
    over everything—

The dead
    do not cough
nor care—

they are going
    exactly where—
are more

like the dogwood
    planted out front
for my son—

rooted, blooming,
    unmoving—
hell of a way

to make a living.

VII. *Usher*

Make of me
a mercy—

This stone-eyed world
I can't see past

To what waits
in the wings

*

The dead wake for nothing.
    Or wake & nothing
is still there.

The wide meadow. Deep grass.
    Vanishing ships.
The far fires

only glimpsed
    from a distance.
Nothing looks back,

blinks twice.

*

Beg the ghosts—
be gone.

Bid the dawn
so long—

Let the day blanch
your bones.

Let the dusk
usher us

Into it—hail
the thick dark

Alongside me,
singing.

*

Finish
me like a fish.

*

Easy then being nothing
    wanting more. Now,
a small something,

I want only
    an end
to the suffering—

to quit this knocking—
    like a boat lashed
tight to the dock, tossed

during storm—
    either cut me
aloose, sent

wild to sea, or yank
    me inland—dry-docked—
spare me this long

longing, tugging
    the leash, moored
in between.

*

I believe no more
in nothing—not yet

in something—
the severed wing

of a bird in the road
still stirs, lifted

by wind.

VIII. *Black Madonna*

The dead multiply
    & punctuate
our lives—

    like doubt
they are damn near
    impossible

to bleach out—
    their stain,
thank Job,

    can't help
but stay. Is the one
    sure thing—

not even the thaw
    the weatherman calls for
arrives on time.

    Seek shelter.
So cold
    my ring won't hold

my fingers. The dead
    are gold
our altars say—

    once their faces
darken
    or fall away, only

clutched hands remain.

IX. *Mantle*

The dead do
    what they want
which is nothing—

sit there, mantled,
    or made real
by photographs

in silver frames,
    or less real
by our many ministrations.

Dusting. Bleach. The world
    swept, ordered,
seemingly unending.

The dead, listless,
    lazy, grow tired
& turn off the tv—

or like a father passed
    out in an easy chair
during the evening news

    what's watched now
does the watching.

x. *Yellowjacket*

The way wasps want
  your house
to be their house,

  so the dead
try & make
  your home

their own—they move in
  promising to stay
only a week, luggage

  stuffed with old
clothes & tinted photographs.
  Building their houses

of paper, buzzing, they draw
  the curtains, desilver
the mirrors till years

  later, look about
& it's your life

  the dead are living.
Wake & rub
  the night

from your eyes—the paper
  fetched wet
from the yard, the paid

  death notices
& ads for living longer
  unread. Mine

not the wings
    for such a flight—

Each day, later than you like,
    the lonely postman
force-feeds words

into the hungry mouth
    of the mailbox—
where this small

dunning bird has begun
    its brittle,
briefest nest.

XI. *Snapdragon*

Of late the dead
    have quit
their midnight

visits. They ask
    to swing by
sometime, without

ringing first—
    Thank you, no.
Think I'll stay here,

friends, in sunlight
    at the start
of summer, the snapdragons

& daylilies bright
    my son plucks.

Down the road
    the dandelions bloom
in a garden of stone.

A garland of souls.

Like the vines
    I'll climb—
like children who join

their limbs to the silver
    maple's, waving

to all who pass on by.

XII. *Faith*

Sky crowded with stars
    I cannot see

XIII. *Buckle*

How badly the body
wants to be

remembered—balding—
the old holes

in the belt buckle
taunt like a god—

Yesterday
is the body's country

Eyes like a banner
lowered—in prayer—

The body's bloody
arithmetic—we multiply

& die & divide—
How divine—

XIV. *Altarpiece*

I've come down with a case
    of Paradise. I've contracted
Eden fever. I'm flush

    with the wish to be allowed
to stay—to watch
    the maples turn

from saplings to trunks
    it takes four men
to topple. I've looked

    around & found myself
like Hell, no more
    livable than believed.

    Like a kite the light
tangled in the trees.

*

The dead won't meet
    your eye—a strange dog
you should greet

fingers tucked under—
    head averted—

The dead don't
    bite, but
bark & claw

your door all night.
    This fever of mine
has no father

to feed it—no end—
    the going—then—
going on—

*

The fury
of bees.

Feed me
till I sleep.

The penny's
lament.

On a long journey
honey the only

thing that keeps.

*

Nobody's good.
Everyone lies.

When I go
the only

mourners will be flies.
They arrive

wearing black robes,
almost polite.

I am reborn
with a billion eyes

& rise—at last
my head

clear & singing
like my wings.

*

I am easy enough
    to find. Look for me

where the rough dirt
    meets paved street,
stones shining your shoes.

I don't mind
    being mistaken for one
of the shadows

courting the sun—how
    it clouds & without seeking
cannot be seen.

Know then the lush cover
    of what might be leaves, rain

like a summons in the trees.

XV. *Grace*

No one's from here.
  Me I'm just
visiting. When I go

don't dare sing *Amazing*
  Grace, that tune
some slaveholder wrote

while at sea, the National
  Anthem of Suffering.
When I'm gone don't

gnash & weep or retch
  like me. What
my life has become

is known above. When I Fly Away,
  don't dare hold no vigil,
no candles—

Just burn the whole
  town on down.

XVI. *Easter Monday*

Almost mechanical,
    the cicada's whine.
The sun slow to arrive.

Sap-light. The bloom
    of the trees, the blues
& greens. Soon the sky a bright

crimson belief—
    as if a thief has cut
his hand breaking

into our house
    uncaught, yet
never whole again—

the scar of the road
    I rode here on. The fog—
or is it the mountain,

the rain who will not leave—
    lingers in the street, the deep
clouds full or empty

with what? The thought
    isn't ever enough
except here's the sun

making its steady sound
    against the drying,
reborn ground.

XVII. *Hereafter*

Once, in winter, I was blessed
by lightning, the plane
sudden struck—the boom

of it, the cabin lit up
& then the air
made metal

in my mouth. It's true,
you can look it up—
we had circled like hell,

*

trying to land
a good while—
once even descended

through clouds of snow,
earthbound, only
to rise again

the last moment
when a plane already
sat there, blinking,

*

on our white runway.
Exiled back
to the sky, we orbited

the airport untethered
    & impatient.
So when lightning threaded

us through, we all knew—
    wrong it turns out,
yet one day

*

true enough, perhaps soon—
    we'd be done.
You should know

that after you ready
    to meet the far,
stony shore, it is not hope

but the strange fire
    of forgiveness
that flares & fights

*

there—not wanting
    to go, hoping only
you'd said so

long to all you knew—
    to the elms
who also know what it means

to be told you'd die
    & survive.
In that emptied, electric air

*

some wept. Others asked
    to help, or for help,
began to act

as if it was merely static
    that snagged
us aloft. How long

did we linger
    up there, in thunder?
Thinking mostly of all

*

I loved, of what
    I'd never write.
Mirror

of my mind. Once we kissed
    the earth again, firetrucks
ushered us

through the open gates
    where the five o'clock news
asked what I'd seen

*

& the woman I loved, picking me up,
    talked a blue streak till she heard
the between we'd been.

Quiet then, we fetched
    my luggage orbiting
the conveyor belt, unspooling

its rosary. We drove
    home in snow deep
as silence. This little

*

living light. Even now
    how to name
just how bright the sky

looked that night & most
    the next day?
Hard to believe

one instant
    you could be beyond
the earth's reach—

*

the next, marveling
    at our singed,
wounded wings.

XVIII. *Rapture*

I want to be awake
when the world ends.
I want to be my friend

who rose to an empty
house, even his grandmother
& her worn cross gone

& thought it was the rapture,
that he hadn't crossed over.
Let me rip my shirt

as he did & tear into the street
hollering. Let me hear
only my blood beat this morning

among the rain before the dawn—
no one on the line.
Later, when they return

let those I love who left
have only gone to the store,
running errands, this errant

unebbing life. After,
let what I've torn—
the myself I mourn—

be mended & start
over, like a scar,
or star.

Spring (& Summer) 2007
Spring & Fall 2008
Winter 2008 & 2009
September 2009
Winter 2010
Spring 2011
Marfa May 2011
Atlanta January 2012
June 2012
January February March 2017
Harlem Jersey Jamaica Chicago New Orleans June 2018
Quarantine 2020
Easter (& Summer) 2023

Acknowledgments & Notes

THE TWO-HEADED NIGHTINGALE: Spoken by Millie and Christine McCoy, conjoined twins born enslaved in 1851 and two years later kidnapped from family to be displayed across the United States, including by P. T. Barnum. Frequently the twins were subjected to invasive and abusive examinations by self-appointed doctors. Together, after the Civil War, the twins' parents sued through the Freedmen's Bureau for their daughters' return. Millie and Christine's father, often removed from earlier accounts, was involved in the custody battle; remarkably, recent scholarship has established that Jacob McCoy went on to purchase his slaveowner's land after Emancipation.

Millie and Christine often spoke of themselves as singular—what I've called "the royal I"—and performed to acclaim across Europe and America, including before Queen Victoria. Photographs and cartes de visite of them often bear a single signature as Millie-Christine. "We have but one heart, one feeling in common, one desire, one purpose," they wrote in one of their several narratives. The poem shifts between these states of selfhood.

Portions of this poem first appeared as part of "The Carolina Twin," the catalog essay for the exhibition *Tales of the Conjure Woman* by the artist Renée Stout that originated at the Halsey Institute, College of Charleston, 2013.

DARKLING: Inspired by Dante's *Divine Comedy,* this sequence's first section, THE DARK WOOD, was originally commissioned for the Museum of Modern Art's Robert Rauschenberg retrospective in 2017. My friend and fellow poet Robin Coste Lewis and I divided up

Hell and wrote our respective versions in response to Rauschenberg's drawings based on the *Inferno*—which he made after a friend read the poem to the artist canto by canto, circle by circle, echoing the oral quality of Dante's original. This "duet" with Lewis—and in turn with Dante-via-Rauschenberg—appeared in a limited-edition catalog, *Thirty-Four Illustrations for Dante's* Inferno (2017).

Afterward, without telling a soul, I decided to continue with the other parts of Dante's poem. I happened to have grown up with the same John Ciardi translation that Rauschenberg heard and in composing my cantos incorporate the that Hell I first encountered as a teenager together with the African American cosmologies and spirituals that have grounded me. The poem "Ditch" also quotes from a 1933 letter from Samuel Beckett found in *The Letters of Samuel Beckett, Volume 1, 1929–1940*, edited by Martha Dow Fehsenfeld and Lois More Overbeck. As in the *Divine Comedy,* each realm ends with the stars—though my *Purgatorio*'s last poem starts there.

A number of these poems first appeared in anthologies, magazines, and journals, online and off. Thanks to the editors for their support:

Adroit: "Cardinals"; "Ditch"
The Atlantic: "All Souls"; "Faith (The Small Birds)"
Best American Poetry: "Diptych (Portraits of Light)"
Bitter Southerner: "Altarpiece"
New American Writing 25 (2007): "Necropolis (Garden of Stone)"; first appeared on quickmuse.com
The New Yorker: "Rapture"
Poem-a-Day: "Ledge"; "Mantle"
Poetry: "The Stair"; "Usher"; "Diptych (Portraits of Light)"; "Hereafter"
T, The New York Times Style Magazine: "Elephant Funeral"
Together in a Sudden Strangeness: America's Poets Respond to the Pandemic: "Shine"; "Resurrection"
You Are Here: "Snapdragon"

CH

"And the weight of the plate didn't bother you?" Duff arched an eyebrow. "Ten kilos isn't terribly light. It's what, twenty-two-pounds?"

"Yeah? So? It did the job. Crushed the back of his skull right at the top of his spine. Caused unconsciousness, paralysis, and an almost immediate spinal infarction that led to a seizure and total respiratory failure."

"What about the weight of the girl?"

"What about it?" Jahnke was getting annoyed.

Duff shrugged and looked at the ceiling. "Sarah Novak is what? A buck-ten, buck-fifteen, tops?"

"So?"

"You think a girl like that can pick up a twenty-two pound weight and swing it with enough force to kill a man?" Duff gave Jahnke his best dumb-guy face. "I'm just sayin', that's like a fifth of her body weight."

"Women her size routinely pick up thirty-pound toddlers, Mr. Duffy."

"Do they beat men to death with those toddlers?"

Fourth and Wrong

An Abe and Duff Mystery

Sean Patrick Little

Published by Spilled Inc. Press, Sun Prairie, Wis.
Printed and bound in the United States

ISBN: 978-1-6671-2303-5

For my dad,
who gave me the idea
for this book when I
graduated from college

ACKNOWLEDGEMENTS

To be honest, when I started this book, I thought it was going to fly out of me and onto the computer. And it did. At first. The first fifty pages were no sweat.

Then the pandemic hit, and plans changed. For most of 2020, I more or less gave up writing. I managed to hack out a rough screenplay and a short story, but those were the only things I finished. I had a number of setbacks professionally in 2020, as so many did. A bunch of disappointments. A lot of things felt like they were in limbo (some still are…).

It was a rough year.

However, writers are supposed to write, so I sat down and forced myself to write when I really felt like I couldn't, because that's the difference between a hobby and a profession. It took a lot out of me, but I got it done, and I'm glad I did. I love these two idiots, and I just want to tell more of their stories.

A number of people helped get this thing together, and I want to give a nod of the head to them. It is literally the least I can do.

First up: my dad. When I graduated from college in 1998, I left UW-Whitewater with a nearly useless undergrad degree, and I was struggling to find a decent-paying job. My dad told me to sit down and write a murder mystery that took place around a Division 3 football team. I gave it a few tries, but everything I came up with at the time was awful. However, that kernel of an idea stayed with me. It only took 23 years, but I finally did it.

While I'm giving thanks to my dad, I might as well tack on my mom and my sister. Also, my wife and daughter. They might not understand why I'm always typing, but they don't complain. Might as well thank the dog and two cats who bother me when I'm writing at home. The cats demand treats. Eddy demands belly rubs. Most of my existence and activities of the past pandemic year has been dictated by the comfort requirements of a somewhat needy 25-pound Heeler/Corgi mix.

Secondly, I'd like to give a big shout out to people who believed in these characters and helped get this book on the road: Ann, Wendy, Jack, Josh, Jena, Carrie, Emily, and a few others. You all know who you are.

Lastly, I'd like to thank you, the reader. Without you, I'm just shouting into darkness. Thanks for being a light in the distance. Thank you for all the reviews you wrote and the little notes you sent asking for more Abe & Duff.

It is much appreciated.

You have no idea.

Sun Prairie, Wis.
June 2021

Fourth and Wrong

1

SO THAT'S IT, then?" C.S. Duffy rubbed his eyes with his fingertips until he saw stars. "After all this time, this is the best we're going to do?" He could not hide the disappointment in his voice, not that he would have ever tried to hide his disappointment. Expressing disappointment was one of his favorite things to do. A light October rain was falling, more a thick, filmy mist that hung in the air like a curtain than actual falling droplets of water. Duff pulled the hood of his black Carhartt sweatshirt over his Milwaukee Brewers cap and buried his hands in the pouch-pocket at his paunchy belly. He heaved a sigh of defeat.

Aberforth Allard, taller and much thinner than Duff, put his hands on his hips and arched his back, stretching until something low in his spine popped. It was only mid-morning, but it had already been a long day, and he was feeling it in every muscle in his body. He flipped the collar of his jacket to keep the chilly mist off the back of his neck. His head was nearly bald, and what hadn't fallen out naturally was shorn as close to his scalp as possible without being razored smooth. He regarded his partner with an apologetic shrug. "That's it. All the days we've put into this, all the searching, and this is as good as it's going to get, I'm afraid. We have to act now." Abe's shoulders were slumped. His chin practically melted into his neck. He shrugged and sighed as well.

Duff shook his head. "Damn shame, if you ask me."

"You could always win the lottery or secure a patent or something, then maybe we could afford something better."

"Oh, sure. I have a few million-dollar ideas in my back pocket right next to my guaranteed-winner Powerball ticket. I just enjoy pretending to be poor for the constant anxiety and overwhelming hopelessness."

Standing before the pair was a dull red 2012 Toyota Sienna LE, almost seventy-thousand miles on the odometer; it was on special on the dealer's lot: $10,500. It was the best deal Abe had found in several weeks of searching. It was not glamorous, but it would suffice.

Duff thumped the back tire with the toe of his shoe. "It's not really the kind thing that single men should drive. We're going to look like total creepers, for sure."

The same thought had already passed through Abe's mind. "How will that be any different than normal?"

"Fair point." Duff beckoned the salesman to approach. The young man had been giving them space to discuss the purchase. "Minivans are the official vehicle of men who have given up, you know."

Abe shrugged. "I thought we gave up decades ago."

"Yeah, but now it's official."

The salesman, a young, round-faced guy who looked like he was about three months out of college ambled back to them. He rubbed his hands together nervously. "Did you make a decision then, gentlemen?"

Abe jabbed his chin, or lack thereof, at the Sienna. "This one, I guess. I suppose it will do."

The kid clapped his hands together and flashed a toothy smile. "Excellent choice, sir. Solid purchase. I have no doubt you'll be happy with this van. Let's go write it up." The salesman led them back into the dealership office. It smelled like new tires, factory plastic, and industrial cleaner with soaked-in overtones of burnt coffee. A forgettable pop song was playing at a barely audible volume on the overhead speakers. In the dull gray of the day, the fluorescent lights of the dealership were too bright, too white. They made everything look sickly beneath them.

As they walked toward the salesman's desk, Duff threw an arm over the kid's shoulder and pulled him close. "Eddie, can I call you Eddie?"

The salesman pointed to a swirl of cursive letters stitched high on the left breast of his dealership-branded polo shirt. "My name's Dalton."

"No, it's not; Dalton isn't a real name. I'm gonna call you Eddie. Is this the best price we can get on that little shitbox, there?"

"It's a fair price, sir. Kelley Blue Book value actually puts it at about a grand more than we're selling it, and this is a no-haggle dealership. We're just trying to move cars at a fair price."

Duff pointed at the Ford sign in the lot. "You're a Ford dealer."

"That's correct; we are."

Duff pointed at the Toyota. "Do you really want a nine-year-old rice-burner like that cluttering up your lot? I don't think you do. You want to move fine American steel. That chunk of ol' Nippon's most desirable is really saying that you don't trust your own product. *Hey, you don't like the Found On Roads Dead we got, then how about you rest your weary mind with something reliable like this Toyota?*"

Dalton frowned. "That's not how car sales work."

"It might be, Eddie. I think it just might be."

"Ten-five is a fair price." Abe grabbed his business partner by the forearm and pulled Duff away from the beleaguered salesman.

"How about you knock off five bills if we pay in cash."

"Ten-five is more than fair," Abe reiterated. Abe just wanted to get out of the dealership with a minimum of confrontation.

Duff scowled at his partner. "You're the worst negotiator ever."

"We need the car, Duff. We don't need to be banned from another sales lot."

Dalton looked perplexed. "You guys have been banned from a sales lot? Is that even possible?"

"Well, to be fair, I've been banned. Abe's probably still welcome." Duff let himself fall heavily into one of the chairs on the client side of Dalton's desk.

Abe gave Dalton a sympathetic nod. "Duff does not always know when to shut up."

"I'm an acquired taste."

"Like raw sewage," said Abe.

Dalton forced a painfully fake smile to his lips. "Well, I hope we don't have to do anything that drastic."

"An extra five bills off the top will keep me quiet, Dalton."

"I just can't do that, sir."

"Ignore him," said Abe. "Ten-five is fine. Write it up." Duff started to speak again, but Abe held up a finger. He spoke with a hard, no-nonsense tone that he only ever used on Duff. "Shut it, Duff."

Duff's mouth flapped closed. He mimed turning a key in a lock at the corner of his mouth and gave Abe a thumbs-up. Then he tilted his head back until he was staring at the ceiling and zoned out of the conversation.

"So, what do you guys do for work?" Dalton started copying down the information from Abe's driver's license onto the sales sheet.

"We run a small private investigations firm."

"Oh, like Hercule Poirot?"

"More like Jim Rockford," said Abe.

"Who?" Dalton's face wrinkled into a confused frown.

Duff's head snapped up, suddenly back in the conversation. "How the hell do you know Hercule Poirot and not Jim Rockford?"

Dalton looked shocked. He swallowed. "I saw that Kenneth Brannagh movie last year, the one with the train. I've never heard of Jim Rockford."

Duff groaned. "Christ, you're young. You've never heard of *The Rockford Files?*"

"Sorry."

"How about James Garner?"

Dalton shook his head again. "Sorry."

Abe chipped in, "He played the old man version of Noah in *The Notebook.*"

The light of comprehension popped into Dalton's eyes. "Oh, him. I know him. My girlfriend loves that movie."

Duff looked at his partner with disbelief. "How the hell do you know who starred in *The Notebook?*"

"I have a teenage daughter. I'm very familiar with the entirety of Ryan Gosling's canon whether I care to be or not."

Duff accepted this explanation. "Ah, yes. You get a pass, then. I was about to yank your man card."

Abe slumped into his seat. "I don't think I ever got issued my man card."

Duff and Abe were quiet for several moments while Dalton finished scribbling out the paperwork. Abe sat quietly trying to clear his mind and not worry about the substantial cashier's check he'd gotten from their bank this morning. It was a sizable dent in their business's meager savings to purchase this van, but they needed a car. They used to have a Volvo that was beaten down more than the Cleveland Browns, but it had met an ignoble end in a horrible car wreck two months ago. Since then, Duff had been largely laid up with pins in his ankle from a break he'd suffered on the same night of the car accident unrelated to the crash. Abe had been taking public transportation or borrowing his ex-wife's Kia Soul when necessary, but the time had come for them to step back into a vehicle of their own. You can't be effective private eyes without some sort of transportation in Chicago. The El and the buses would only get you so far, and taxis and Ubers were not ideal when trying to maintain a low profile.

Abe glanced at his partner out of the corner of his eye. Duff's eyes were darting from object to object, taking in the little knick-knacks on Dalton's desk. Abe knew what he was doing. Duff was looking for something to use to know the kid better, to possibly damage the kid. That's how Duff worked. His powers of observation were scary. He could size someone up at a distance and give them a Sherlock Holmes-esque dressing

down that would leave them reeling. Like Holmes, Duff usually used his powers for good, but he had no qualms about upsetting someone's personal apple cart for no reason. It was never done maliciously; it was just born from Duff's own lack of personal awareness and social skills.

Abe lifted his index finger to his lips and shook his head slightly. Don't say it, he silently implored his partner.

Duff responded by jabbing two fingers at his eyes and then pointing those fingers at the photographs mounted on Dalton's cubicle wall. Abe's eyes followed Duff's fingers and saw what his partner saw. Like his partner, Abe was no slouch when it came to powers of observation. Abe's resume was padded with a B.A. with a double-major in Criminal Psych and Pre-Law. In his CrimPsy classes, he developed an easy affinity for reading people by their posture, their expressions, their movements. His own observational abilities complimented Duff's logical puzzle-piece methods in that Abe understood relational complexities between humans very easily, except when it came to him personally. With anything having to do with him, Abe was utterly clueless and unable to see the forest for the trees. With other people, he was a marksman of subtext and personal peccadilloes.

In several of the photos at which Duff pointed, Dalton was standing with his arm around a pretty young woman. She looked to be Dalton's age. From Dalton's position, it was clear that he was in love with the girl. His round face was smiling with a genuine smile. His position was one of protection, of possession. The girl, on the other hand, was not reciprocating. She leaned away from him in each picture. It wasn't overt, though. It was a subtle posture, a tilt of the head, or slope of the shoulders. Her eyes were duller, less involved than Dalton's. To the average person, they might have looked like a lovely couple. For someone with the observational abilities of Duff and Abe, she might as well have been screaming for help. She did not want to be there. She was not in love with Dalton, not the way he loved her. To Abe, the photos made it clear that she was not making long-term plans to stay with Dalton.

Abe felt a familiar hollow in his stomach. It was the same sort of feeling he'd felt when he learned that his wife of nearly twenty years was a lesbian who had been hiding her true inclinations for the sake of their marriage and their daughter. Had Abe been objective, an outside observer of his marriage, he would have seen it years before. Since he was emotionally involved, his observational powers had been dampened by his love for the mother of his child and he had not seen the hammer dropping. Now, as he looked at the pictures of Dalton and his girlfriend, he saw the same expression that Katherine had in a lot of their old photos, a lot of the same body posture. Katherine loved Abe platonically, of course. They were good friends,

perhaps best friends. She was just not attracted to him sexually, and she never had been. The same postures and facial expressions were present in the girl in the photos hanging on the walls of Dalton's cubical.

Duff, seeing Abe had come to the same conclusion as he had, cleared his throat, and prepared to inform Dalton his relationship was over, even if he didn't know it. Abe shot Duff a death glare and gave a quick shake of his head. It was not their place to ruin this guy's life. Duff snorted and folded his arms across his chest petulantly.

Dalton, completely unaware of his customers' silent actions and glances, finished writing the write-up sheet and smiled at them. "I'll just take this up to management and get them to check off on it, then we'll get you through the business office in two shakes of a lamb's tail. Did you need to finance this vehicle?"

Abe shook his head. He pulled out a folded check from the breast pocket of his maroon polo shirt. "I took the liberty of getting a cashier's check earlier today. This should cover the purchase price, tax, title, and license."

Dalton glanced at the check and nodded. "It will, indeed. This should speed things along nicely." He nodded his head at the investigators and walked over to the closed-door office of his superiors to get the final stamp of approval on the sale. At this point in the proceedings, it was a perfunctory gesture.

Duff leaned over to Abe. "We gotta tell him."

"Not our circus, not our monkeys, Duff."

Duff snorted again. "*Puh-leese*. Remember how screwed up you were when Kath dropped her news on you? We're just saving this kid from that. He's still young. He's got a whole life ahead of him. You want him to go through what you went through? The rejection in bed? The constant feelings of being alone even when he's with her? The depression?"

Abe hated being reminded of those days. No, that was a lie— he could never be reminded of those days because he could never forget those days to begin with. They were on a permanent loop in his head, the feelings of inadequacy, sadness, and fear. He hated when Duff was right about something. "Fine. We can mention it. But, let me do the talking, will you? You're as subtle as a bull moose."

Duff mimed locking an invisible lock at the corner of his mouth again.

When Dalton came back, he had a signed contract, a guaranteed sale, and the finance department was already gathering up the necessary paperwork. The young salesman put the detail crew on stripping out the protective plastic and polishing up the interior of the car. "Everything looks great, fellas. We'll have you up and out of here and on the road in no time."

"That's great, just great." Abe licked his lips and cleared his throat. "Hey, uh, Dalton? Can I bring up something sort of personal with you?"

"Sure, Mr. Allard, whatever you like." Dalton settled himself into his desk chair and laced his fingers over his stomach. "What can I do for you?"

"Please, call me Abe." Abe paused. There was no easy way to say it. As much as he didn't want to do it, he was about to shatter this boy's world. "Uh, my partner and I noticed your photographs on that wall next to you."

"Oh, yeah?" Dalton sat up in his chair, a big smile spreading across his face. "That's Caroline. These were taken at an End-of-Summer Party a friend of ours threw a couple of weeks ago."

"Fiancée?"

Dalton shook his head. "Not yet, no. I think we're headed in that direction, though."

Duff could not stop himself. "Think again, big guy."

Dalton's left eyebrow arched. "What?"

Abe slapped Duff in the chest with the back of his hand. "What my idiot friend is trying to say is that I'm a specialist in reading body language. It's pretty clear from your photos your gal isn't really into you. I'm sorry to be the bearer of bad news."

"Say what? That's… What?" Dalton looked like he was stuck in the corner of the ring during a heavyweight fight. He was confused and reeling.

Abe pressed the situation even though it pained him to do it. "Let me guess: You barely have sex anymore, right? You tell yourself it's because you're both tired, but it's not. Not really."

The kid was red in the face, eyes large. "How? What?"

"You don't really talk anymore, do you? It's all Netflix and then passing out on the couch, right? Is she making excuses for everything? Has she said that it's not you, it's her?"

"She...what? Mr. Allard, I don't understand what you're saying."

"Jesus. Call him Abe, first off. Mr. Allard sounds so uptight." Duff waded into the fray with all the grace of a hippo ballet. "What my esteemed compadre is insinuating is your girl has already mentally checked out of the relationship. She's moved on. She's finding someone else. She just hasn't told you, yet."

The kid was rocked. His eyes were rolling their sockets. He looked like a stiff wind would knock him down.

"I only bring it up because I was there not long ago." Abe pulled out his wallet and produced the last picture he and Katherine took together before she came to terms with her sexuality. He had been meaning to throw the picture out, but he could not bring himself to do it. In the photo, Katherine had the exact same look on her face Caroline did in Dalton's photos. Her

body posture was similar, as well. Abe flipped the picture to Dalton's desk. "This is just before my wife of nearly two decades figured out she was a closeted lesbian. Notice anything familiar in her pose?"

Dalton picked up the photo. He compared it to the ones on the wall. "Caroline is a lesbian?"

Abe shrugged. "Maybe. Maybe not. I couldn't tell you that. I can just tell you that she's ready to move on from you."

A secretary walked up to the cubicle at that moment. "Mr. Allard? We have all the paperwork ready for you to sign if you'd care to follow me to the finance office."

Abe and Duff stood. Abe took his photo from Dalton and returned it to his wallet. "Just think about it for a while. It's a hard thing to admit, but it's better to learn it while you still have time to live a different life. Believe me, I know."

Abe and Duff followed the secretary to the office. The finance guy was a trim, fit, middle-aged man whose biceps strained the material on the sleeves of his polo shirt. His hair was gelled to perfection and his smile was gleaming white and well-veneered. He walked Abe through all the paperwork, and Abe signed everything he was told to sign. After ten painless minutes of paperwork, the finance guy handed Abe the two sets of keys. He shook hands with Abe and Duff, thanking them profusely for their business. "Enjoy the van!"

"Not likely," said Duff.

"I'm sure it will be fine," said Abe. "Thank you."

When they walked back out to bid farewell to Dalton, the kid was slumped in his chair. Any sense of pride or bravado he'd had earlier in the day was gone. He was a hollow-eyed shell of a man.

"Everything okay, Dalton?" Abe kept his voice low. He already knew what transpired while they were signing the papers.

Dalton was stunned. "You were right. I called her, confronted her, and she broke down crying. She said she's been sleeping with some guy in her office for months, and she thinks she's in love with him."

Abe felt a familiar pain in his chest. He patted the kid's forearm. "I'm sorry, Dalton."

"Yeah. Tough break, kid. You deserved better."

Dalton was silent for a moment. "Thanks... thanks, to both of you. I wouldn't have seen it coming. I didn't see it coming."

"Go out, get stupid drunk with some close friends, and then realize that there are a lot of fish out there. That's all I can tell you," said Abe.

"Is that what you did?"

"No. I don't really drink."

"Did you find another fish?"

Abe shook his head sadly. "I think my fishing days are long past. And I was never a good fisherman, anyhow. You're still young enough to cast another line."

Abe and Duff walked away from the kid leaving him to stew in sad silence. When they were out of earshot, Duff leaned toward his partner. "I'm impressed with your fishing metaphors. I didn't think you knew enough about fishing to string those together."

"I sometimes watch the Outdoorsman Channel on TV. I've seen fishing."

"You like fly fishing?"

"Who fishes for flies? You fish for fish."

Duff thumped Abe on the back. "There's my guy."

The van was waiting for them in the lot. It was usually a tradition for the salesman to follow them out and give them a final walk-through of the vehicle, but Abe knew Dalton was in no shape to do his job. Besides, it was still chilly and misty, and there was no need for that poor kid to get wet for their sake.

They walked to the Sienna and climbed in, shutting the doors and silencing the din of traffic outside the dealership. A light patter of rain drummed a steady cadence on the roof. "You nicknamed the Volvo. What are you going to name this one?" Abe stuck the key in the ignition. The van jumped to life with a light turn. There was no sputtering or protest from the engine. Abe might be able to get used to that. The Volvo started like a Russian tank.

Duff sniffed the air. It smelled heavily of whatever cleansers the detailers used to spruce up the cloth seats and the faux leather of the dash. "I'm going to treat it like a military pilot call sign."

"How so?"

"I'm going to give the van a training name, something simple. When it earns a new name, I will change it."

"What name are you going to give it?"

"Not *The Pussy Wagon,* that's for sure. This thing is the vehicular equivalent of chemical castration."

"I don't think I could drive a vehicle called *The Pussy Wagon* in good conscience."

Duff thought for a moment, hand on his chin. Then, with a flourish, he decided. "To start, we shall call her *Rose,* as in rose-colored glasses. Get it? Because she's red. We're going to be overly optimistic about the quality of this beast until she's off the lot a while and shows us her true nature. When we find out what sort of shitbox she really is, I'll gloss her with her true

name."

"*Rose* it is. For now." Abe angled the van off the lot. It drove differently than the old Volvo did. There was a lot more rocking. The bucket seats rode high and made him feel less stable.

"I still can't believe we're in a minivan," said Duff. "So uncool."

"Cool was never part of our game."

"Still. This is a whole new level of uncool for us. We'll never get chicks in a ride like this."

"We could never get chicks before, either."

"And would we really want to, anyhow? Drive on, MacDuff."

THE DEALERSHIP WAS only a few blocks from their office. Abe thought about taking a considerable detour to get a feel for the new vehicle but decided against it. He'd drive it later when Duff wasn't next to him to annoy him with a steady stream of acid-tongued observances about people on the street. Testing cars around the small streets in Chicago was always tough. He'd taken the van on the highway for too brief a moment to see how it handled at speed, but he needed more practice. The Sienna was boxy, and it felt tippy. The Volvo had been a rattletrap of a tank, grinding low to the ground and heavy-bodied. The van was more elegant but was going to be a while before Abe felt completely comfortable driving it.

Abe pulled into a spot on the street next to the apartment complex that housed their office. He killed the engine. "Feels kind of nice to be in a sorta-new vehicle again."

At that moment, a large green city works pickup truck came from behind them on the street. The truck's extended passenger-side rearview mirror clipped the minivan's driver-side rearview mirror snapping it off cleanly and launching it thirty yards down the road in a tight spiral. If the driver of the truck noticed, he didn't care. He didn't stop. He quickly hung the next corner on squealing tires and vanished from view.

Duff patted the roof of the van by the passenger door. "Perfect. Now it looks more like our car."

Abe was heartsick over not being able to keep a vehicle looking decent for more than ten minutes, but Duff was right. The old Volvo, which Duff had called *The Fucking Embarrassment,* had been a cranky, touchy heap of mismatched, rusty panels and broken parts, scars earned from two decades of Chicago winters and repairs made with spit, bondo, and prayer. A minivan missing a mirror was par for the course. Abe sighed and put the keys in his pocket. He left the mirror on the road. Why even bother with it? "At least it looked new for a couple minutes, at least."

"So did you, once. Nothing to be done about it now." Duff clapped Abe on the shoulder. "C'mon, I'll buy you a taco."

"Gonna need at least two to bury this sting."

"Two it is."

The office of Allard and Duffy Investigations was on the second story of an apartment complex. It was technically a one-bedroom apartment that was not zoned for a business, but since Abe and Duff had been there for twenty years and never missed a rent payment, the building manager looked the other way. On the first floor of the building was a couple of commercial spots, including a taquería called El Muro that subsisted largely on Abe and Duff's daily patronage. Cesar Salazar, the portly owner of the shop, had known the boys since they hung out their shingle. He credited Duff's purchases alone with helping him put his oldest daughter through college at Notre Dame.

Cesar was working the window when they walked up. He shot the duo a big smile. "Heya, fellas. How goes the gumshoeing?"

"Another day, another lack of a dollar, amigo." Duff stepped up to the window. "Dos al pastor, and dos asada, por favor."

"You got it, boss," Cesar called out the order to one of the guys working the grill. "Drinks today?"

"Lime Jarritos for Abe. I'll take a fruit punch."

"Done deal." Cesar didn't bother to tell Duff the total. Duff knew the total. Hell, Duff could have worked the grill and made his own food by now. Duff handed Cesar a twenty, and the shop proprietor handed over the change. He propped two ice-cold glass bottles of Mexican soda on the counter. The tacos were served up a second later, steaming hot with onions, cilantro, and salsa verde on top, a lime wedge on the side. "You guys take 'er easy, eh? And if she's easy, take 'er twice!"

"Always." Duff and Cesar bumped knuckles, and Duff started to walk away.

"Oh, hey. I almost forgot." Cesar called them back. "There was a dude here looking for you a little while ago. I think he might have left."

"What kind of dude?" Abe asked.

"Big sumbitch. Gringo. Tall, blonde, looked like a fuggin' lumberjack, eh?"

Duff and Abe exchanged a worried glance. In their line of work, a big sumbitch was often someone who was angry about something that they had a hand in recently. It also meant that the big sumbitch was likely to attempt to loosen their teeth with his fist. Duff scratched at his jaw, still feeling the punch from the last time that happened. "Did we bust anyone cheating in their marriage lately?"

Abe shook his head. "Haven't done that since last year."

"Anyone we busted get out of jail recently?"

"Maybe." Abe glanced nervously at the portal that led to the second floor. There was no door, just an archway where a door once stood. In the twenty years they had rented that office there had never been a door. It made the hallway very cold in the winter. "Did he go upstairs?"

Cesar shrugged. "Maybe. I didn't see. He didn't buy no tacos, so fuck him."

Abe took a bite of one of his asada tacos. "Well, if you hear gunshots in a second, call the police."

"You got it, boss." Cesar made a finger-gun and clicked the hammer at Abe.

Duff and Abe walked toward the door. Duff shoved the second half of his first taco in his mouth. Through a mouthful of al pastor he said, "Let me go first. I'll be your meat-shield."

"That's a pleasant thought." Abe let Duff enter the stairwell first. Just as Cesar said, there was a tall, broad-shouldered man standing at the door to their office at the top of the stairs.

With the hallway light behind him, his face was bathed in shadow. He was wearing well-worn jeans and a flannel shirt, heavy leather work boots on his feet. His hands hung easily at his sides. They were empty, which was a good sign, but they were huge. The fingers were thick and calloused, a working man's hands. The man's frame filled the narrow hallway.

Abe swallowed hard. The bite of taco he'd been chewing felt like a stone in his throat. "Are you waiting for us, sir?"

The man said nothing.

Duff took a couple of gimpy steps up the stairs favoring his still-healing ankle. "We're Allard and Duffy if you're looking for an investigator. If not, I suggest you move on, pal."

The man spoke with a voice like a distant rumble of thunder. "Hello, Clive."

Duff froze. The man had known his given name. He didn't like that. It meant the man knew him. He craned his neck to the side and looked hard at the lumberjack in the hall.

The man, realizing that he was in shadow, took a step back. As he did, the ambient light washed his face. A broad chin, slightly chubby cheeks, and a pronounced brow. His eyes were small and intense. He had a good head of hair, blond and thick. He looked to be middle-aged, mid-forties like Abe and Duff, or maybe early fifties if he was aging well.

"Abe?" Duff did not move. He kept his eyes trained on the man at the top of the stairs.

"Yes, Duff?"
"Go get my gun, please."
"Why?"
"Because I'm 'bout to shoot this motherfucker in the goddamn face."

2

THE MAN AT the office door offered Duff a sad smile as if he expected that comment. "I wondered if you would remember me."

"I remember everything," Duff said indignantly. "Whether I want to or not, I remember everything. Always. Believe me, Hank, if I could permanently purge your shitty face and every last thing about you from my memory, I would. I'd do it in a heartbeat."

Abe cleared his throat. He'd not seen that level of agitation in Duff in a long time. At least, not since Taco Bell discontinued the Mexican Pizza. "Old friend of yours, Duff?"

Duff shook his head. "Not by a long shot. His name is Henry Novak. This is the prick who used to beat the shit out of me on a daily basis at Bensonhurst."

"Oh." It was all Abe could say. Duff did not talk about Bensonhurst much, and sometimes Abe thought Duff might have thought of the place as something that all kids had to endure, even though he was in a very rare circumstance. When Duff was thirteen, he'd found his best friend— only friend, really— and her parents murdered in their home. It was a seemingly random murder, and the police, according to Duff, badly botched the investigation to the point where there was never a suspect and the investigation quickly ground to a stone-cold halt. Duff's obsessive-compulsive disorder flared, and he spent nearly every second of the next year trying to solve the crime to the point where he could not focus on anything else, and the situation derailed his promising academic career. His

parents had him committed to a psychiatric hospital for teens somewhere out in the backwoods near Timmons, Ontario, Canada for several years in order to get a handle on his illness. He never completely got over the murder which remained unsolved to that day, and he never forgave his parents.

"I owe you a huge apology for that," said Novak. "I was an out-of-control teenager with rage issues. That's why I was in Bensonhurst. My parents couldn't contain me. I'd gotten kicked out of three school districts and been arrested a dozen times. I had a lot of pent-up anger, but that is no excuse for how I treated you. If it helps at all, the people at Bensonhurst eventually helped cure me. I'm a different person now. Honestly. I am truly sorry for how I treated you. I wish I could take it all back."

"Save the apology for someone who cares." Duff walked up the stairs and keyed the door to the office. "Then, go to hell. Tell the devil I said hello. Remind him that he owes me six bucks."

Abe followed his partner into the office. "Nice meeting you, Mr. Novak." Abe started to close the door to their office apartment, but Novak stuck out his foot to stop it. Abe opened the door wider.

Novak was contrite. If he'd had a hat, it no doubt would have been in his hands. "That apology is long overdue. I wish I could do more than an apology. I don't expect forgiveness. I don't want to erase the past. I was an asshole then, and I deserve your scorn for what I did. However, I'm not that stupid, messed-up kid anymore. I need you to know that, to believe it. I came here because I need your help."

"Take a number. Everyone needs our help. I'm not a shrink, though. That's the kind of help you need." Duff strode across the small living room/office. He slumped into a well-worn chair and kicked his feet onto his desk. He stuffed half of his second taco into his face and chewed angrily staring daggers at Novak.

"Still stress-eating, I see." Novak chuckled uncomfortably. "This guy used to take all his commissary points and spend them on vanilla Zingers and Zebra Cakes. Then, he'd power-chow them whenever he got upset. I'm talking six-to-ten at a time, one after another. He didn't even seem to enjoy them. He just inhaled them."

"Sounds familiar," said Abe.

Duff scowled with pure hatred radiating from him in waves of intensity. If his eyes could have shot lasers at that moment, they would have burned off Novak's face. "Gee, I wonder why I would have had reasons to stress-eat, you dumbass. I still remember with vivid clarity that day you broke my orbital bone. Remember that? Do you have any idea how much pain that caused me? It hurt to fucking blink for weeks."

Novak held his hands out to his sides, palms out, and bowed his head in a penitent gesture. "I am sorry. Truly. I could prostrate myself before you and flagellate myself with a cat o' nine tails if that's what it would take for you to help me."

Duff considered this for a second. "It'd be a good start."

"How can we help you, Mr. Novak?" Abe was not getting any sense of deception or aggression from the man. He looked melancholy and compunctious. Whatever he had done in the past, he was currently projecting every indication that he was truly aggrieved of his actions. Abe offered the man the chair in front of his own desk. Duff snarled and finished his taco.

Novak accepted the chair. He lowered himself into it like a man who had not slept in days. His large, powerful frame seemed to melt into the cheap faux-leather. He was exhausted, defeated. He ran a hand through his hair and took a deep breath. "I don't know if you saw the news about the quarterback at the University of Wisconsin-Rockland who was murdered last week."

"Only what scrolled across the bottom of the morning news." Abe really had only seen a headline. Nothing else. Wisconsin and Illinois did not share too much between newsfeeds, but a young athlete being murdered on a college campus was a big story. Abe settled into his own desk chair. He picked up a legal pad and a pen and poised to start writing. He did not need to take notes. His memory was more than adequate to listen to a client and absorb all he needed, but he found that taking notes helped clients feel more respected and made them share more.

Novak was silent for a moment. Then he swallowed hard. "Well, my daughter was the girl who was arrested and charged with that young man's murder."

"Apples don't fall far from trees, I guess." Duff did not try to hide the venom in his tone.

Novak shook his head. "You've got her wrong, Clive—"

"Duffy," Duff corrected him. "I will only answer to Duff or Duffy. Nothing else. Never call me Clive again."

Novak accepted the criticism with grace. "As you wish, Duffy. My apologies." He reset himself. "Sarah is a good girl. She's sweet. She's kind. She loves puppies and kittens. She wants to be a pediatric nurse. She is incapable of murder. She's not like I was, never has been. She's like her mother."

Abe stepped in to play peacemaker. "Why would the police arrest her, then?"

"She had been seeing Nate Riegert, they had an on-again/off-again

relationship and had just broken up again, and her cell phone was found at the crime scene."

"So, she had motive and something that pins her at the scene of the crime. Do they have any evidence other than the phone?"

"Nothing concrete. Nate was bludgeoned with a plate from a set of weights. One shot that crushed his spine where it met the skull. As I understand it, there were too many fingerprints on the plate to get a clean impression. The lawyer she was assigned from the state told me the police were testing hair fibers found on Nate's clothes, but they had only broken up two days prior to his murder. Her hair is most likely on his clothes."

"Sounds like she's screwed." Duff was sitting up in his chair suddenly interested. This was not uncommon for him. He loved puzzles as much as he detested most of humanity.

A single tear welled into the corner of Novak's right eye. "That's my fear. You know how juries are. If police tell them that someone was the only person to have committed the crime, they convict regardless of evidence or a lack of evidence. I'm scared her whole life is about to be ruined for something she didn't do."

"Any other solid evidence? There have to be some security cameras somewhere."

"There are, but I'm told they neither confirm nor deny her presence at the football team's facilities on the night of the murder." Novak swiped at his eye with the back of his wrist. "My little girl didn't do this. She's being held at the county lock-up and was not permitted bail for the time being. The detectives in the county sheriff's department think it's open and shut. They're saying she could get twenty years, maybe thirty. She's eighteen. That's her youth. That's her time to have children. I'm scared shitless over here."

"You want us to find the real killer?" Abe offered a box of tissues to Novak.

Novak refused the tissue with a small wave of his hand. He used the back of his wrist to swipe the tears welling in his eyes. "Yes, please. I've followed your career for the last couple of years, Duff. I'd almost forgotten about you until you solved that murder in Green Bay a couple of years ago. Once I saw your name in the papers, I've paid attention to your career down here. I'm glad things worked out for you."

Duff gestured at the lousy little slum sublet of an office/apartment around them that was, for all intents and purposes, the full extent of Allard & Duff Private Investigations. "Oh, yeah. Worked out real well, as you can tell. Got a Lamborghini in the garage, too."

Novak's cheeks flushed red. "I just meant—"

Duff waved him off. "I don't give a shit what you meant."

Novak swallowed and coughed. He tried to regroup. "Yes, well. I'm doing okay for myself. I have a general contracting company up north, a lot of carpentry. I keep about twenty guys employed year-round doing framing, builds, remodels— that sort of thing. I've got decent funds. I would like to hire you two gentlemen to get my little girl clear of these accusations."

Duff did not hesitate. He popped his middle finger out at his old bully. "Sorry, our caseload is full."

Abe's eyes darted involuntarily to the small, framed picture of his own daughter's most recent school photo. Fifteen-year-old Matilda was a beautiful girl with a smile full of braces and a wild mane of red hair. She had her mother's features, and Abe was always grateful for that. He knew how he would feel if Tilda was in jail. "We'll do it."

Novak's face spun from Duff to Abe. "Really?"

Duff looked shocked. "I just said no."

Abe ignored his partner. "And I just said we're doing it." Abe turned back to Novak. "I have a daughter, too. I know I wouldn't want her in jail. We will help get her out. If she's innocent, at least."

Novak exhaled a shuddering breath. "Thank you, Mr. Allard. Really, I meant it." He stood up to shake Abe's hand. "Can you start right away?"

Abe looked at the clock. It was early afternoon. Even if they hustled, it was at least three hours to UW-Rockland, maybe four depending on traffic. The courts would be closed until the morning. He could probably get in to see the girl in jail if he took over her legal case. Abe shook Novak's hand. "We can."

"Do I get a say in this matter?" Duff stood, as well.

"No," said Abe. "Think about what you'd do if it was Tilda in her place."

Duff was silent for a moment. He swore under his breath and punched a stack of papers on his desk. "Fine. We'll do it."

Novak exhaled as if he'd been holding his breath since he entered the office. "Thank you. Thank you so much." Novak went to shake Duff's hand. Duff just stared at him coldly until Novak pulled his hand back. "Well, thank you, again."

"Will you be staying in Rockland, Mr. Novak?"

Novak turned back to Abe. "Yes. My wife and I are at the Super 8. Should I get you both a hotel room, as well?"

"Please," said Abe. "We'll be up there as soon as we can. Mr. Novak, I'll be taking over as Sarah's lawyer, as well."

"Really? You think that's a good idea?" Duff knew Abe had crippling stage fright in a courtroom; it was what kept him from being a lawyer in the

first place, despite easily passing the State Bar.

"If we can figure this case out quickly, I won't even have to go before a judge."

Duff played Devil's Advocate. "What if you do have to go before a judge?"

Abe's mouth gawped like a trout for a moment. He did not have a smart answer for his partner. "I guess we'll figure it out when we have to."

Duff flopped back in his chair. "Sure. We're good at winging things. Why bother having an actual plan, right? Can we at least charge this man for doing this, or are we going to do this pro bono like a couple of chumps?"

"I can pay," said Novak.

"A thousand a day, plus expenses," said Duff.

Novak nodded. "Cost is not an option."

Duff's lip curled angrily. "I should have said two grand."

"We'll meet you at the Super 8, Mr. Novak," said Abe. "We just need to pack."

Novak let himself out of the office. When the door clicked closed, Abe and Duff looked at each other. There was a horrible moment where Abe feared that Duff might get angry or shout. Abe did not like confrontations. Duff just shook his head. "I'm doing this for the girl, not him."

"That's all I need you to do."

"And I'm only going to do it because of Tilda. If you hadn't boned your wife without a condom sixteen years ago, I would've told him to hit the bricks."

Abe nodded. "I understand. He must have been very cruel to you."

Duff hesitated. He spoke in a low voice. "You have no idea. He used to punch me every day just because he could. When he'd flip into a rage, he'd lash out and pummel me. Broke my orbital bone when he hit me in the face with a chair." Duff tapped the bone near his eye with a finger. "Guy was a prick then, and I'm not convinced that he's not a prick now."

"People can change, Duff."

Duff huffed an angry breath through pursed lips, arms crossing defensively over his chest. "Then why haven't we?"

THE DRIVE TO Rockland, Wisconsin was pleasant. For the first time in twenty years, Abe was driving a car with a working air conditioner, even if the weather did not necessarily call for it. The van's shocks were still in decent shape, and there was almost no extraneous noise from the body. The joy of driving something that wasn't a complete hunk of junk almost made Abe forget the fact that the driver's side mirror was missing.

Duff read over what little information there was about the case from the newspapers. He read it aloud so Abe could process it as well.

The Chicago papers had precious little to go on outside of the barest facts of the case: Nathan Lee Riegert, 19, the sophomore starting quarterback for the UW-Rockland Owls, was found murdered in a corner of the football team's athletic facility, the back of his head cracked by a twenty-pound iron plate which lay nearby. A cell phone found at the scene of the crime belonged to Sarah Amelia Novak, the quarterback's ex-girlfriend with whom he'd had a public row with earlier that day. Sarah Novak was booked on suspicion of murder and was currently being held in the women's facility of the Waukesha County Jail.

Duff knew that jail well. Having grown up in the City of Waukesha, he had hounded the Waukesha Sheriff's Department for months after Becca Sigrud's murder. The cops had gotten so tired of him pestering them they arrested him for trespassing, disorderly conduct, and being a public nuisance a few times. That was part of the reason that Duff's parents sent him to the Middle-of-Fucking-Nowhere, Canada. Out of sight, out of mind.

Duff looked up the quarterback's stats on the Wisconsin Interscholastic Athletic Conference website. The school had only played five games before he met his untimely demise. Duff checked his quarterback rating, his total yards, touchdowns, and interceptions. He let out a low whistle. "Holy shit."

Abe did not take his eyes from the road. "Good news?"

"Great news. This kid was shredding the WIAC. Like, unholy shredding."

"What does that mean?" Abe did not follow any sports. Without a father in his life while he was growing up, sports never became a point of interest. He knew only the most basic aspects of all sports. Any football jargon beyond "touchdown" was a mystery to him.

"I mean he was slinging the ball all over the yard."

"I assume that's a good thing."

"With stats like this, it's a great thing. This kid should have been in D-1 if he's this good." Duff scrolled down a list of the late quarterback's achievements. "In five games, he's thrown for twenty-three hundred yards and change, fourteen touchdowns, no interceptions, and he's got a completion rate of better than eighty percent. He rushed for another buck-fifty and four touchdowns. This kid is unreal."

"Unreal is good." Thanks to having a teenager, Abe was not entirely slang-deficient.

"Unreal is great. This kid was a human highlight machine." Duff kept scrolling and summarizing the article. "Apparently, he went to a really small high school up north that didn't have a football program because they did

not have enough kids in the school to play. He was recruited to UW-Rockland as a baseball pitcher but looked into walking onto the football team last spring. The coach was impressed with his arm, his poise, and knowledge of the game."

"Is this unusual?"

"Highly. Kid like this, if he'd played football in high school like he's playing in Division Three, he would have been recruited for any number of upper-division schools. The Wisconsin Badgers would have been salivating for a kid who could rack up numbers like this kid could. In D-3, a QB like this would pretty much guarantee you a trip to the Stagg Bowl."

"What's that?"

"It's the championship game for Division Three schools. Try to keep up, Abe." Duff tried to find more information about the victim, but only found a few old articles from the kid's hometown newspaper about his pitching skills. "I guess he was a solid baseball player, but not a superstar, maybe a future minor-leaguer, at best." Duff found a point of information in one of the articles and let out an envious groan. "Oh, man. His nickname in high school was *The Rocket*. Nate 'The Rocket' Riegert. I always wanted a cool nickname like that."

"Duff is a nickname. So is Abe."

"I know, but they're not cool. Like, we should get some badass nicknames. I should be something like Hawk or Iceman, and you could be Vulcan."

Abe's face wrinkled involuntarily. "I don't think anyone in their right mind would ever call me Vulcan."

Duff fluttered his eyelashes at Abe. "I would."

"I stand by what I said: No one in their right mind would call me that. I don't think I could call you Hawk, either. That sounds like the nickname of someone who could do at least two push-ups in a row, and you don't qualify."

"Technicalities."

THEY PULLED INTO the parking lot of the Super 8 in Rockland, Wisconsin three hours and a handful of minutes after they left the office in Chicago. They might have made it in under three if traffic had cooperated, but given that it was Chicago, the traffic never really cooperated.

The new minivan performed admirably for its maiden run as Abe's new vehicle. By the time he wheeled it into a parking space at the hotel, it felt like he'd been driving it for weeks, not hours. Duff seemed to be enjoying his new arrangement in the shotgun-spot, as well. The seat reclined almost flat,

the glove box was much bigger than it had been in the old Volvo, and he'd praised the center console between them for its drink holder depth.

The parking lot of the hotel was nearly empty. There were a couple of nondescript sedans occupying a few spaces, a battered Dodge Neon straight out of 1998 that was clearly begging for euthanasia, and a Chevy 2500 diesel laden with the contractor package in the bed, a steel monstrosity with doors and drawers for holding tools and a ladder-rack laden with ladders on the top. The doors were wrapped with a shingle that said "Novak Builders, LLC" and displayed a website URL and phone number beneath it. A fancy hand-painted script along the rear quarter-panels on both sides of the truck bed said, *Building Your Dreams and Beyond.*

"How can someone build beyond your dreams? That doesn't make sense. *Building Your Dreams* is a pretty sketchy statement to begin with. Can he build the dream where I got attacked by a twenty-foot Kathy Ireland, but she had crab-claws for hands, yet gave a strangely sensuous massage with them?" Duff stepped out of the van. He reached back and dragged his old Milwaukee Brewers duffel bag out of the middle seat of the van. The old vinyl bag was the same baby blue as the club's 1978 uniforms, and it was duct-taped heavily along every seam. The M/B ball-in-glove logo was almost faded away completely. The bag was the same one Duff had used to take a few meager belongs with him to Bensonhurst when he was fifteen. Abe had pleaded with him to get rid of it a few times, even buying him a brand-new Brewers bag as a birthday present a few years ago, but Duff refused.

"I don't know. Maybe he just means he over-delivers on his promises." Abe pulled his own luggage out of the car, a simple black Protégé hardsider with an extendable handle and little wheels on the bottom that never rolled properly unless the surface was perfectly flat and smooth. Thirty bucks at Walmart.

"Like what? You wanted a desk with a drawer, and he's like, *'No, wait! I gave you two drawers!'* Dream big, I guess."

A thin woman in a large white shawl-collar sweater and jeans emerged from the hotel. She wrapped the sweater tightly around her frame and trotted over to Abe and Duff. "Are you the detectives Henry hired?"

Abe pulled a business card from his shirt pocket. "Allard and Duffy Investigations, at your service."

The woman took the card. "I'm Maggie Novak, Henry's wife. It's very nice to meet you."

Abe took a good look at the lady before him. Even wracked with sadness and worry as she was at the moment, she was beautiful. Her mouth was stretched into a thin line, and it looked like she was fighting to hold back

tears. Her eyes and cheeks showed the wear-and-tear that many crying jags over the last few days could do. "It's nice to meet you, as well. I have a daughter almost the same age as yours. I'd like to do what I can to help."

"Henry told me to rent you a room. The hotel is going through a remodel at the moment, so they don't have a lot available."

"I'm sure we won't complain about whatever it is we get," said Abe. He pointed at his partner. "This is Duff."

Maggie looked confused for a moment. "Duff Duffy?"

"Just Duff," said Duff. "Or Duffy if you must. No mister."

She held out a hand to Duff. "It's nice to finally meet you. Henry has spoken of you occasionally over the years. You must have made a big impression on him."

"He made a lot of impressions on me." Duff ignored her hand. "Mostly on my face with his fist."

Cheeks reddening slightly, Maggie pulled back her hand. "I know. He's told me. And I'm sorry."

"For what? You weren't there. You couldn't have stopped him."

"I'm sorry for him. And for you. And for what you had to endure. Henry's been very honest with me from the beginning. I know about his issues as a teenager. He worked very hard to get past them. He still works very hard to get past them."

Duff, only slightly chastened, looked down at his toes. "Yeah, well. Thank you."

"I know it was difficult for you in Canada. I know that Henry made it worse for you." Maggie put a hand on Duff's shoulder. To Abe's surprise, Duff did not shrug her touch away. "I want you to know that Henry has spoken of you with nothing but admiration since I've known him. He has not spoken of you much, but every time he has, it was to speak of your intelligence, and how much he marveled at your brilliance. He said he did not know how to channel his amazement at how you remained so detached and intelligent in the school, so he lashed out."

"Or— alternate theory here— maybe he lashed out because he was a gigantic douchebag."

"Don't try to appeal to his softer side, Mrs. Novak. He doesn't have one." Abe picked up the extendable handle to his hardsider and started toward the hotel, bag bouncing behind him on the pavement. "Let me stow my bag, and then I'd like to get to the jail to speak with your daughter."

"Are you really a lawyer?" Maggie trotted after him.

"Licensed to practice in the quad-state area," said Duff. "But I would never call him a lawyer. That'd be an insult to both him and the profession."

Maggie led them to a room on the first floor. She gave them the plastic

keycards for the room. "Henry and I are next door if you need anything."

Abe keyed into the room. There was a single king-sized bed.

Maggie looked embarrassed. She bit her lip. "I'm sorry about the bed situation. This was all they had. I asked if they could bring another bed into the room, and they said they'd work on it."

Duff shrugged. "We've had worse, believe me." He pushed into the room and tossed his ratty duffel onto the bed. "I call right side. I also call Little Spoon."

Abe tried to assuage her. "I'm sure it will be fine. I will go see your daughter and let you know what I think."

"Do you think you can free her? They wouldn't give her a bond at her arraignment on Monday morning."

Abe hated this part. The parents were always certain their little angels had to be innocent. "No. And I don't know if I want to, yet. At this moment, all we have are the facts of the case, and they're pretty alarming. She might have done it. That's what I want to assess."

Maggie did not seem put-off by Abe's statement. Her face grew harder, and she straightened herself, drawing herself to her full height. "She did not kill anyone, Mr. Allard. My little girl won't even swat flies or squish spiders. She never even fought with her brother. There is no bigger pacifist on the planet."

"With all due respect, Mrs. Novak— even pacifists have emotions, and sometimes emotions can take someone by surprise."

Maggie's face fell, and that immediately made Abe feel guilty. He tried to take another tack. "I'm not saying she's guilty, either. It's just... questionable."

"People get framed for murder, don't they?" Maggie looked up at Abe with red-rimmed, but hopeful, eyes.

"Yes. Certainly. It's just... rare. It's hard to frame someone. It does not happen like it does on the TV shows. People try all the time, but hiding a trail is harder than successfully framing someone."

Duff piped up from the bed where he still lay spread out like a starfish. "Usually, if someone gets wrongly convicted for murder, it's a systemic breakdown or full conspiracy from the act, to the cops, to the prosecutor, to the judge, and quite frankly, your daughter is neither the correct gender nor skin color for that to happen."

"What does that mean?"

"It means that statistically if someone is going to be jailed for a crime they did not commit, they're a young, Black male. The courts usually favor pretty, young, white girls."

"They favor women in general," said Duff. "Women, on average, receive sentences sixty-three-percent shorter than the sentences for men who do for

the same crimes."

"That's horrible. And sexist. And racist." Maggie looked shocked.

"Facts cannot be sexist or racist. They are merely facts. They can be horrible, though. So, you're correct there."

Abe knew what Maggie was feeling. It was one of the reasons he first tried to become a lawyer, because he wanted to change things. It was also why he was not a practicing lawyer, because he quickly learned the system was set up the way it was for a reason, and nothing he could ever do would change it. He was not the main character in a Grisham novel; he was only a tiny, pointless cog in that horrible machine. "That's another reason I'm not a lawyer: the system is an untamable beast." He stepped into the room. "Get some rest, Mrs. Novak. I will go see Sarah. I'll give you a full report when I return."

Abe closed the door as politely as he could. "Well, as far as initial meetings go, I feel like that was a somewhere between the Hindenburg Disaster and Reichelt's parachute test off the Eiffel Tower."

"Hey, give Reichelt some credit— dude put his money where his mouth was."

"Are you going to wait here when I go to the jail?"

Duff sat up. "No way. I have things to do."

"You can't come into the room with me. You'd have to wait in the—"

"Hey, you do you, big boy. I have other things to do in Waukesha."

"Will I have to call Bensonhurst whenever you're done doing whatever it is you think you have to do?"

Duff shrugged. "Put 'em on your speed dial just in case."

THE COUNTY JAIL in Waukesha was a monument in government brown. It was long, low, and imposing, as jails are meant to be. It was strangely situated, though, lying just off West Moreland Boulevard in Waukesha, near a golf course and some suburban neighborhoods filled with duplexes and Little League ballfields. The county courthouse was in front, open and accessible to the public. The lock-up lay beyond it, housing the adult male and female lawbreakers of the county.

When Abe rolled up in the van, most of the parking lot was empty. It just after five, so most of the courthouse staff had cleared out for the night. There was an all-hours door where he could access the jail, after going through the usual barrage of checkpoints and metal detectors, of course.

Duff got out of the van and stretched. "Any questions?"

"Not yet. I just want to interview the girl, see if she's lying at all."

Behind the low, gray clouds that had peppered them with rain off-and-

on all day, the sun was already setting. Fall in Wisconsin did not screw around. Once the late summer suns of September disappeared, darkness tended to descend promptly at quitting time. Throughout the winter months, the whole state suffered a lack of Vitamin-D which most residents tried to remedy with cheese, brats, and beer. Particularly beer. And perhaps brandy, straight-up, if the Packers or Badgers were playing football like they had their heads up their asses which they did a little too often for most residents' tastes.

"What are you going to do?" Abe zipped up his coat. A chill wind was blowing.

"Stuff." Duff wore a thinly insulated, black Carhartt duck jacket over his black Carhartt sweatshirt. The jacket remained open, but he shoved his hands deep into the pockets of his coat and pushed them down to pull the coat together.

"Becky stuff?"

"Just stuff," Duff reiterated. "I can do stuff. I'm an adult."

"Only by the the strictest interpretation of the legal definition." Abe already saw the wheels turning his partner's head. He was hunting again. "Let her go, Duff." Abe knew that suggestion would fall on deaf ears. Duff would never let her go. She was his Quixotic fixation.

"I'll see you back at the hotel, eh?"

"How are you getting back to Rockland?"

"It's not that far. I can call an Uber or maybe hitchhike."

Abe's eyes narrowed. "Hitchhike? Did you not read the Gary Ridgeway biography like I told you to?"

Duff snorted and waved his partner off. "I read it. I'm almost six feet tall and three-hundred-and-way-too-many pounds. I'm not really fitting into most serial killers' victim profiles."

"Well, if you end up decapitated at the bottom of the river and someone is wearing a vest made out of your flesh, don't come crying to me."

"I'll put the lotion in the basket, buddy." Duff strolled away. No goodbyes. No see-you-laters. He just drifted into the pale golden lamplight along the sidewalk.

Abe watched him go. Abe knew that Duff was heading in the direction of his old childhood home, of Becky's old home— the scene of her murder. He also knew that whatever Duff was going to get into, it probably wouldn't be for the best. What could he do about Duff's obsession, though? Abe had been friends and business associates with Duff for twenty-two years. Working with Duff was actually a good warm-up for having a toddler, only the toddler threw fewer rage fits when her Legos didn't fit together properly.

Abe walked into the receiving area of the jail. The transition from the burgeoning dark to the sickly white fluorescent lights of the jail hurt his eyes. There was a large desk in the entry and a pair of large, locked doors next to a metal detector. The floor had two long, industrial carpet runners. A chubby, bored-looking middle-aged woman in a dark brown county sheriff's uniform was typing away on a computer at the front desk. She looked up at Abe with tired eyes and sighed. "Visiting hours are over. Come back tomorrow at ten."

Abe pulled his Wisconsin Bar card from his wallet. "I'm a lawyer. I was just hired by Sarah Novak's parents, and I'll be taking over her case as of now. I'd like to see her immediately."

"Did you clear this with the district attorney?"

"Not yet. I just got into town."

The woman, whose nameplate on her uniform read "Givens" shrugged and sighed. "You're the boss, I guess." Givens typed some things into her keyboard, made a few strategic clicks with a mouse, and printed a sheet from the laser printer behind her. She handed Abe a lanyard with a visitor's badge hanging from it. "Go to the metal detector. You know the routine."

Abe tossed his keys and wallet into the metal detector. He unthreaded his belt and kicked out of his loafers, added them to the bin. He passed through the metal detector successfully his first time and quickly put everything back on his person. The woman at the desk pressed a button and buzzed Abe into the entryway beyond the doors. Another clerk, a broad-shouldered young Latino man met him at the door. "I'm Officer Hendrix," he told Abe. "You a lawyer?"

"I am. Abe Allard."

The kid gave a short laugh. "Funny name. Did kids call you 'All Lard' when you were little?"

"They tried, but I was always underweight when I was young, so it didn't make sense."

"When I was in school, everyone called me 'Chicken Dick.' *Hendrix*—get it? 'Cause *drix* sounds like dicks, and hens are chickens."

"My condolences. I suppose it didn't help to point out that hens are female, and therefore never possess male genitalia."

"Nicknames like that aren't nicknames because they're factually accurate."

Hendrix led Abe to an interview room. It was painfully spare. No decorations. A small, square table, two chairs, and a video camera in one corner that oversaw the room. There was a second door to the rear of the little room, presumably that door led to the jail area. "These doors lock once you're inside. A guard will be outside this door when you want to leave. The

camera is video-only, no audio. It's just for safety. Any questions?"

"Nope. I just need my client."

"We're getting her. She'll be in restraints. That's not negotiable. She has to be cuffed. Her hands will be locked to that ring on her side of the table, too."

"Fine." Abe took a seat. He opened his coat slightly. "Thank you, Officer."

"You're welcome. I'll bring you a bottle of water." Hendrix shut the door behind him. There was a resounding click as the door closed and the safety lock engaged. The room fell into a heavy silence, walled off from the ambient noise of the jail.

Abe sat and waited, anxiety rising in his chest. He wasn't a lawyer. He was never a lawyer. It was one thing to pass the tests and know the material, it was another entirely to actually practice law, to be the guy who knew what to ask and when to ask it and how to phrase it. Abe was never that guy. When the spotlight was on him, he got tongue-tied. His ex-wife, Katherine, used to compare him to Austin Pendleton's performance as a badly stuttering legal eagle in *My Cousin Vinny*. Abe tried to reassure himself if he and Duff could do their jobs correctly, this whole case would be over quickly, and it would never go to trial. He would never have to stand before a judge and pretend to be something he was never able to be.

Keys jingled in the door opposite Abe and a stocky, blond, female correctional officer opened the door. She held the door open and nodded at someone around the corner of the door. A second later, Abe got his first look at Sarah Novak.

The girl was eighteen, but looked slightly younger, as so many young people did to Abe nowadays. She also looked sad and scared—wide eyes framed by mousy brown hair that hung on the sides of her face in limp, poorly-kept tendrils. She was dressed in the dull green oversized jail smocks all new inmates had to wear. It hung off her thin, petite frame like a scarecrow's frock. She had to hold the waist of the pants with her hand to keep them from falling around her thighs. She crept into the room with her head down, but face up, her shoulders hunched as though she expected someone to hit her at any moment. She stayed close to the wall.

The CO entered the room and attached the cuffs Sarah wore to the ring on the table. To Abe she said, "When you're done, just knock on that door." She pointed at the door they had just come through. "Someone will be outside at all times."

"Thank you." Abe tried to give the girl across from him a confident smile, but he doubted it was convincing. He wondered if the girl could sense the worry he felt.

The other door opened, and Hendrix came in with a bottle of Kirkland

water. He set it on the table. "Can I get you anything else?"

"No, thank you, Officer Hendrix."

Hendrix left without another word. The big steel door clicked shut behind him. It was just Abe and Sarah in a deadly silent room. Abe was struck by a wave of paternal fear, a desire to get that poor girl out of the room. He saw Matilda sitting across from him for the briefest of seconds. He could only imagine what Henry and Maggie Novak were going through.

Abe slid a business card to her across the table. "I'm Abe Allard. I'm a lawyer. Your parents hired me to get you out of here."

Sarah Novak's eyes immediately started leaking tears. "Can I leave now?"

Abe's heart broke. He could feel the fear radiating from her. "I'm afraid not. This is just an initial meeting, a fact-gathering mission. Since I'm taking over as your lawyer, I want you to know that I need you to be completely honest with me at all times. Nothing you say will ever be revealed to anyone, not even your parents. You have total confidentiality with me."

"That's what the public defender said, too."

"It's a standard practice in law. Courts cannot compel me to tell them anything you said. Neither can the cops. If you killed Nathan Riegert, you could tell me. I will still be legally bound to never reveal that fact, and to use everything in my power to get you acquitted of the crime."

Sarah immediately went into the defensive. Her eyes went wide and pleading. "I didn't! I didn't kill him! I would never kill him!" Her fragile emotional wall broke, and she burst into sobs burying her face in her hands. With a muffled breath, she whispered, "I loved him."

Abe's fatherly instinct almost overwhelmed him. He wanted to rush to her side, wrap her in his arms as he would have if it had been Matilda crying like that. He felt himself start to get out of his chair but forced himself to stay professional. He needed to be clear, be level. He ran through his own observational processes, going down the mental checklist that was second nature to him now. He looked at her posture. He watched her hands. He processed every moment he witnessed since she walked into the room. He ran through every glance, every gesture she made. He was looking for a chink in her armor. Liars, no matter how good they were, always gave hints, a bad poker player's tell. It was usually in the eyes. People can't control involuntary twitches in the eyes. It's also around the mouth, little microexpressions that belie the mask a liar tries to wear. Abe could always see them, even on practiced liars. On a naive, frightened eighteen-year-old, tells would stand out like semaphore flags.

Abe saw none. The body, her face, the crying— it was all authentic. She wasn't lying.

However, not telling a lie did not mean she was innocent. Abe had a degree in criminal psychology. He had more than twenty years of experience dealing with some of the most questionable elements of humanity. Abe knew the best liars were never aware they were lying. Trauma could create false memories. She might have killed Nate Riegert but buried the memory of it so deeply in her mind that she simply could not force herself to remember it. Abe needed her to talk, to open up to him. He needed to see more.

"Tell me about him." Abe pulled his little spiral-bound notebook from his pocket. He clicked his favorite Parker Jotter and poised it over the notebook.

Sarah's eyes would not stop leaking tears. It was not crying, per se, but more of an overflow of too many emotions fighting to be released at once. She was grieving Nate Riegert. She was scared of what might happen in the future. She was scared of being in jail at the present. She missed her parents. She wanted to leave the county lockup. In the span of a few days, her entire world had been yanked from her and she was sent spinning into a chaotic nightmare.

"I know it's difficult." Abe reached across the table and patted her hands. "But, I need to know what happened. Where were you that night, and how did your phone come to be at the murder scene?"

Sarah's lower lip was quivering at a hundred-and-twenty beats a minute. She bit into it with her upper teeth to steady it. She had bright, white teeth that lined up with the perfection that only several thousand dollars of orthodontia could grant. She squeezed her hands into tight fists and inhaled sharply through her nose. "Nate and I started dating pretty much the day I moved into the residence hall in mid-August. He was one of the football players volunteering their time to help carry things. He smiled at me. I smiled at him. Next thing I know, later that night he and I are making out in the lounge in the basement of the hall."

"He was a charmer, then."

"Charm. Looks. He had a great body. He was funny. I was flattered by his attention. I don't know." She hesitated. "You seriously can't tell my parents anything?"

"Lawyer-client privilege is absolute. You're over eighteen, so you're an adult. Not even a judge could force me to tell them something you haven't given me express permission to tell."

Sarah hesitated another moment, before launching back into her story. "I had broken up with a guy I was seeing back in Marinette because we were going to two different colleges, and we knew we weren't going to be able to stay faithful to each other. It felt really nice to find a new guy so quickly, you know?"

Abe didn't know, but he could guess. "Validation from the opposite sex feeds the ego. It builds confidence."

"Exactly. I felt like I was sexy and adult. Nate and I got physical quickly. Like, that first night I was in college, right? Don't tell my dad, whatever you do. I'm sure he thinks I'm still a virgin, but I started having sex when I was sixteen. There wasn't much else to do in my hometown other than get drunk and have sex."

Abe's mind could not help but flash to his almost-sixteen-year-old daughter and her boyfriend, Magnus. Were they physical? Would it matter if they were? Abe shuddered and put the thought out of his mind. He was not his daughter's overlord, he reminded himself.

Sarah's face darkened. "I thought Nate and I were on the same page, but it got messy. And stupid. We were both immature. He thought we were just hooking up, and I thought we were going to be exclusive. I'd see him flirting with some girl on campus and get angry. We'd fight. We'd end up having sex. He'd go back to flirting with other girls, so I'd flirt with other guys, making sure he saw me do it, trying to make him jealous. And it worked. It always worked. He'd get jealous, so we'd fight some more. And that always took us back to sex. He was living off-campus and had his own room, so there was always a place for us to do it. It wasn't healthy, but it was like we were trapped with each other."

"That's a recipe for a powder keg."

"It's a recipe for stupid." Sarah leaned forward to wipe her tear-stained cheeks on the back of her wrists. "I wish I'd just told him to go to hell and moved on."

Abe had to nudge her forward. "Now, take me to the day he was killed."

Sarah's jaw trembled for a moment. New tears sprung to her eyes. "It was Friday. We fought that afternoon, right before he went to football practice. They had a walk-through for Saturday's game."

"What did you fight about?"

"Nothing important. Just...stupid shit. I found out he was screwing some new girl, and he was acting like it was no big deal because I screwed some other guy two weeks ago."

Abe remembered college, but he did not remember the rampant sex. He knew it must have been going on, but he had been dating a deeply closeted lesbian whom he later married, so sex had not really been a major part of his agenda. Maybe that's why he finished college early, he thought. "And then what happened?"

"I went back to my room and drank half a bottle of vodka, cried, and passed out. I woke up when two cops barged into my room and put me in handcuffs. That's it. I swear."

"Your phone was found at the scene. How?"

Sarah's shoulders bounced in a shrug. "I don't know. I was literally unconscious from drinking. Someone could have come into my room and taken it. I don't remember locking the door that night."

"That's your whole story?"

Sarah looked exasperated. "It's the only story I have! I told it to the fucking cops. I told it to my parents on the phone. I drank half a bottle of vodka; I was lucky I didn't die. I mean, the cops gave me a breath test when they brought me in that night, and I was still at like a point-one-eight. I couldn't even form a coherent sentence that night."

That was an important point. It wasn't a fatal flaw in the police's version of the murder, but it might be something Abe could work at and winnow into something important. He could worry the edges of that fact and turn it into a gaping hole that would prevent the prosecution's case from holding water. "Well, let me ask you this, then: who else would have wanted Nate Riegert dead? Who else could have killed him?"

Sarah's eyes rolled, and she gave a petulant huff of breath. "I don't know. There were probably at least a dozen girls on campus who hated him. There was probably another dozen guys, at least. Maybe more. He was a player. He liked sex. He liked to sleep around."

"But this was at a college campus. Isn't that sort of thing pretty common?"

"Maybe. I don't know. I know that Nate made enemies pretty quickly. He could be super charming when he wanted to be, but he also had this weird aura about him, like he was better than everyone and they should kiss his ass for deigning to lower himself to our level."

"Anyone else?"

"I don't know. Nate kept his life pretty locked up. It was one of the things we argued about. I was an open book to him, willing to tell him anything he wanted to know, but when I tried to get answers from him, he wouldn't say anything."

"No one on the football team?"

"Maybe. Nate was a red-shirt last year. He took the starting spot from some senior who was supposed to start this year. Maybe that guy could have done it."

"Do you know his name?"

"Robbie Conroy."

"Anyone else?"

Sarah thought for a moment. "No. No, that's it."

Abe closed his notepad. "Thank you, Sarah. You've been very helpful."

"Can we go now? Are you getting me out of here?" Sarah's eyes opened

very wide. She looked hopeful.

Abe had to break her heart. "I can't do that. Not yet. You're stuck here for a while because it's a murder charge."

Sarah started crying again. "I hate it here. It smells so bad. It smells like people just piss on the floors. And the women here— they're horrible. They say the worst things, and they're so fucking stupid, and they're so mean."

"I know, I know." Abe fought with every fiber of his being not to sweep her into a hug. "It will be okay. I promise you my partner and I are working to get you out of here. It won't be much longer."

"I miss my mom."

"I know. I'll tell her that for you."

Sarah had to lean forward to wipe her tears again. "Will I see you again soon? They won't let my parents visit me in person. I have to see them through a window."

"I'll be back very soon. Tomorrow, possibly. I'll keep you apprised of what's going on out there."

"Can you bring me real food? The mess hall here is fucking disgusting."

"I'll see what I can do."

Sarah bit her lower lip and tried to put on a game face. "I hope you figure this out. I didn't do it. I know I didn't."

"I believe you." Abe stood and knocked on the door behind Sarah to signal for the guard.

"Are you saying that because you *really* believe me, or are you saying it because you're my lawyer and you have to?"

Abe saw no reason to doubt her. "I really believe you."

That response garnered Abe the tiniest of smiles, a slight upward twitch of a lip. "Thank you."

The stocky female correctional officer opened the door and entered the interview room. "You all done here?"

Abe nodded. "I think we are for now. Thank you."

The guard walked Sarah out of the room and the big, heavy door clicked shut with an ominous clank that seemed to linger in Abe's ears for several, long seconds.

Officer Hendrix opened the other door. "All good here, Mr. Lawyer?"

"As good as it gets, I suppose."

Abe tossed his visitor's badge on the counter and walked out of the courthouse to the new van. He wanted to see Matilda. No— he *needed* to see Matilda. He fished his phone out of his pocket. The battery was down to fifteen percent. He thumbed the icon for Facebook Messenger. He had three contacts in that list: Matilda, Katherine, and Duff. That was it. His social circle was painfully small.

The app took its time connecting, but after eight rings, Matilda answered. Her face took up most of the screen, but to one side of her head, Abe could see the kitchen of his former home behind her. Katherine was hunkered over the stove cooking while next to her the hulking form of Tilda's football-playing boyfriend, Magnus Veit, was eating carrots and dip and telling Katherine something. Abe could hear the low murmur of his voice but couldn't make out the words. Matilda's face lit up when she saw her father. "Hi, Daddy! Mom made a mountain of chicken alfredo. You and Duff want to come over and get some? There's garlic cheese bread, too."

Tilda was always trying to get Abe back to the house since the divorce. Abe stayed away, partly out of respect for Katherine and her newfound single life, and partly out of the fact that he still loved his ex-wife and knowing they could no longer be together caused him physical pain. "I'd love to, Tildy, but we're not actually in Chicago. We're up in Waukesha, Wisconsin at the moment working a case."

Tilda's right eyebrow arched when Abe said *Waukesha*. She knew the significance of that city to her uncle-by-proxy. "Is Duff okay?"

"He's fine."

"Is he going to relapse? Should Mom and I start looking at treatment facilities?"

"No." Abe paused and reconsidered that idea. "Maybe."

"You know how he gets."

"I do. Don't worry, I'll keep him grounded."

"Where is he? Is he in the car with you? Did you get a new car?" Tilda realized Abe was calling from a decidedly different vehicle.

"I did. It's a minivan."

"Are you and Duff adopting kids?"

Abe smiled. "Maybe."

"Mom says that a minivan is the official vehicle of giving up."

"Well, your mom knows I gave up years ago."

Tilda gave Abe a forced smile. She had handled her parents' divorce better than they had. It was a testament to her maturity and foresight. In many ways, she showed the shrewd, practical, analytical mind that made her father a good private investigator. "Well, the van looks nice. What color is it?"

"Red. And it's already missing a review mirror."

"Wouldn't be your car if it was pristine."

"That's a true enough statement." Abe's phone suddenly displayed a low battery warning. "Are you okay? Everything good with you and Magnus?"

Upon hearing his name, the broad-shouldered teen glanced over at Tilda. He waved. "Hi, Mr. Allard!"

Tilda smirked over her shoulder at her paramour. "I told you that you can call him Abe."

Abe said, "No, I like Mr. Allard. Stick with that."

Tilda's face filled the screen again. "Everything is fine with us. Why?"

"Duff and I are working on that case at UW-Rockland where the girl killed the football player." Abe felt sheepish suddenly. It felt like he was almost accusing Tilda of going down that same road.

"Oh, that case." Tilda was suddenly interested. "I've been reading about that. There's not a ton in the news, but it sounds like that guy who got murdered was going to be great."

"Duff said something about that. He said his stats were good."

"His stats were unreal. I've seen some rumors on Twitter that he was getting offers to play at some Power Five universities next year. He could have had three years playing in D-1."

"What's Power Five?"

"Every school is in a conference, right? The Power Five are the five biggest conferences in college athletics. You went to two different Big Ten schools, Dad. How do you not know this?"

"I was too busy earning a four-year degree in two-and-a-half years, I guess."

"Sure. Rub that in."

"Why does it matter than he might have been going to a Power Five school?"

Tilda rolled her eyes. Her father's inability to understand sports was a point of contention between them. "In college sports, if you play for one D-1 school and want to transfer to another one, you have to enter the transfer portal and wait a year to play. However, you can transfer from a D-3 school like UW-Rockland to a D-1 or D-2 school and play immediately. Basically, with stats like his, this Nate Riegert was going to be a big deal next year. Whatever school landed him would have an instant, big-play starter with possible NFL potential."

None of this meant anything to Abe, but he was glad Matilda was alert and alive. He would have listened to her talk about anything.

The screen on his phone suddenly went dark.

"Daddy? I can't see you." Matilda's voice still came out of the speaker for the moment.

"My battery is almost dead. I think it killed the camera to conserve energy."

"Oh, okay. Well, Mom almost has dinner ready. Do you want to say anything to her?"

Abe did, and then he didn't. He had nothing important to tell her, and

since their divorce he hated starting a conversation just because he missed her voice. It was all for the best, but the wounds were still bleeding. "No. Just tell her I say hello."

"I will."

"Tilda, I just want to let you know that I love you."

Abe waited for a response but got none. He looked at his phone. It was completely dead. Frustrated, Abe tossed it at the cup holders on the dash console. It missed and clattered to the rubber floor mat on the passenger side. Abe just let it lie there.

3

DUFF WALKED STEADILY down a familiar sidewalk in Waukesha. That's not entirely accurate; he limped more than actually walked. He should still be walking with a cane, but he hated that stupid stick. It made him feel ancient and infirm. Canes were for old guys in Florida who wore black socks with sandals and pulled their Bermuda shorts up to their nipples. Duff used it as little as he possibly could, and eventually just decided to cast it aside. It made his ankle hurt more, but at least he could bullshit himself into thinking he was still young. With the cane in hand, it was a lie he simply could not buy.

Despite having a body that looked like someone haphazardly stuffed sweatshirt and faded blue jeans with three hundred pounds of sentient liverwurst, Duff liked to walk. He did it often. As long as he was in the act of walking, he never felt the bone stress or joint pain that was commonplace to big men. When he stopped, it would flood into him, a nightmare of aches and pain no amount of Advil could cure. So, the logical plan was just to never stop walking. It had been easier prior to him blowing up his ankle by leaping out a second-story window back in August. Now, the pain was a constant and permanent reminder that he was, despite all his efforts not to be, an old man. It did not stop him from walking, though. It was just another pain he had to carry. He was used to it. What's another straw for the camel's back, anyhow?

The neighborhood he was in was older, filled with narrow, two-story homes that stood just far enough from the one next to it to fit in a single-lane driveway to the garage behind the house. The front yards were all

postage stamps. The oldest trees lining the street denoted a neighborhood which had been around for at least a hundred years. It looked like any other older neighborhood in Wisconsin, right down to the vehicles which lined the streets and perched in the driveways. There was a wide assortment of Fords and Chevys, all manner of trucks and plain-looking sedans. No leather seats or moon roofs in this neighborhood. All the vehicles were base package models. Nothing fancy. Blue-collar. Bought used, not new.

Duff had walked these streets before, many years ago when he was a kid. They had not changed. The boxy Ford Granadas and Chevy Impalas of Duff's youth had gone away, replaced by the much less impressive Focus and the sleeker, redesigned Impala, but the F-150s and Silverados were the same, just fancier. The streetlights glowed with the same pasty yellow light. They hummed the same locust-drone buzz they'd hummed when Abe was a kid. David St. Hubbins of Spinal Tap was right: "*The more things stay the same, the less it changes.*"

Duff had two stops to make that night. The first would be short. He paused in front of a house which looked like all the others on the street. A small porch on the front of the left side of the house, a big picture window on the first floor, right side. There was a glow from beyond the picture window. Dancing lights denoted the shifting colors of a television playing somewhere beyond the gauzy curtains that blocked any view of the people inside. A red Chevy Outlander minivan sat in the driveway of the house. A silver Hyundai Elantra was at the curb. The house was alive again. People were inside making it a home. That was good. It deserved to be a home.

The last time Duff had seen that house, he was trying to piece together the murder onto which he had unwittingly stumbled. Cursed with an excellent memory, every gory detail of the three bodies splayed out in the living room with bullet wounds to their heads haunted him. The dried blood in pools around the vacant, surprised, dead faces. Frozen forever and living permanently front-and-center in his waking brain were the piercing blue eyes of Becky Sigrud. She died with her eyes open. When Duff fetched the spare key to open their door because he *knew* something was wrong, she had been staring directly at the door with her dead eyes, her mouth in a look of shock, almost as if her corpse was imploring Duff to tell her what just happened. Almost every minute of every day, that image of her face popped into Duff's mind unbidden. Like the pain in his ankle, he carried that image, too. All things considered, it was impressive Duff had not drunk himself into catatonia on a daily basis since then.

Duff did not linger on the former Sigrud house. He had other things more important in line for that night. Besides, there was nothing the house could tell him now that he did not already know. This was just an act of

paying respects. Becky and her parents had been cremated by their extended family, their ashes scattered somewhere. Duff never found out where. He didn't care. They were only ashes. Whatever made Becky the person she was had died in that house, snatched away forever by a single, well-placed bullet.

Duff wished he were sentimental enough to say something, to make some sort of speech. He watched enough ghost hunting shows on TV to make the concept of an afterlife a plausible but distant possibility to his painfully logical and pessimistic mind. Maybe Becky's ghost was staring out that second-story window, the one that had been her bedroom. Maybe she was watching him at that very minute. Duff's eyes darted to that window, but it was dark. No ghostly face peered back at him. She was gone. She would always be gone. There was nothing that would ever change that.

Duff walked away from the house and tried to push all thoughts of the morning he found her body out of her mind. He used all the coping techniques the doctors at Bensonhurst taught him during his six years in the asylum. He visualized that morning, put it into a mental "balloon," and released it to the sky. The doctors at the hospital thought that exercise was supposed to help. It never did. Maybe it worked for someone with an average IQ and normal mental health. However, for a genius-level IQ with severe, overly specific Obsessive-Compulsive tendencies, it was a laughable attempt to heal him. Still, Duff tried it because he was willing to try anything to purge that morning from his mind.

Duff limped his way to the end of the block, cut through a small city park, walked down another street, turned right, limped two more blocks, and up a different street. He did not follow the street signs. He moved on instinct. He still remembered the way to get where he was going. He would never forget it.

The neighborhood was newer than the neighborhood where Becky's house had been. Most of the homes were built in the late 1960s or early 1970s. They had that HUD-home look that so many homes of their era had, a plethora of plain, homely, single-level ranches with an attached single-car garage or split-level ranches with the two-car garages under the bedrooms. Duff had lived in one of those split-level deals when he was a kid. He remembered how the floor in his bedroom would vibrate when his mother or father would come home and hit the garage door opener. It was a sound and vibration that meant the tension in the house was going to increase tenfold. He would be quizzed. He would be given reading assignments. He would be harshly judged for his shortcomings and mocked for his non-academic interests like fantasy-fiction novels and *Dungeons & Dragons*. Just remembering that noise made Duff feel a little bit sick to his stomach.

This was not the neighborhood where Duff lived, though. That was several blocks east of this neighborhood, closer to where Becky had lived. He had come to this neighborhood for an entirely different purpose.

Duff limped to a familiar house, a single-level ranch with a long, low, covered porch on the front side and a two-car attached garage on the right side of the house. The house had been a horrendous Seventies' yellow when he was a kid, a sickly mustard color that went away for good when neutral tones overwhelmed suburbia in the early Eighties. The house's vinyl siding had been updated since then. The wide panels had been replaced with a narrower, more modern slat, and the yellow was purged completely for a mute, dark gray tone and white siding. It looked far better than it had in his youth, but Duff would never get the yellow out of his mind.

Duff walked up the driveway, climbed the single step to the porch, and rang the doorbell. He could hear the clang of an electronic bell somewhere inside the home. Duff backed off the porch and stood in the yard, his hands jammed in his pockets.

After a moment, the interior door opened and an older man in his mid-seventies peered out through the screen door. He squinted at Duff and pulled a pair of glasses out of the breast pocket of his plain, white t-shirt and put them on. Duff gave the old man a half-hearted wave.

The old man opened the screen door and stepped onto the porch. If he was cold, he did not show it. He was sporting a round beer gut, but his arms were thick. He had once been a man of action. He gave Duff a slow once-over and pulled the glasses from his face. "Clive Duffy?"

Duff nodded. "Just Duff, now. No Clive, please. How are you, Sheriff?"

"Jesus Christ." The sheriff hung the vowels almost like a southern drawl. *Jee-hee-zus Keer-eyest.* He slipped his glasses back into his shirt pocket. "I got all your emails, of course, but I haven't actually seen you in person in what, twenty years?"

"More than that." Duff knew the exact amount of time that had passed since the last time they had laid eyes on each other, of course. He knew it down to the minute, but he kept that to himself because most people frowned when he was overly pedantic.

The retired sheriff shook his head in disbelief. There was a long silence. Then finally he spoke. "You got fat."

"Yeah, well, so did you." Duff inclined his head toward the sheriff's ample and well-rounded beer belly.

The old man did not bat an eye. "When you got a tool as big as mine, you gotta build a shed over it."

Duff expected the joke. "I wish I had that excuse. I look like this because I pretty much exclusively eat a diet consisting of foods typically

found on a carnival midway."

"Did you come to badger me about the Sigrud murders in person again? Those were the good old days."

"No, I have an entirely different murder to badger you about now."

"That little girl who killed her boyfriend over in Rockland?"

"That's it."

The former Waukesha County Sheriff, David Einar Olson, better known as "Buddy" to everyone in the county for reasons Duff never bothered to learn, sighed and rubbed a hand through what was left of the thin, wispy, white hair on the top of his head. "You drink beer?"

"I've been known to when the mood strikes."

"Then you might as well c'mon in. I've got a fire pit in the backyard." Buddy held the screen door open for him.

"You got decent beer or Colorado piss water?"

"Spotted Cow outta New Glarus."

Duff shrugged and walked into the house. "I don't turn down Spotted Cow."

"Spoken like a true son of the Badger State." Buddy clapped Duff on the shoulder. "It's good to see you again, boy. Damn good. How's your mom?"

"Don't know. Don't care."

Buddy shook his head and chuckled as he shut the front door and led Duff toward the screen door in the dining room. "You haven't changed at all, have you?"

"I've heard people like consistency."

FIRE PITS WERE not a solely Wisconsin construct, but for some reason they were a very Wisconsin tradition. Growing up, it seemed to Duff that almost every home had a fire pit or a brazier in the backyard where friends would sit in fold-out camp chairs and swill beers while chatting around burning logs until the small hours of the morning, especially on pleasant summer nights. Plenty of people in other states had fire pits, but in Duff's mind the three things that made Wisconsin what it is were beer, an intense, burning hatred of anything Minnesota-related, and fire pits.

The few happy memories Duff had from his childhood centered around a fire pit. When he was very young, he had fond memories of sitting around the Sigrud's adobe brazier in their driveway and roasting marshmallows with Becky while her father told them ghost stories. Becky's family always had the sort of vibe that Duff imagined when he was in first grade and read stories about families like the Quimbys in Beverly Clearly's

classic *Ramona* books or the Hatchers in Judy Blume's *Superfudge*. Duff's house was cold and quiet and serious. His parents were academics with little time for games or stories. They had research to do, books and papers to write, papers to grade, and classes to teach. Duff was simply an accoutrement to them, a piece of research they undertook for the experience, not the joy. He was a hastily scrawled footnote in the bibliography of their lives. That's why it had been so easy for them to send him away when he caused them more trouble than they cared to have in their lives.

Buddy handed Duff a green-and-black camp chair and a brown bottle wrapped in a black koozie advertising Sobelman's Pub & Grill. A red-and-black camp chair was already set up next to a square fire pit rimmed with plain cement blocks that were stained black by years of smoke and soot. The backyard of Buddy's house was nothing fancy. A birdhouse stuck on a tree was the only decor outside of the fire pit in the center of the lawn. A six-foot wooden privacy fence rimmed the yard. A stack of corded firewood was in one corner of the yard. Once, there had been a dog that roamed the fenced-in yard, but that dog was long dead and never replaced.

The retired sheriff grabbed four logs, tented them into a little pyramid, and used a piece of newspaper lightly tagged with canola oil as a wick for the tinder he placed beneath the four logs. In less than two minutes, the dried firewood was starting to burn, great plumes of white smoke coming off them at first, but quickly dwindling to a thin, twisting stream of smoke the night wind swept into nothingness.

Buddy flopped into the weather-beaten red-and-black chair with a groan of old age. He popped the cap on his own beer with a bottle opener on his keychain, casting the bent top into the flames where it joined many of its half-melted, soot-stained brethren. He passed Duff the opener. "Well, you came all this way. What do you want to know?"

Duff popped his own cap and handed the keys back. He held the cap in the fingers of his left hand and let the cap roll over them in a practiced act of legerdemain, the only holdover from several months of trying to practice magic as a kid. "I want to know what you know, I guess. I got hired by the girl's father to prove her innocence."

Buddy shrugged. "You know I'm not a cop anymore, right?"

"It's arguable that you never really were."

Buddy took Duff's ribbing in stride. "You might be right. I liked putting away bad guys. I was never good at all the politics that being sheriff brought about. Maybe I should have stayed on patrol in the local P.D. I wouldn't have made nearly as much money, but I bet I would have been happier."

"You could have just stopped running for the office, you know?"

"Really? You can do that?" Buddy took a long pull on his Spotted Cow. "Honestly, I just let my staff handle the details. My secretary was the one who put me up for reelection every four years. I never said no, but I never told her to do it, either. I don't think I campaigned once after that initial election. I ran unopposed a lot, so I figured I was doing a good job. Or more likely no one else wanted to do it."

"You been back in the building since you retired?"

Buddy thought about it for a minute. "Once or twice for PR stuff, but nothing important."

"I know you, though. You've got someone inside feeding you info when you need it, don't you?"

"Oh, I still have people I can call when I need to, but I try not to need to."

"What do you know about this murder?"

Buddy stuck his feet toward the fire and crossed them at the ankles. "What makes you think I know anything?"

"Logic, mainly. You never married, never had kids. The job was everything to you. It was your whole world. That's why you kept running for the office. What else were you going to do, right? You might be retired, and I use that word loosely when applied to you, but I'm confident that you know before the newspapers do if something hinky goes down in your county. Retired doesn't mean dead."

Buddy chuckled before taking another swig of his beer. "Damn shame you didn't become a cop. Your drive, your mind— you would have been one of the greats."

"Yeah, I'm sure I would have been a poster boy for the department, what with my rampant hatred for authority and this thing—" Duff slapped his protruding stomach. "What do you know about the Riegert murder?"

"Right to business, then?"

"Right to business."

Buddy was quiet for a bit. "The detective assigned to the case wasn't one of my hires. She's one of the new sheriff's guys. Or girls in this case. She's young and eager, desperate to make a name for herself. This is a big case for her, and she's willing to roll it all on some pretty thin evidence just to prove she can make an arrest before the blood has dried."

"Doesn't seem like she cares about truth and justice, then."

"You know how it is: close the case fast, whatever it takes. This murder seems pretty cut-and-dried, doesn't it? Teenage romance in the middle of hormone central. It's no stretch to think some young gal got her panties in a bunch and took out her anger on some young Lothario who jilted her."

"That's usually the first thing I would consider."

Buddy took a big pull on his beer. "You know what bothers me about

this case, though?"

"The phone." It was a statement, not a question; Duff knew the answer.

Buddy nodded. "The phone. I've seen these kids today forget to put on shoes, but they never forget their phones. They're almost surgically attached to them."

"It does seem mighty convenient, doesn't it? Direct piece of evidence to tie someone to the scene of the crime. Almost like someone put it there on purpose."

Buddy tapped his fingertip on the end of his nose. "Without that phone, there's not a single thing to tie that girl to the crime scene. No one saw her there. No security cameras on campus have her going there."

The camera issue bugged Duff. Everything was being recorded now. How did the cameras not exonerate her? "How is the D.A. going to get around the security cameras?"

"None of the cameras in the fieldhouse were working the night of the murder. They were down for most of the week to an unrelated technical issue. They had a scheduled service ticket set for Monday. Rockland does all their IT stuff in-house because they have a good IT program there. Things just get backed up sometimes."

"What about the rest of campus?"

"There are a few streetlight cameras, nothing fancy, nothing specific. It's almost November, so pretty much every kid is wearing a jacket or sweatshirt. They all look the same. You can't pick out any individual faces. Not to mention half of them are wearing the same types of sweatshirts all branded with UW-Rockland insignias. Plus, most of the kids on campus clock where the cameras are on their first day. If you want to avoid being seen on camera, there are plenty of places on campus where you can walk without being picked up."

"Cards on the table, Buddy. Do you think this Novak girl killed the kid?"

"I'm not really involved in the investigation, little buddy. I'm an old man with a few too many crazy ideas."

Duff laughed out loud. "I'm calling bullshit with that. I know you; you have your theories."

Buddy poked at the fire with a long stick he lifted from the ground near his chair. The end caught alight, and Buddy snubbed it out in the damp grass. "All I know is most of the campus knew Nate Riegert was an asshole who thought he was too good for them. From what I hear, he laid more pipe in his freshman year than I have in my lifetime. He had a long string of heartbreaks behind him and a bright future playing for a big school ahead of him, maybe even a future with the NFL. And he knew it. He was like Jupiter

and there were a lot of moons in his orbit. Guy with a head that big— there are all manner of people looking to knock him down a peg."

Duff was hearing what he thought he would hear. "That's what I figured."

"You really going to prove this girl is innocent?"

"Maybe. Maybe not. As far as I'm concerned, they could give her the Chair, and I'd still sleep soundly." Duff took a long pull from his bottle.

"They don't have the death penalty in Wisconsin."

"I guess being a Badger fan is penalty enough."

"Truth." Buddy held out his bottle, and Duff clinked his own bottle against it.

"You want to come with us when we go see the scene tomorrow?"

"What? And leave all this?" Buddy waved his hand at the plain, empty yard.

"We'll stop by and pick you up."

"Don't show up too early. I like to sleep in now."

4

BUDDY GAVE DUFF a lift back to the Super 8 in Rockland after they demolished another beer and talked about life, the universe, and the Packers chances of winning the Superbowl. Buddy was optimistic, but Duff felt that the front office had not done enough to give Aaron Rodgers a decent set of downfield weapons. Either way, they both agreed the team would make the playoffs and then choke in a big moment.

Abe was propped up in bed in his pajamas when Duff keyed into their room. He was watching a *M*A*S*H* rerun on TV, the one where Trapper and Hot Lips got trapped in the supply closet during the bombing attack.

"You look like Ricky Ricardo in those things." Duff closed the door behind him and kicked off his shoes. "Seriously, it looks like you're wearing a cheap suit to bed. Did you wear those when you were married to Katherine? Between those pajamas and her being a closet lesbian, I know the answer to why you only had one child."

"These are nice pajamas. Ralph Lauren." Abe straightened the collar. They were rather formal for sleeping, but they made Abe feel strangely manly. The male leads in all the TV shows he watched as a kid wore pajamas like that. Those were his father-figures. Other kids had actual dads; he had Rob Petrie and Darrin Stephens. "I like these pajamas. Katherine actually gave me these for Christmas last year."

"Why? Was she mad at you?"

"I think you're just jealous."

"Sure. Let's go with that." Duff undid his pants and let them fall to his ankles. He stripped off his Carhartt hoodie and dropped it on the ground

next to him. Clad in black boxer-briefs and a faded Milwaukee Brewers t-shirt, he took two steps forward and collapsed onto the bed, falling heavily across Abe.

"Jesus, you're a load." Abe grunted and tried to shove Duff away. "I think you're breaking my femurs."

Duff crawled over Abe and lay next to him in the bed, using two pillows to prop himself up. "I should brush my teeth."

"You should also shower and use deodorant. Use mine, if you have to. Be considerate, man."

"I showered this morning, so you've got that going for you."

*M*A*S*H* went to commercial, and Abe muted the TV. "I think the girl is really innocent."

"Good meeting, then?"

"I saw no indication of deception in her story. It's possible she just convinced herself she didn't do it, or maybe she has no memory of doing it, but I don't think that's the case. She got really drunk the night of the murder. For someone her size, if she drank as much as she says she did, she's lucky she didn't get alcohol poisoning. She was in no shape to kill a man, especially a man much, much bigger than she was."

"We need to see the crime scene photos."

"I'll get those tomorrow from the DA. I'll get everything they have so we can see the timeline." Abe wanted to ask about where Duff had gone, but he knew it was a silly question. He knew that Duff had gone to the Sigrud house. Abe knew that Duff had probably walked the streets of his childhood. Duff also had a way of not answering Abe's questions about personal issues. Despite them being partners for more than twenty years, there were still aspects of Duff's world that were dark spots to Abe. Duff meted out information in drips, not torrents. If one was going to spend time with Duff, one had to be content with what was given, and not demand more. Matilda was really the only person on the planet who could make Duff talk about things when he did not want to, and that was only because she'd had him wrapped around her little finger since the day she was born.

"We're going to have a tag-along tomorrow." Duff scratched idly at his belly. "I told you about David Olson, right?"

"The sheriff?"

"That's him. I went and saw him tonight. He said he'd help us get in at the Waukesha Sheriff's Department."

"He didn't throw you in jail for being a pest again?"

"He never did that. It was always his dumbass detectives and deputies."

"Did you go past—" Abe let the phrase hang in the air. It did not need

to be made more concrete than that.

"Yes." Duff's response was curt, a tone that fully indicated that he did not want to share more about it. Abe pressed the situation anyhow.

"How was—"

"It was still there."

"Did—"

"No."

Abe stopped talking. Hawkeye and Trapper were back on the screen, so Abe unmuted the TV. Neither of them said anything more.

ABE WAS AWAKE before the alarm he programmed into his phone could go off. He almost never slept all the way to the alarm anymore. Part of that was the fact that he was no longer comfortable in a bed alone. After more than twenty years of sleeping next to Katherine, regardless of how little physical contact they typically shared at night, getting used to being a solo sleeper again was taking more adjustment than he thought it would. Having Duff in the bed next to him was not the same. The big man snored and kicked frequently, sometimes murmuring something incoherent, probably fighting off whatever demons tormented his dreams.

Being in a hotel did not help, either. Abe never slept well in a hotel. The weight of the blankets never matched the weight of the blankets on his own bed, a constant reminder he was not at home. Plus, there was the smells, the sounds, and the strange feel of the sheets. Abe also had trouble convincing himself that the sheets were truly clean, given the potentiality for bedroom-based activities people might have participated in betwixt the very same sheets in which he now slept. Sure, the water they used to wash the sheets was blistering hot, and they threw in plenty of bleach and detergent, but there was something deep in Abe's puritanical core that skeeved him out about hotels.

Abe slipped out of bed trying not to wake Duff. He did not know why he bothered. Duff did not wake easily. Abe could have turned on every light in the room and crashed a couple of cymbals together, and it probably would only have made Duff roll over to his side.

In the dim morning light creeping through a small crack in the blackout blinds, Abe pulled on a pair of sweatpants and laced up his Asics running shoes. He pulled on his favorite Northwestern hooded sweatshirt and crept out of the room taking only a keycard. He pulled the hood over his bald pate to keep his head warm.

A few months back, Abe needed to run during a case, and it only proved he was desperately out of shape, not that he was ever really in shape

to begin with. He was trying to get back into some semblance of health, even if that only meant he could run a half-mile without stopping. Abe hated running, though. He hated it with a passion. He did not like it when he was a child. He did not like doing it in gym classes when he was in school. He hated everything about it. However, it was about the only athletic activity which required no real standard of coordination, so it was the only thing resembling a sport he could actually do.

Contrary to the previous day's oppressive skies and misty rain, the new day had a brilliantly blue late fall sky, and the sun crested the horizon with a display of pink and orange hues. Abe walked outside and took in a deep lungful of southern Wisconsin air. It was crisp and smelled sharp and clean in that way only the last gasp of fall weather could. He could not get that scent in Chicago. In Chicago, every breath he took smelled faintly of gasoline and tacos, but that had a lot to do with living so close to a busy street and a taquería.

Abe started to stretch his calves against a wall, pressing his toes to the wall and leaning into it. He did not understand how to really stretch before a run, but he always saw people doing it in movies before they went for runs, so he figured he should at least make an attempt.

The automatic doors of the hotel swung open. Abe turned his head to see who was coming out. Maggie Novak walked out in a windbreaker, tight capri-length yoga pants, and a pair of Nikes that looked like they had seen many, many miles of road. She was surprised to find Abe standing at the door and jumped a bit. "Mr. Allard, I was not expecting to find you out here."

"Sorry if I scared you. I have that effect on a lot of people."

Maggie straightened her windbreaker. "I'm sorry. That was rude of me. I'm just not used to other people being out this early."

"I'm not usually up this early. Just couldn't sleep."

"It's hotels, isn't it? I can't sleep in them, either." Maggie put a foot up on a yellow cement bollard near the doors and leaned into a thigh stretch. "Are you a runner, Mr. Allard?"

"Please, call me Abe. And not really."

Maggie smiled at him. "You didn't strike me as a runner."

"Athletics were never a passion."

"I can understand it. I imagine sports are like any other hobby. You either like them or you don't, and there's not much you can do about it if you don't." She leaned toward her toes, stretching everything in her lower body taut. Abe tried not to stare, but she was exceptionally toned, and it was making him a little light-headed. While she was reaching over her toes anyhow, Maggie retied her right shoelace. "I like running. It's simple. It's

honest. You can either put in the work, or you can't. Truly great marathoners might have some genetic boosts that help them, but anyone can be a runner as long as they commit to putting in the work."

Abe did not know how to respond to that. It was a statement, not a conversational lead. Abe was not good at small talk. Abe had grown up as the only child of a single mother who worked sixty-hour weeks to keep him fed and housed. This led to Abe spending the first eighteen years of his life studying alone in front of a TV and never interacting with other human beings. As an adult, he'd married a woman who was uncomfortable with herself, so they never socialized with other couples much, and there had been a lot of silence between them. Abe could not make conversations flow and ebb. When they hit a point where he could not see a logical next sentence, he froze, or he said something inane. After a few seconds of silence, Maggie looked up at him from her stretch and smiled.

Abe tried to smile back. "Running is good." Immediately he winced in his own mind. *You idiot.*

Maggie was nonplussed. If she thought it was an awkward statement, she did not react as though she did. In fact, she echoed the statement with a cheerful smile. "Running *is* good! Would you care to run with me today, Abe?"

"Uh, sure. I'm not sure if I'll be able to keep up with you, though. If I'm slowing down your workout, feel free to leave me in your dust."

"This isn't competitive, Abe. We're just out to have fun and be healthy." She started jogging in place with light, bouncy steps showing she was no stranger to working out. "C'mon, it'll be fun!"

Abe tried to smile at her, but his smile never worked properly when it was a manufactured gesture. Abe fell into step behind her, his big feet slapping the pavement gracelessly.

Maggie was one of those runners who moved like water in a calm stream. She flowed. She was loose and easy. She made movement look natural and effortless. Her steps were impossibly light, and her pace made it seem as though she could run all day without tiring. Abe's gait was closer to Karloff's lumbering stagger as Frankenstein's monster.

Maggie slowed to fall back to Abe's pace. "Are you going back to see Sarah today?"

Abe had informed the Novaks of his visit with Sarah the previous night. He did not tell them anything specific, and he did not tell them that he was not certain of her guilt or innocence, but he let them know that she looked well, and she wanted to come home. Maggie had cried when he'd said that. "I'm not certain. If there is time later, I'm going to try to see her again. She said she wanted real food. Apparently, jail food is as bad as television and

movies have led us to believe."

"Did she do it, Abe?"

"Did she eat? I don't think she's eaten much."

"Did she kill that boy?"

Abe glanced at Maggie out of the corner of his eye. She was staring straight ahead. There was no look of worry on her face. Abe decided to press for more information. "Do you think there's a chance she did?"

"Oh, no. No. I didn't mean it like that. I just… I don't know for certain. I have never seen her be violent. I've never seen her hit anyone, not even her little brother, not even when he probably deserved a punch in the head. She's a good girl, but you have a daughter, right? You know how it is. You always think there's something she's holding back from you. Those teenage girls, they get so secretive."

Abe did know that. He knew it all too well. The distance his divorce drove between Matilda and him had not helped that feeling.

"I found out a few weeks ago that Sarah was sexually active and has been for a few years, now. I sat her down before I sent her off to college to give her a big, long sex talk, and she probably could have given me pointers." Maggie barked a half-sob, half-laugh. She started running a little harder. Abe had to push himself to keep up with her. "I mean, I just do not know everything about her, and that's what scares me. I honestly believe she's not violent, but I could not swear on that before God. If you asked me if I were completely certain of her innocence, I could not honestly say yes. No matter what, there's always a little part of me that knows she might be capable of some dark things."

"Duff says that your husband had a problem with violence when they were teens. Do you think it could be some sort of inherited trait?"

"I doubt that." Maggie jogged in silence for a moment. "Henry was a real prick when we first met. He'd just gotten out of Bensonhurst. He was still having issues adjusting to normal society. He was full of himself."

"You said he was changed, though."

"He is. He's never been violent with me or the kids. I've never seen him lose his temper. He was just an asshole, bragging about his strength, bragging about the money he made. He did not know how to be a decent person, how to interact with other people on a human level."

"That sounds like Duff."

"He and Henry had some difficulties in the past, didn't they?"

Abe could not speak to that. "I don't know. Duff never really mentioned your husband until yesterday."

"Really?"

"Really. Duff doesn't just share information like that. He has to have a

reason to talk about it. I knew he had been abused at Bensonhurst. He talked about taking almost daily beatings from some of the other teens there but never mentioned names and never went into further details."

Maggie glanced at the Fitbit on her wrist. Abe knew that some people used that to monitor their heart rate. Abe's version of monitoring his heart was to assume that as long as it did not explode in his chest, he was probably fine.

"Henry used to tell me stories about the other people in the hospital with him. Some of those stories made it sound like hell on Earth."

What little information about Bensonhurst Duff let slip would confirm that assertion. "Duff just said it was the worst time in his life." Abe's partner was prone to pointing at various scars on his body and attributing them to beatings suffered at the hands of violent teens and orderlies at the asylum.

"Henry spoke of Duff with a mixture of fear and awe. He said that he used to resort to violence with him because it was the only way he could be superior to him. He said that Clive— that's what he was called at the hospital, I guess— was just too smart. He said he knew everything about everyone just by looking at them."

"That sounds like Duff."

They were silent for a few beats. Only Abe's labored breathing and their regular footfalls could be heard.

"Teenagers, right? Adult bodies, simple minds. That's why I'm so worried about Sarah. That little voice of doubt in the back of my head keeps telling me, *What if she killed him?* I'm not ready to visit my little girl at Taycheedah for the next thirty years. To have to turn her over to the prison system, to see her only during certain weekend hours in the cold, bland visiting room— I don't think I could handle it."

Abe was suddenly thinking about Matilda being in the same situation. There was no doubt in his mind, seeing her wasting the best years of her life in a prison would probably push him over the edge. If fear and worry did not break his heart, he wondered how long he could keep pushing on with life if he knew that Matilda's whole potential would be sacrificed.

Maggie wiped away tears with her fingers as she ran. "I don't think I could go on, Abe. I really don't."

Abe fully understood.

ABE AND MAGGIE finished their run. They parted at their respective rooms. Abe showered and dressed. Then, he woke Duff, a task that was never pleasant but sometimes necessary.

Duff showered and dressed. The big man was not a fashion plate. He

only had one outfit, and that consisted of a pair of Lee jeans, a usually black t-shirt advertising a sports team, a beer, or classic rock band, and a hooded sweatshirt. The sweatshirt was always Carhartt, and it was always in heather gray or black, although he did have a dark maroon one for special occasions. The jeans were the only pair he owned. When they got holes in them, he would buy a new pair of the exact same brand and color, and then he would throw the old pair in the trash. Abe was just grateful Duff changed his socks and underwear every day. Mostly.

They drove to Waukesha and picked up Buddy Olson. Duff climbed into the backseat for the old sheriff, a gesture to which Abe did not draw attention, but he noted how it clearly showed the level of respect Duff possessed for the old man.

The trio headed straight for the detectives' bureau of the Waukesha County Sheriff.

There is a distinct similarity in detective bureaus across the country. They are like airports that way. No matter which station Abe and Duff were in, the stations all looked enough alike that the duo did not need any sort of guide or orientation. The desks, the ringing phones, the faint smell of stale or burned coffee— they were always the same. Waukesha was not an exception to the rule. The pale beige desks with faux-wood tops looked like they had not been updated since 1972. The walls and carpeting had a light gray neutral tone that screamed of a design aesthetic straight out of 1992, which was probably the last time they were updated. And before that update, it was likely they looked like something straight out of 1962 because municipalities tended to save money by only updating facilities every twenty or thirty years.

Buddy walked to the reception desk where a civilian worker was standing. She was a middle-aged woman, pretty for a Midwesterner, wearing a pastel sweater and black skirt. She had a short bob cut and a no-nonsense face that plainly showed the wear and tear of two decades of hearing bad cop jokes and dealing with the pissed-off public. The woman broke into a broad smile when she saw the retired LEO waddle through the door. "Sheriff! What an unexpected surprise. What brings you in today? Business or pleasure?"

"Howdy, Janie. All business today. I'm escorting a pair of detectives from Illinois who were hired to look into that Nate Riegert murder." The retired sheriff pointed at the men trailing him. "That's Abe Allard. This is Duff. Fellas, this is Jane Hustvedt. She keeps this place running like a top."

"Just Duff?" asked Jane.

Duff nodded. "Just Duff."

"Just a single name like Cher?"

"I think mononyms will be all the rage soon. I'm trying to get ahead of the curve."

Abe stepped forward and offered Jane a business card and flashed his private investigator's license and Wisconsin State Bar card. "We were hired by Sarah Novak's parents to research this murder and represent her in trial, if necessary."

"Hey, if Buddy vouches for you, that's good enough for me." Jane peered at the proffered ID. "Isn't it a little unethical to be both a lawyer and a PI?"

"I'm not really a lawyer."

"Me neither," said Duff. "I'm a prima ballerina."

"And an asshole," said Buddy. "We'll need to see Pam, Janie."

"She's in her office. I'll let her know you're coming." Jane picked up a phone and started dialing an extension.

Buddy walked through the door which separated the offices from the public lobby. Buddy lowered his voice and spoke to Abe and Duff as they passed through the door. "Mind your Ps and Qs, Clive." Buddy used Duff's proper name as a way to drive home his point a little harder. "Pam's a decent detective, but she's still new at this and she doesn't feel like she's made her bones yet, so she's wound tighter than a Russian clock."

Buddy walked them back to the office of Pamela Jahnke, who was standing behind her desk waiting for them. She wore a plain, dark gray pantsuit with a mauve blouse beneath it. No necklace, no rings. Her fingernails were short. Her dark hair was cut short in a professional bob. She had the bearing and stance of someone who only recently shed the uniform for the plain clothes. She was still young, still out to show the world she was invincible. Her shoulders were square, and she stood like she was ready to spring into action at the slightest flinch. She gave the retired sheriff a professional smile and held out her hand. "Hi, Buddy. You come to make sure I'm filling out the right forms?"

Buddy shook her hand. "Hi, Pammy. I just came to introduce you to an old friend of mine, and his friend. They're here about the quarterback murder." Buddy pointed out the detectives filing into her office behind him and made the pleasantries. "They're going to need to see what you have. Abe, there, is the young gal's lawyer." His work for the day finished, Buddy flopped into one of the extra chairs in the office. He kicked his feet out in front of him and crossed his hands over his ample belly.

Jahnke's disposition darkened when Buddy said *lawyer*. Abe could tell she had a policeman's stereotypical distrust of defense attorneys. She tried to play nice, though. She sat in her desk chair, opened one of the drawers on her desk, and pulled out a murder book, a sort of scrapbook detectives compiled for cases. She flopped it onto the desk. "You can make copies if

you want. The district attorney already has everything we have. They're charging her with second-degree murder, although you could probably get them to plead down to third pretty easily. It was clear the girl was drunk out of her mind on the hooch."

Abe heard Duff start to speak— no doubt about to attack her use of the word *hooch*— but Abe cut him off. "Thank you. We'd like to ask you some questions if you have a few minutes."

"Sure. Nothing I love more than wasting my time debating the merits of an open-and-shut case." Jahnke's eyes stayed level, staring hard at Abe. "We got motive. We got means. We got opportunity. We got evidence tying the girl to the scene. What the hell else do you need?"

"She's right, Abe? What the hell else do we need?" Duff took the other available chair in the office, leaving Abe to have to stand in front of Jahnke's desk. "Well, for starters: how 'bout fingerprints? I'd like to have fingerprints, if I were you. Do you have fingerprints? How about witnesses? Are there witnesses who can positively ID the girl at the scene? What about conclusive video evidence?"

Abe rocked back and stomped on Duff's toes. "Excuse my friend. He was raised by television and rabid opossums."

"Opossums almost never get rabies." Duff yanked his foot out from under Abe's heel.

"Which makes yours all the rarer." Abe gave the detective an apologetic smile. "The murder weapon was a weight plate, yes?"

"Yes. A ten-kilo Weider standard plate with Hammertone finish. The finish is rough and pitted, and it has only been handled by a few thousand students in its lifetime. Finding a definite set of fingerprints on it which would have held up in court would have been impossible."

"And the weight of the plate didn't bother you?" Duff arched an eyebrow. "Ten kilos isn't terribly light. It's what, twenty-two-pounds?"

"Yeah? So? It did the job. Crushed the back of his skull right at the top of his spine. Caused unconsciousness, paralysis, and an almost immediate spinal infarction that led to a seizure and total respiratory failure."

"What about the weight of the girl?"

"What about it?" Jahnke was getting annoyed.

Duff shrugged and looked at the ceiling. "Sarah Novak is what? A buck-ten, buck-fifteen, tops?"

"So?"

"You think a girl like that can pick up a twenty-two pound weight and swing it with enough force to kill a man?" Duff gave Jahnke his best dumb-guy face. "I'm just sayin', that's like a fifth of her body weight."

"Women her size routinely pick up thirty-pound toddlers, Mr. Duffy."

"Do they beat men to death with those toddlers?"

"He wasn't beaten to death, Mr. Duffy. It was a single blow to the back of the skull. A girl her size could have lifted the weight above her head when his back was turned and let the weight itself do most of the damage."

"Huh. I guess she's guilty as hell then. Give her the Chair!"

Jahnke leaped to her feet. She leaned across her desk menacingly. "You got a problem with my case, Mr. Duffy?"

"Nah, I'm sure you're brilliant." Duff sat forward in the chair. He appraised Jahnke for a moment. "UW-Oshkosh or UW-Milwaukee? Oshkosh, right? Maybe two years at a tech school, first?"

This caught Jahnke off-guard. She pulled back and looked confused. "What?"

"Which one did you attend?"

Jahnke looked around her desk. There was nothing there to identify anything personal about herself. It was all business. No personal mementos, no photos, no diplomas. "Oshkosh."

"Makes sense. Still working on the ol' Master's degree, aren't you? Might finish it in a year or two, maybe three."

"How?" Jahnke looked rattled. She got defensive. She crossed her arms in a strength position. She rocked backwards. Abe could see all the classic signs of someone trying to protect themselves, trying to put up a wall. Jahnke's eyes narrowed. Her lips got thin as she pressed them together. "How did you know?"

Buddy intervened. "Pammy, this is that weird kid I used to tell stories about, the young Sherlock Holmes wanna-be who pestered my detectives until they locked his insolent self up."

Jahnke's face relaxed a bit, but not much. "This is that guy?"

"The one and the same, thirty years later."

"Still a pain in the ass, I see."

Duff gave her a sheepish grin. "I play to my strengths."

"Why were you asking about the colleges."

"Just trying to figure out where you went to college so I could email their Criminal Justice program chair and tell him he needs to update the curriculum."

Jahnke's eyes narrowed. "Fuck you."

Abe side-stepped to block Duff from Jahnke's view. "Detective, I'm sure your work is thorough. It's just, given what we've learned about this case, it seems a little circumstantial to pin this on a girl who was heavily intoxicated that night. Your own notes here say that when you finally got her a preliminary breath test the morning she was arrested, she still blew a 0.172. Legally intoxicated is less than half that. It's entirely conceivable that this girl

was in no state to walk, let alone walk a fair distance, unnoticed, to brain someone with a weight."

"So, plead down to murder-three, then. This isn't my responsibility. I laid out my case, the DA agreed with it, and they filed charges." Jahnke's voice was stressed, she was agitated. Her hands balled into fists and went to her hips. Her stance widened. It was a power move. She was trying to present confidence and certainty.

In conditions where someone was escalating a stressful situation, Abe and Duff behaved differently. Duff's attitude was normally to antagonize and belittle, usually getting the aggressor stressed enough to punch him. Abe retreated and became compliant. He did not like stressful situations. When it was an issue of arguing with someone at the business, he let Duff do it. Duff could tell someone off to their face and take a nap directly afterward. Meanwhile, Abe was still losing sleep to verbal missteps he made in elementary school.

Abe needed the detective to stay professional and willing to talk to them. He took a half-step back. He let his shoulders slump giving him the look of a beaten man. "Duff, could you and Buddy step out? I'd like to talk to the detective alone for a minute."

Duff snorted. He crossed his arms like someone who was not going anywhere. Buddy, wiser and more seasoned in the arts of interpersonal politics, knew instinctively where Abe was heading. Buddy pushed himself out of his chair and grabbed Duff by the elbow. "C'mon, Squirt. Let's let the adults talk."

"I'm not going anywhere. I still have questions."

"They can be answered in the murder book. We'll go make a copy of what the good detective gave us."

"I told you, I'm not—"

Buddy was insistent. "I'll buy you a Coke."

Duff's lip curled, but he realized he was not going to win this argument. "Fine. But there better be doughnuts in the break room."

"This is the modern police force. They have carrot sticks and protein snacks." Buddy pulled Duff from the chair and gave him a playful shove through the door. He grabbed Jahnke's murder book from Abe's hands.

Duff scowled darkly as he exited the office. "No wonder there's so much police brutality. You hand me almonds and pecans instead of a cream-filled Bismark, and I'd hit someone with a stick, too."

Abe gave them a moment to clear out of earshot before addressing the detective. He sat down in the chair Duff vacated. It was a psychological move. The detective was standing. Abe was sitting. He let her have the height and power advantage. He looked to the floor. He was a supplicant

before her. Abe cleared his throat. "Detective, I'm sure your work was thorough. My partner has a few rough edges, and he was insinuating that maybe you might have taken the easy route and overlooked other possible suspects."

Jahnke huffed an angry breath out through her nose. She stayed standing, but her hands relaxed. She put them on the desk before her. "Murder is typically a crime of passion or gain. You know that."

Abe did. Most people either murdered out of love, hate, or because they stood a chance to make money or elevate their standing because of someone's death.

Jahnke continued, "The kid was only nineteen, still a few months from twenty. He had no money. No one would gain from his death. So, that cuts the motive to passion. The Novak girl thought she was his girlfriend. He had a lot of hookups. She got angry, got drunk, and hit him with a weight. I'm sure she did not *intend* to kill him, but that is what happened, and now she's got to pay the price. That's just life."

Abe felt the detective was taking a very narrow look at murder and all the myriad reasons— or lack thereof— someone might commit the crime. True, it was often as simple as passion or gain, and those were the simplest ones to deliver. Abe's conversation with Maggie Novak popped into his head. He had no proof Sarah Novak *didn't* kill Nate Riegert. What if, in her drunken state, she was capable of murder? Was Abe being too dismissive of Jahnke's investigation because he believed the girl was telling the truth? Abe had to take a big mental step back. Assume nothing, he told himself. Look at the evidence. So far, the only evidence was that phone at the crime scene.

Abe smiled at the detective. "Perhaps you're correct. Did you interview anyone else about this murder?"

"Several. It's in the book."

"Were there any other suspects?"

"Do you mean did anyone hate Nate Riegert?"

Abe nodded.

"A bunch of people disliked him, maybe even hated him. Apparently, Mr. Riegert was an asshole. The people we talked to said he and Sarah Novak had a screaming fight at least once a week. They also said he had a swelled head and thought he was too good for UW-Rockland. He was a prick to teachers and administrators, and he had a trail of broken hearts and used condoms a mile long behind him. Frankly, Mr. Allard, I didn't even know the kid, and I still wanted to slap him just from hearing the stories."

"That's what I hear, as well." Abe stood up from the chair. "Thank you, Detective. I'll be on my way. I'll be sure to get your book back to you when we've made the copies." Abe started to leave the office.

"Mr. Allard."

Abe stopped in the door and turned back to Jahnke. She was still sitting at her desk. Her eyes were narrowed to slits. "I'm a good detective, Mr. Allard."

"No one said otherwise, Detective."

"Your friend did. I could hear it in his voice. He might not have said the words, but he implied it, and I do not care for his implication."

"I'll be sure to let him know." Abe started to leave.

"Mr. Allard?"

Abe stopped.

Jahnke regarded him for a moment, her cheeks flaring red. "How did your partner know I went to Oshkosh? How did he know it?"

"That's what he does. Sometimes I know how he does it. This one, I'm at a loss as well, I'm afraid."

"Buddy says your friend is the best detective he ever saw. Is he that good?"

"He's very good. I don't know about best, but he connects a lot of dots and sees things most people don't. He and I have made a living in Chicago for two decades doing this. Maybe not a good living, but it's been a living. Not many PI's can say that."

Jahnke's fingers drummed on her desk in a single, four-beat cadence. "I'm a good detective, Mr. Allard."

Abe nodded once, and he left her office.

"SHE'S A HORSESHIT detective." Duff wasted no time weighing in with his opinion of Detective Pamela Jahnke.

Ever the diplomat, Buddy tried to play referee. "Pammy's alright. She's a little high-strung and a little desperate to make a name for herself, but other than that, she's a fine detective, I'm sure."

They were back in the minivan and Abe started the engine. "How did you know she went to Oshkosh?"

"Fast logic, really, an educated guess. She's got the typical Sconnie accent, so I knew she was in-state. She did not look like the type to go too far from home, so I figured she stayed in the area she felt familiar with. The three best Criminal Justice programs in the southeastern Wisconsin area are in Oshkosh, Milwaukee, or Carroll College in Waukesha. She didn't look like she had money, so I knew it had to be a state school. If you pressed me to guess Milwaukee or Oshkosh, I figured she wasn't a big city girl. Something about her hips and butt said horse-rider to me, so I figured if she grew up in the country, she would have gone to Oshkosh."

Buddy chuckled. "Sounds like you haven't changed a lick." He leaned over to Abe. "Back in the day, I watched this idiot discombobulate my detectives on the regular. He could always tell where they'd had lunch and what they'd had. He's freaky that way."

"Oh, he's freaky in a lot of ways," said Abe.

Duff started scanning through the copied sheets from Jahnke's book. "The crime scene is probably taken down by now. Not much there, anyhow." He handed a copy of a photograph to Buddy. The picture showed the victim face down on a rubber mat next to a weight bench. There was no blood. A circular weight lay next to the victim. A cell phone lay a conspicuous distance away from the body. That was all there was to see.

"She barely interviewed any other suspects. Almost one-hundred percent of her focus was on Sarah Novak."

"I can't blame her." Buddy returned the crime scene photo to Duff. "Not much else to think given the evidence at the scene."

"But the cell phone at the scene does not prove the girl was there. It only proves that someone, possibly her, dropped her cell phone there." Duff pulled out another picture, a photocopy of a professional headshot of the quarterback from his high school yearbook. Duff let out a low whistle. "This dude is handsome as hell. He looks like Ryan Gosling, like a damned clone of Ryan Gosling. I totally get why he got as much tail as he did. I mean, I don't bat from that side of the plate, but I might have considered it for this dude."

Duff extended the picture toward the dashboard. Abe diverted his eyes from the road for a fraction of a second, just long enough to glance at the photo and see that Duff was not exaggerating. The kid was a top-notch human specimen with the sort of face that tended to make women swoon. Abe felt a pang of jealousy. Life was harder for homely people. He was glad Matilda was cute, perky, and popular. It always seemed to Abe that those sort of people had a much better time in life than sad-eyed misery sacks like himself and Duff.

"Well, what's the next step, then?" Abe saw the sign pointing travelers toward UW-Rockland.

"We need to get into Sarah's residence hall room, and it'd be good to see if we can go through Nate's things, too. We need to approach the case like we don't have a suspect and see if the cards still fall the same way."

"The quarterback had an off-campus apartment. I know where it is," said Buddy.

Duff punched the old sheriff lightly on the shoulder. "I knew you were already deep into this case."

"I wouldn't say I'm deep into it." Buddy lifted his faded Waukesha

County ball cap from his head and ran a hand over his hair before resetting the cap. "I'm just a curious bystander, is all."

5

THE TRIO KNOCKED on the door to the apartment where Nate Riegert lived with his roommate and fellow Rockland Owls teammate, Oliver Coleman. It was situated in an off-campus apartment complex which had been around at least twenty years, maybe more, and was showing the wear and tear of being the home for scores of college students who would live in its rooms for a year or two, studying hard and partying harder the whole time, before moving on to bigger and better things after graduation. The hallways possessed the heady funk of time, unwashed humanity, and questionable cooking choices. Near the garbage bins at the end of long halls, stacks of empty pizza boxes and 55-gallon Hefty bags of crushed beer cans were piled like a small fortress after the weekend's socializing. The cans were all of the cheapest brands, Wisconsin collegiate favorites like Hamm's, Busch, and Natty Light; no fancy microbrews for perpetually poor students. The complex parking lot was filled with cars in various stages of falling apart. Getting drunk was more important than vehicle maintenance. Better cars could be purchased once a coveted post-college job was found.

Riegert and Coleman lived on the second story of the three-story complex. They had a choice corner room with a balcony that overlooked an intramural field, one of the best views in the building. Chances were they had inherited the lease from a pair of graduating seniors the previous year. The best apartments tended to be handed down to friends that way. Abe never lived in an off-campus apartment until he was in graduate school, but the room he rented in a house just off the UW-Madison campus should have been condemned. To find the best rooms, you needed connections or

big money and those were something Abe continually lacked.

Buddy knocked hard on the door to the apartment. It was a cop knock, hard and loud. There were muffled voices inside, sounds of movement. "Sounds like we're disturbing them," said Buddy. "I hear a high-pitched voice and a low voice. There's a girl in there."

"I guess Riegert's death isn't affecting young Master Coleman too badly." Duff rapped on the door. "Private detective. Can we talk to you?"

"Coming!" A man's voice called out from within the apartment. The door muffled the sound.

"I'll bet he was," said Duff.

"I miss college," said Buddy. "Plenty of gals for every occasion."

"Maybe for you," said Abe. "I remember college differently."

"Didn't you attend college before they let women in?" said Duff.

"I'm old, but not that old," said Buddy.

The door opened. A blushing young woman skirted past them while pulling on a jacket. She had disheveled brown hair. "Sorry. I was just leaving." She shoved her hands deep into her jacket pockets and headed down the stairs to the parking lot.

A sheepish-looking young man was standing in the living room in nothing but a pair of basketball shorts. The kid was tall and stocky, built like a barrel. Thick thighs and calves propped him up. His arms hung at his sides like sides of beef. His hair was cropped short, so it was not disheveled. "Sorry about that. That was just my girlfriend."

"Mind if we come in and ask you a few questions about Nate Riegert?"

The kid shrugged at Abe. "I guess. I mean, I don't know. Do I need a lawyer?"

"Did you kill Nate?" asked Duff.

Oliver looked taken aback. "No. Of course not."

"Then you're fine, champ. We're coming in."

Buddy took a step inside the apartment. "Smells like sex in here."

Duff followed the sheriff. "I'll take your word for it."

Abe walked in and handed the kid a business card. "You're Oliver Coleman, I take it? Nate Riegert was your roommate, yes?"

Oliver squinted at the card. "You're private detectives?"

"Our meerschaum pipes are at the cleaners." Duff moved a couple of shirts off a recliner in the room and took a seat. "You mind if I sit? My ankle is pretty busted up."

Oliver was unphased. "Oh, go ahead man. Make yourself comfortable. Mi casa es su casa."

Abe and the sheriff remained standing. "You were Nate's roommate?"

"Yes, sir. We played football together. I play center."

"Have a seat, get comfortable." Duff gestured at the couch along the wall with the windows.

The kid looked confused. He wasn't any sort of dim bulb, but they had awakened him too early for him to be thinking at full capacity. He sat down on the couch and grabbed a T-shirt, tugging it on. It was a Milwaukee Brewers shirt.

"Damn shame about the Crew this year, eh?" said Duff. As per usual with Milwaukee, they battled valiantly but came up short of the playoffs. If you can be anything, be consistent.

The kid gave Duff a smile of commiseration. "Right? I don't think I'll see them play a World Series in my lifetime."

"Me neither," said Duff. "Were you and Nate close?"

"Pretty close. I mean, we weren't going to be each other's best man at our weddings or nothing, but we roomed together last year, and he was my quarterback."

"Wasn't he everyone's quarterback here?" Abe was confused.

Duff explained to his partner, "The quarterback/center relationship is usually pretty tight. The snap is the part of the play where miscommunication can lead to fumbles if the center pulls the trigger early or the quarterback tries to leave his crouch too soon. Centers and quarterbacks have to be on the same wavelength."

Buddy sat on the couch next to Oliver. "I used to be the Waukesha County Sheriff until a couple years ago. I used to get over to watch games on Friday night while serving on safety patrols. Your name sounds familiar to me. Didn't you play over at Hamilton High School?"

Oliver nodded. "I did. I had a chance at a couple of minor school scholarships, but I hurt my knee the second week of my senior year, and a bunch of them dried up. I came here hoping to make some people notice me, maybe transfer to a bigger school next year."

"You had an older brother, Damon, right?"

"Yep. He played for two years at UW-Platteville before he blew his ACL. He's in agricultural finance now."

Buddy reached out a hand and patted Oliver's shoulder. "That's good. Good for him for getting the degree. He was a helluva lineman. If you stay healthy, I bet you got a good shot at D-2, maybe even D-1."

"I did with Nate playing, that's for sure. He made everyone look better."

"Was it true that Nate got D-1 offers?" asked Duff.

Oliver nodded his head hard. "Oh, yeah. Half a dozen, at least. Probably more. Maybe even as high as fifteen or twenty letters showed up. I tried not to pay too close attention. He took a lot of phone calls, too."

Abe interjected, "Would anyone other than Sarah Novak have a reason

to be angry at Nate?"

Oliver's eyebrows raised, and he looked to his left without thinking, a dead giveaway the answer was yes. "I'm sure there might have been a couple."

Abe pulled out his notebook and pen. "Who?"

Oliver thought for a second. He scratched at the three-day stubble on his chin. "Well, there were a few girls who were angry at him. He liked to have sex with them and then ghost them."

"Do you know names?"

"Oh, um—" There was a lengthy pause. "I know some first names if that helps: Maggie, Mikayla, and Abby. Maybe Jessica. There were a couple of others who were leaving as I was coming home a few times. It wasn't like we became pen pals or anything. Nate liked the ladies, and the ladies loved Nate. He was a magnet."

"Who else?" asked Abe.

Oliver shrugged, his big shoulders bouncing once. "I dunno. Maybe Robbie Conroy."

"The backup quarterback." Duff snapped down the footrest on the recliner and leaned forward. "Tell me more about him."

"Well, it kind of sucks for him, right? He was on the team for four years now. He greyshirted his freshman year to get an extra year of eligibility. He enrolled in graduate school this year thinking he was going to finally start for the team, and Nate came out of nowhere with his super-arm and took his spot. Now he's hosed, right? All that time practicing, all those hours, for what? A few nothing snaps in mop-up time."

"Was Robbie angry when Nate was named the starter?" asked Buddy.

Oliver nodded again. "Disappointed. Angry. Frustrated. A few of the older guys on the team took him out to Larry's for beers and helped him get over it, though."

"Who's Larry?" asked Abe.

"Oh, it's not a who; it's a where. It's a local bar. Most of the guys on the football team like it there. Larry Panner is the guy who owns it. It's just called Larry's Bar and Grill. They have good burgers."

"Noted," said Duff. "Abe, write that down. It will be lunchtime at some point."

"I've been there many, many times," said Buddy. "He's not wrong. The burgers are pretty impressive."

"That's two votes for Larry's, Abe."

Abe was used to Duff thinking with his stomach and getting sidetracked; it was a common event. He tried to put the investigation back on the rails. "After the guys took Robbie to the bar, did he seem okay with Nate taking

over the starting position?"

"Oh, yeah. Robbie's a good team guy, always willing to do what's necessary for the good of the team. Besides, it's only Division Three. It's not like he was going to the NFL or anything. If he was lucky maybe he gets a job at the bottom of the coaching ladder next year, but more than likely he finishes his MBA and gets a real job."

"Did you notice anything weird about Nate the last few weeks?" Abe wanted to know if the quarterback's personal habits had changed at all. That was usually a sign that they might have known something bad was coming, or they were getting into territories that might have led to his death.

Oliver thought about it for a moment. "Can't say that I noticed anything, no. But it's not like we hung out all the time. He spent a fair share of nights in other beds, and I would go over to my girlfriend's apartment if I knew he was bringing someone back here."

"Have his parents come for his things, yet?" asked Buddy.

Oliver shook his head. "No. They asked if I would box them up for them. They did not want to have to do it. I told them I would."

"Have you started yet?" asked Abe.

Oliver shook his head and pointed to a flattened stack of U-Haul-branded cardboard boxes next to the door of the apartment. "My girlfriend and I were going to do it together later this afternoon."

Duff forced himself to get out of the recliner. Several of his joints popped and cracked as he did. "Do you mind if we go through his things for a minute?"

Oliver looked confused. "Why? Don't the police already know who killed him?"

"They know who they think likely killed him. They don't have proof. We need to see if there is anything that might tell us someone other than Sarah Novak did it."

Oliver scratched his head. He looked confused, but he quickly resigned himself to the strangers in his late roommate's bedroom. "In that case, go ahead."

Oliver walked the three men to the bedrooms off the main room of the apartment. Like most collegiate apartments, the two bedrooms were barely big enough for a bed. If the occupant chose to go with a modest twin bed, there might be space enough for a dresser and a small desk. However, like anyone who might be expecting company in his or her respective bed, most students forced a queen mattress into their bedroom, or a full mattress at the least. This left barely enough space to walk around the bed to the closet.

Duff angled himself around the bed awkwardly, moving side-straddle to the closet. "I'm betting Nate just climbed over the bed."

"He did," said Oliver. "We all do. It's easier."

Duff threw open the closet. It was stuffed with clothes of all sorts: a pair of suits, several pairs of jeans, a large section of sports jerseys and t-shirts. A shelf above the bar where the clothes hung was full of all kinds of baseball hats from different colleges and pro teams. On the floor of the closets was a jumbled mess of towels, shoes, and dirty clothes in a laundry basket. Duff wasted no time in sorting through the clothes. "Hey, he's got one of the new Brewers jerseys, the second alternate road jersey. Even got a Brent Suter number thirty-five jersey. Clearly Mr. Riegert was a gentleman of taste."

Duff pulled the jersey out of the closet and held it up to his chest. His 3XL bulk was clearly never going to fit in the much-smaller large-size jersey. He tossed the jersey to the bed with a heavy sigh.

"Nate got a lot of stuff the last few weeks. A lot of gifts."

Abe, Duff, and Buddy all perked up at the G-word. In the world of private investigations, *gifts* was often a code word for favors owed to someone. A failure to repay said favors could result in things like injury or death, depending on to whom the favors were owed.

"Gifts, you say?" Buddy crossed his arms and leaned against the door jamb.

"Yeah. Lots of packages. Lots of deliveries. Recruiting gear, mainly. A lot of D-1 schools were hot after Nate. Even a few D-2 schools. Lots of jerseys from big schools. Lots of hats, water bottles, and notebooks."

"Must be nice," said Buddy.

Oliver's face was impassive. "I just wish I were a pretty-boy skill position player so I might have been able to fit into some of that stuff. When you're an O-line guy, no one sends you the fat guy swag."

"Preach, brother." Duff was dragging out more jerseys. He pulled a Wisconsin Badger football jersey out of the closet, one of the home reds. It had been customized with Riegert's name on the back. He tossed it on the bed next to a dark blue Notre Dame jersey.

"Do you think any of those D-1 schools might have been pushing the bounds of recruiting violations with some of those gifts?" Buddy's methods of questioning never felt overly invasive or pushy. It was just a good ol' son of Wisconsin making friendly conversation over the Friday night fish fry. It was part of what made him a good cop back in the day. People felt comfortable around Buddy, even when he was in full uniform.

Oliver shrugged. "Who knows? I mean, probably. He was getting a ton of stuff, but when you look on Instagram at other guys getting recruited, they're always posting pictures of the piles of shit they get from schools. If it wasn't above board, you'd think the NCAA would crack down more."

"That's true," said Duff. "You can't really keep recruiting violations like that a secret in the digital age. Kids are too stupid about that stuff. They will do anything for a few hundred Likes on the 'Gram."

Abe did not understand college recruiting; he had to trust Duff did. To Abe, it made no sense that a young man would base his college choice off which school offered him a scholarship instead of which school had the best academic programs. The likelihood of a college athlete making it to the professional level was astronomical. The likelihood of someone getting a college degree was far more attainable and practical. Abe liked practical.

Abe was sorting through a stack of textbooks on the little desk in the corner of the bedroom. It looked like most of the books had never been opened. There was still plastic shrink wrap around half of them. A pair of notebooks and a leather-bound day planner on the desk were completely clean, not a single mark in or on them. They did not even look like they had ever seen the inside of a backpack. It was abundantly clear that Riegert did not take his scholarly pursuits seriously. At least, not during football season.

Abe looked on the shelf above the desk. There was a single copy of Stephen King's The Stand wedged next to a bottle of skin lotion and a collector's tallboy of Coors Light. A bookmark was barely sticking out of the pages. Curious at where Riegert had stopped reading, Abe plucked the book off the shelf and opened it. The slip of paper was between pages 568 and 569. It was not even between chapters. There was not even a clean paragraph break on those pages. Likely, the bookmark had been jammed into the book for safekeeping rather than marking a page of reading.

Abe turned the bookmark over. A few numbers and letters were set in printed boxes on the sheet. Abe saw the names of professional football teams and a date. Abe plucked his reading glasses from his breast pocket, slipped them onto his face, and looked at the slip harder. On one end of the slip was a cash amount, $200, and a payoff figure. Abe was not a gambler, but he knew a bettor's slip from a bookie when he saw one.

Abe held it out to the guy he knew dabbled with wasting money playing odds on rare occasions. "Duff, does this look like a bookmaker's receipt to you?"

Duff flopped forward onto the bed and bounced across the mattress like a seal trying to beach itself from the surf. He squinted at the slip. "Looks like one to me. How 'bout you, Buddy?"

The retired sheriff adjusted his own tinted bifocals and looked over the slip. "Certainly does."

"Who's making books in this town?" Duff's eyebrows knitted together in thought.

Buddy knew. "Strangely enough, Larry Panner over at Larry's Bar and

Grill."

"How long?" asked Duff.

"Long enough."

"And you never busted him?"

Buddy held his hands out in a so-what gesture. "He never got too big for his britches. People are going to gamble if they're going to gamble. As long as he kept his bar from attracting too much of the wrong element, I was content to let things lie."

"Translation: You gambled there, too."

Buddy winked at Duff. "Give a lonely single man his vices, won't you? Larry kept his side business low-key. He had a grand limit, and he never took crazy odds he could not pay off. He was smart about it. Cash upfront. No loan sharking."

Abe had been searching through the textbooks while Buddy and Duff spoke. He had discovered at least ten or eleven slips from Larry's bookmaking business. There were probably more around the room. The amounts of the bets placed ranged from fifty bucks to a grand. A bit of quick math showed that Riegert had placed bets totaling more than ten grand in the last four months. That did not sit well with Abe. He remembered far too many nights at college where spending a single buck for a six-pack of microwavable ramen noodles seemed like a luxury. "Where does a broke college kid get more than ten grand to gamble with?"

"If he's a good gambler, maybe he made it from successful bets," said Buddy.

Duff took the tickets in Abe's hand. He was looking at the match-ups and the bets. "Loser. Loser. Loser. Loser. Loser." He shuffled through the rest of the slips. "All these are losers. He lost over ten grand here." Duff sat up on the edge of the bed.

"What does that mean?" asked Oliver.

"It means that we now have a potential new suspect in the murder of your roommate," said Abe.

"If your pal was betting on credit and was five-figures deep into Larry, maybe Larry sends a thumb-breaker who takes his job a little too seriously to try to milk some cash from Mr. Riegert."

Buddy pooh-poohed that theory. "I never knew Larry to have a thumb-breaker."

"How'd he get money from guys who drew bad beats?"

"I told you: No loan sharking; he never let it get too big. I never saw Larry spot a guy. If you did not have cash in hand, you didn't bet. It was that simple."

Duff was still suspicious. "Seems sketchy."

"Larry is a small-time bookmaker, not a mafioso."

Duff looked to Oliver. "Did Nate have a lot of cash on hand?"

Oliver's face was blank. "I have no idea. He never really sprang for pizza, if that's what you're asking. When he bought beer, it was always cheap shit. Never got the good stuff."

"Do you know what his parents did?"

Oliver thought for a second. "His mom's a nurse, and his dad was a house painter."

"Not exactly big money professions," said Duff.

Abe was already to the logical end of Duff's questions. "So, the question remains: who was giving him all the cash?"

Duff pointed at the closet full of collegiate and professional team swag. It was not inconceivable to think some college or zealous booster might have padded the lad's wallet a time or two to entice him to play for their school. "Recruiting violations, anyone?"

6

LARRY'S BAR AND Grill did brisk business at lunch. It was fast and convenient. There was plenty of free parking behind the building and easy access from the street. Plus, they slapped together a tasty burger with a side of fries in almost the same amount of time it took to run through a McDonald's drive-thru line. Guys on their lunch break could get a burger far better than the average fast-food slop for a few cents more, check out the scrolling ticker on ESPNews while they did it, and Monday-morning quarterback whatever the Packers did wrong on Sunday.

Larry Panner was the current owner and namesake. It had gone through a half-dozen iterations before he took over the place in the mid-Nineties. Prior to being Larry's Bar and Grill, it'd been Dave and Maureen's Bar 'n' Grill, the Rockland Grill, Marty's Place, and a few others forgotten to time. Before he became a restaurateur, Larry had been a residential painting contractor, and before that he'd done a stint in the Army, four years doing data and communications stateside. Easy work, but dull as watching a dryer cycle. The Army loses its gloss pretty quickly when the world travel the recruiter promised never materializes, and the only exotic location you get to see is the underwhelming glory that is Fort Monmouth, New Jersey.

Larry was gifted when it came to running a bar, though. He was gregarious to a fault, told jokes with a perpetual smile, and kept the beer flowing. He was knowledgeable about all things sports and politics, and he was one of the guys who served as a touchstone for all the local happenings. Next to Buddy Olson, Larry was probably the most well-informed man in Waukesha County.

Larry also worked almost all the time the bar was open. He was an institution now, and people just expected him to be there whenever they were. He was hustling food and drinks to waiting customers like usual when Buddy Olson pushed open the tinted-glass door to the bar. A pretty-faced blond twenty-something in a tight tank top branded with the bar's logo greeted Buddy at the door. "Hey, Sheriff! Long time, no see. You want to sit at the bar like usual?"

Buddy winked at the girl. "Hey, Abby. I'll take a table today. I'm entertaining." He gestured to Abe and Duff.

"Sure thing!" Abby's smile was perma-plastered, unwavering, to her face. She walked them to an empty table along the wall. As the men took their seats, Abe and Duff on one side of the table, the sheriff on the other, Abby asked if anyone wanted coffee or something else to drink.

Buddy looked over at the taps behind the bar. "What's new?"

"Last new thing we got in was a keg of Capitol Brewing's Oktoberfest. It's heavy and hearty."

"I'll take it."

"I'll just have water," said Abe, who was not a drinker.

"Diet Coke." Duff only drank diet Coke, Jarritos, and the occasional beer. Abe could not even remember Duff drinking water unless there were no other options. Abe wasn't even entirely certain if Duff used water when he brushed his teeth.

"Tell Larry I need to talk to him when he gets a chance. No rush," said Buddy.

"Will do!" Abby whisked off to get the drinks.

Like most small bars in Wisconsin, the menus were pinned between the wall and the condiment caddy on the far side of the table. Duff grabbed them and distributed them to his compatriots.

Abe barely glanced at the menu. Like he always did when he entered unfamiliar surroundings, whether consciously or subconsciously, he was watching the patrons at the bar and learning what he could from observing them. Abe knew that Duff had already learned everything he could learn from just a glance. Abe was not that fast; he was more thorough. He concentrated on Larry behind the bar. He watched his face, his posture, and his micro-expressions. By all indications, Larry Panner was a genial, happy fellow who truly enjoyed what he did. His smile was genuine, not forced. He did not have any breaks in his expressions. He did not favor one customer over the other. He really enjoyed being behind the bar and the relationships that came with it. Many people were fiercely loyal to their local watering hole, and Larry did not take their loyalty lightly. Every man and woman at the bar were greeted by name or nickname, lots of handshakes and back-

slapping, friendly inside-jokes, and questions about health, parents, and spouses. Larry had the long memory and instant recall that made for a good bartender.

While Abe watched, he saw a man hand a slip of pink paper over to Larry along with two bills. Abe did not catch the denomination of the bills, but if he had to guess, he suspected each one sported a bust of Benjamin Franklin.

Larry palmed the slip and the bills like a skilled magician. They simply disappeared from view. Larry took the bills down to the end of the counter and disappeared through a door just past the end of the bar. When he came back, he was all smiles and jokes again. Abe kept watching the door. A few seconds later a middle-aged woman in jeans and a hooded sweatshirt branded with the bar's logo emerged. She walked to the guy who had given Larry the slip. A bettor's receipt emerged from the front pocket of her sweatshirt, and the guy took it from her, folded it once, and slipped it into his shirt pocket. She made a joke, they both laughed, and she returned to the office behind the bar.

Anyone not paying attention would not have noticed anything wrong. No one who was not looking for the betting would have seen it. It could have been a transaction over a bar tab. It was subtle and effective. Abe was certain that betting happened in every bar in the country, but this was a different level of betting. Most bar bets were parlor games or friendly wagers. This had organization. This had structure. Abe wondered how much under-the-table money Larry made from this endeavor. If the IRS ever got a hold of proof of this under-the-table betting, surely there would be a major investigation. Abe also wondered at why Buddy Olson would let such a thing continue. Did the current sheriff of Waukesha County know this was going on? Did he care?

Abe leaned toward Duff and spoke in a voice low enough to not carry across the table to the sheriff. "Did you see—"

"I saw." Duff spoke in an equally low voice. His eyes were still staring at his menu, but Abe knew Duff was on the same page. Twenty years of being partners gave them a pretty tight mental connection. Duff was sometimes erratic or secretive, and Abe sometimes had problems following his leaps in logic, but they spent most of their time together weaving along the same wavelength.

"I don't know why I look at the menu." Buddy tossed the plastic-covered sheets to the center of the table with a flip of his wrist. "I always get whatever the special is."

"What is the special?" asked Abe.

"Meatloaf sandwich with grilled onions and a side of chili." Duff's eyes

did not leave his menu.

"Where do you see that?" Abe saw no listed specials on his menu.

"It's on the board behind the bar back there." Duff pointed toward the corner of the bar behind him.

Buddy chuckled. "You still doing that observational stuff?"

"He can't help it," said Abe.

Buddy leaned forward smirking. "Close your eyes."

Duff looked up at his old mentor, an eyebrow arched. "Seriously?"

"Seriously. Humor an old man."

Duff shrugged and closed his eyes.

Buddy looked around the bar. "How many blue shirts?"

Duff did not hesitate. "Three."

"How many ball caps?"

"Seven. Two trucker-style, five cloth."

"How many people aren't wearing jeans?"

Duff hesitated. "At least three, including Abe. Possibly four."

"Possibly?"

Duff pointed toward the bar. "The girl behind the bar. She's too short for me to see what she's wearing from the waist down. However, I'm going to wager that she's likely wearing those skin-tight leggings, probably black ones. She seems like the type at first glance. I can't be certain, though."

Buddy looked toward the diminutive woman behind the bar. He called out, "Hey, Shelly?"

The girl's eyebrows raised as she sought who called her. She saw Buddy's raised hand. "Yeah, Buddy?"

"You wearing jeans or tights?"

"Yoga pants. I'm lazy today."

"What color?"

"My yoga pants? Black."

"Four people not in jeans, then," said Duff. "I knew she didn't look like the jeans type."

"It still amazes me, that whole see-the-whole-room observation thing." Buddy leaned back in his chair and crossed his arms over his expansive belly. "I wish I could have trained my detectives to do that. We could have closed a lot more cases, I think." Buddy turned to Abe. "You know, I always hoped this joker would have grown up, gone to the academy, and become a cop so I could have hired him as a detective for my team. You never saw someone so bulldog-determined to solve a case as this guy."

Abe was very familiar with Duff's OCD when it came to solving crime. "I can imagine."

Abby the waitress returned to the table with their drinks and a green pad

to scrawl down their orders. "What'll you guys have today?"

"Gimme the special," said Buddy. "And whatever these guys want. Put it on my tab."

"You got it." Abby looked at Abe and Duff expectantly.

"Bacon cheeseburger," said Duff. "Side of the fried cheese curds, please."

"You want ranch with that?"

"Is there any other acceptable dipping sauce for cheese curds?"

The girl shrugged. "Some people like barbeque sauce or ketchup. Saw one guy dip them in soy sauce once."

"Absolute philistines. Ranch or nothing." Ranch dressing was practically communion wine in Wisconsin.

Abby winked at Duff in that way that waitresses have winked at pain-in-the-ass customers for decades. "You got it, hun." She turned to Abe. "And you?"

"I'll try the club sandwich," said Abe.

Duff tossed his menu in disgust. "Why would you do that? We came here for the burgers, man. We talked about the burgers."

"That's a lot of red meat."

"But deli turkey is an improvement? That's a ton and a half of sodium and nitrates. You're literally trading one devil for another." Duff turned to Abby. "Give him a burger."

"Are you his wife? Let the man have a club sandwich, Clive," said Buddy.

"He always does this, though. We go somewhere to get a particular item. He changes his mind at the last second, orders something he's not happy with, and then he regrets it."

Abe hated to admit it, but Duff was not wrong. "That's true. I do that a lot."

Abby looked confused. "So...club or burger?"

Duff sighed. He already knew what Abe was going to do. "You know you're going to hate the club sandwich, but you're not going to be able to complain about it because you'll know I was right."

Abe put his menu on the pile. "Club sandwich, please, with a side of cottage cheese." He added the side just to ruin Duff's day.

"Get fries, at least! You don't go to a bar and order cottage fucking cheese!"

"Cottage. Cheese." Abe crossed his arms.

"You're trying to kill me with your stupidity, aren't you?"

Larry Panner walked over to the table at that moment. He moved fast for an older, bigger guy. Conditioned from years of waiting on customers in a busy bar, there were no wasted movements in his gait. He crossed from

the bar in a few wide steps. "Buddy, how's the world treatin' you?" Panner stuck out a paw and clasped Buddy's hand.

"Repeated kicks to the crotch, like usual. How's your world?"

"Busy." Larry gestured at the bustle around the bar. "Busy, busy, busy, just like always. Better to be busy than not, though. It makes the day go by fast. I'm not complaining."

"Have a seat. These jokers and I need to have a few words with you." Buddy pulled out the empty chair next to him.

Panner checked the bar. The two young women he had working for him were holding off the crowd on their own. He sat. "I guess I can take a load off for a couple of minutes. What's up?"

"These boys are private detectives from Chicago. They're looking into the murder of Nate Riegert."

Larry's smile fell. "Damn shame, that. Kid had a bright future."

"We found your stubs in his apartment, Larry." Buddy nodded at Duff and the portly sleuth dropped the betting slips on the table.

"Hey, I didn't do nothing." Larry put up his hands defensively. "I'm not that kind of guy. Besides, they gotta pay up front. He wasn't in debt to me. You know the rules, Buddy: no cash, no bet."

"I know, but we got questions," said Buddy.

"Where did the kid get the cash?" said Duff.

Larry glanced around the bar for a moment. "Grab your drinks and come on back to the office. We'll talk there." He pushed back from the table and waved at Abby. "I'm gonna take the boys back to the upstairs office. Bring their food there, yeah?"

"You got it!" Abby shot Larry a big smile. "Should be up in a minute."

Larry led them to the kitchen at the back of the bar. A pair of cooks were slapping together meals at a blinding pace, steel spatulas flashing across the flat top grill. Neither of them acknowledged the group. Larry headed up a narrow staircase in the corner of the kitchen. The stairs were built pre-code, as so many things in those old buildings were. They were so narrow that Duff just barely fit, bouncing his shoulders from wall to wall with each step.

The stairs emptied into a dusty hallway the length of the building with two doors on either side. Larry went to the first door on the right. Beyond was a good-sized conference room, an oval table was in the center of the room with six matching office chairs around it. Around all the walls were bookcases laden with old accounting books, receipt books, and other accoutrements of a world before computers when all financial records had to be kept by hand. Many of the books had writing on the spines. Some were designated only by years. Some were identified by various months.

The four men took seats around the table. Larry leaned back in his chair and let out a groan. "I'm getting too old to be on my feet all day."

"Sounds like it," said Buddy. "Maybe you should do a little yoga in the morning."

Duff was scanning all the accounting ledgers on the shelves. "Looks like the records in here go back to the Forties, at least."

"Some even earlier," said Larry. "They were all here when I took over the bar in the Nineties. Never had the heart to throw them out. I spent some time going through them, and it's like a little glimpse into the world of Rockland through the ages. There are receipts for milk delivery from a dairy that hasn't existed since the early Sixties. That's just sort of cool. I thought about donating some of these things to the county historical society, but I imagine most of this stuff would just get thrown out, and I'm too much of a pack rat to let that happen."

"Do you mind if I—" Duff gestured at the books.

"Help yourself," said Larry.

Abby appeared in the doorway with a stack of Styrofoam containers. "Easier to get these up the stairs than a tray. I hope you don't mind." She placed the containers on the table.

"I'm sure it's fine," said Buddy. "Thanks so much, Abby."

"Can I get you anything else?" She pulled a bottle of ketchup from the pocket on her waist apron.

"We're fine, thanks." Buddy dismissed the server with a smile. Abby backed out of the room without another word closing the door behind her.

"So, what do you fellas need to know?" Larry leaned back in the chair and laced his fingers behind his head. "I've got nothing to hide and no reason to lie."

"Gambling is illegal in Wisconsin," said Abe. "At least, off-the-books gambling like you're running out of this bar is."

Larry shrugged. He glanced over at Buddy. "I made no secret about it. I don't really make a profit from it. It's just harmless fun that keeps my regulars engaged. Sometimes they win. Sometimes they lose. No one is missing a mortgage payment over it."

Buddy chimed in. "If it wasn't happening here, it'd be happening somewhere else."

"Exactly," said Larry. "Before I took over this bar, it was run by some guys who had some shady connections down in Chicago. Guys were getting their thumbs broken when they went in the hole. I changed the system, made it safer and easier. Cash up front. Cash payouts when you win. No loans. No one needs to get beaten up anymore."

"You can't stop all gambling, so I preferred it run fairly like what Larry

is doing. If he gets in trouble with the IRS for it, that's his look-out. I was only concerned with the actual crime in town." Buddy took a big, galumphing bite of his meatloaf sandwich. Through his chewing he added, "A few guys betting on the Packers game isn't crime in my book, and I'm not going to tie up the courts with it. Cost us more in tax dollars than it's worth."

Abe opened his own food container and saw the club sandwich and cottage cheese. The sandwich was limp and more bread than meat or lettuce. There was a thin spread of mayo on it. It paled in comparison to Buddy's meatloaf. Instantly he wished he had ordered the cheeseburger, but of course he could not say that aloud. "Do you know how Nate Riegert had the money to keep betting on games?" Abe gamely took a bite of the sandwich. Duff was right; the burger definitely would have been better.

Larry shrugged. "I didn't ask. Figured he must have a rich daddy or something."

"College kids aren't in here betting on games much, are they?" Abe took a bite of the sandwich. It was lackluster, at best.

"Not too often, no. Every few semesters I might get a guy in here who has a few bucks left over from his student loans and he tries to parlay that into a good chunk of next semester's tuition, but it's rare."

Duff was scanning through old record books. Without looking back at Larry, he asked, "Do you think it's possible that Nate Riegert had a loan shark?"

Larry rubbed a hand across the top of his scalp. He considered this for a moment. "Anything is possible, I guess. I would hope he didn't. If I knew he had one, I would have talked to him about it, tried to steer him right."

Abe frowned. "Didn't you see how much money he was spending?"

"I don't take all the bets. I don't go over the slips. That's more Dorothy's domain. And she doesn't worry about who is betting what. She just records the bets and pays out when they win."

Abe was feeling like the betting slips were a dead-end. Could Nate have been killed for getting into debt? Maybe. Was it a solid lead? No.

There was a knock at the door. Abby stuck her head into the room. "Larry, there's a call for you. It's Finsky."

Larry's eyes widened. "Oh, hot damn. Thanks, Abby. Go tell Finsky I'll be right there."

Larry pushed away from the table and stood. "Fellas, I have to go take this call. Please excuse me. Feel free to stay here to finish your lunches. Just leave the containers and glasses on the table when you're done. Abby or I will get them later." He breezed out of the room before they could ask another question.

"Thoughts?" asked Abe.

"I think you hate that club sandwich." Duff was still scanning through the records.

"It's perfectly fine."

"That's code for you hate it."

"I don't think Larry did anything wrong. We're at a dead end here," said Buddy. He took a mouthful of his meatloaf sandwich. Gravy dripped down his chin.

"I agree. Sarah Novak's phone being at the scene points to someone who had access to her things and knew of her history with Nate Riegert." Abe took a bite of his sandwich. "Some loan shark's professional hitter wouldn't have known that. He also would have used a gun."

"Larry didn't do anything having to do with this case. I just find it weird that he didn't bother to learn where this kid kept coming up with big bills for gambling." Duff turned back to Abe and Buddy. He had a large record book with the year *1989* written on the spine. He brought the book to the table and dropped it next to Buddy.

"What you got there?" The old sheriff adjusted his glasses on the bridge of his nose and peered down at the book.

"This is the year Becky was killed."

"I remember. I was there. I don't have dementia yet, knock on wood." Buddy rapped the table with his knuckles.

Duff flipped to a page in the middle of the book. "This appears to be the former owner's records. The guy who owned this place in '89, what do you remember about him?"

Buddy shrugged. "Not a ton. Italian guy. Big belly. His name was Michael Pizzarelli, but everyone called him Mikey Pizza."

"Wouldn't be a good Italian gangster without a good nickname, right? Did you know if he was mobbed up?"

Buddy shook his head. "Not directly, no, but I assumed he was. It was a safe assumption for an Italian guy from Chicago who was running books out of the back room of a bar."

"What are you getting at?" Abe asked.

Duff pointed to a name in the ledger. *Hal Sigrud.* "That's Becky's dad. He was betting money."

"So? So was I," said Buddy. "Doesn't mean that Mikey Pizza killed the Sigruds."

"But it's a lead, isn't it?" Duff's voice elevated slightly. His normally droll, sarcastic tone was replaced with something slightly more alive, edgier. Abe recognized that tone instantly. It meant that Duff was hunting. He found a new clue.

Duff's method for solving crimes was to use his OCD and relentlessly piece together clues and hunt down leads until answers revealed themselves. He was a bulldog worrying at a bone until it broke to the marrow. It could break his mind, though. Duff having a new potential lead meant the fires of investigation were being stoked in his brain. Abe knew from experience this usually ended poorly.

"Did you even look into Hal Sigurd's gambling?"

Buddy closed the record book. "There was nothing concerning in his finances. He had plenty of money in his savings and checking accounts. He didn't get murdered because of gambling."

"But, how do you know if you didn't look into it?" Duff picked up the record book, clutching it to his chest.

"It was not an issue." Buddy's tone was firm. "His bank accounts were golden."

"But, you didn't look!" For an instant, there was something adolescent about Duff's posture, his expression. It was as if he was reverting to that angry, grieving fourteen-year-old trying to solve the murder of his only friend in the world.

"Duff." Abe used a sharp, parental tone he used to use on Tilda when she was small and on the verge of a tantrum.

Duff was not having it. "You hate that sandwich. Admit it."

"Duff, focus. I need you here, now. Sarah Novak is in jail."

"So go get her out. Get the judge to set bail." Duff turned to Buddy. "Mikey Pizza. Is he still alive?"

"I have no idea, honestly. If he is, he's my age, maybe a little older."

"I have to make a phone call." Duff grabbed his jacket and left the little meeting room still clutching the record book to his chest. He slammed the door behind him like a teenager angry about being grounded. The force of the slam felt as though it rattled the whole building.

Duff's burger sat untouched in the Styrofoam clamshell on the table. That worried Abe more than anything. Duff might occasionally forget to put on pants, but he never forgot a meal.

Buddy and Abe looked at each other. Buddy took a bite of his meatloaf sandwich as if nothing happened. Abe cringed inwardly and felt as though he should apologize for his partner. "He's touchy about…you know."

"Oh, I know. You think he's touchy now, you should have seen the little prick when he was fourteen."

"Was he really that bad?"

"I'll put it this way: I got a vasectomy six months after meeting him for a reason."

"Ouch."

"Indeed." Buddy popped a French fry into his mouth. "It wasn't so much the surgery that hurt, but having to put bags of frozen peas on my nuts for a week is something I'd like to never repeat."

DUFF STORMED OUT the back door of the bar being careful not to let either of the cooks in the back see he was carrying something. The rear door of the bar emptied into a back alley lined with garbage dumpsters and a couple of cars that looked as if they had seen better days. People who worked in restaurants really could not afford the luxury of cars which were not falling apart. The alley smelled rank, a mixture of stale beer, spoiled food, and moldering grease. Even the chilly weather did little to dampen the baked-in smell of the alley.

Duff reached into his pocket for his phone. He scanned through his contact list until he came to the name of his landlord. Duff hit the man's name and the phone automatically dialed the number. A woman answered after two rings. "Meyer Himmelman's office. This is Judy."

"Judy, this is Duff from Allard and Duffy Investigations."

"Oh, hello Duff. I haven't seen you in a long time. How are you?"

"Is Meyer in today?"

"Sure. You know him. He doesn't like to go out in the cold if he can help it."

"Does he have thirty seconds free so I can talk to him? I'll be brief."

"I'll check. Please hold." Without waiting for Duff to answer, Judy hit a button on her phone and muzak began playing in Duff's ear, a swirly, gentle trumpet-led instrumental version of Stevie Wonder's "You Are the Sunshine of My Life." The song was just sliding into the chorus when Judy returned. "Mr. Himmelman says you can have two minutes, three if you make him laugh."

"I'll only need two."

"Hold please."

The phone clicked to silence, then it rang again. Himmelman picked up on the first ring. "Duff, my boy. How are things?"

"Real good, Meyer. I need some information from you if you don't mind."

"For you, I never mind. You and Abe, you're good boys." Himmelman was in his late sixties, a diminutive, slightly-built Jew with a paunchy belly, squinting eyes, and a bad hairline. He owned the building that housed Duff's apartment, the taco shop Duff visited almost daily, and a few dozen apartments rented by other people. Himmelman also owned at least twelve or thirteen more buildings just like it. Duff didn't know how much money

Himmelman had, but he knew it was a lot. Despite that, Himmelman still dressed like a flood victim and drove a black 1988 Cutlass Supreme with red vinyl interior.

Himmelman was also connected. Abe and Duff both knew Himmelman had contacts deep within Chicago's Jewish mobsters, but they did not know exactly how deep his connections ran. He might just be the guy who knows a guy who knows a guy. He might know more. They heard rumors Himmelman might be one of the heads of the Kosher Nostra in the Windy City, if not the main guy. They had no evidence of it, of course. Getting close enough to get evidence on someone like Meyer Himmelman was a good way to end up bobbing face-down in the Chicago River in questionable circumstances that would inevitably be labeled a *suicide* by the Chicago Police.

Duff was not scared of Himmelman, though. He liked the old man. The old man was always good to him. "I'm in Rockland, Wisconsin."

"The murder of that quarterback, right? I heard you and Abe went up there."

"You heard?"

"I keep my ear to the ground. You know how it is."

"Well, I'm at a bar called Larry's Bar & Grill. They're running numbers out of the back office."

"Oh?" There was a hint of life in Meyer's voice. Duff had touched a subject to which he had a direct interest.

"It's not major league stuff. It's just sports betting, small-time. No shylocking."

"Oh." Meyer's voice deflated.

"This bar, it used to be run by an Italian guy, a guy called Michael Pizzarelli. They called him Mikey Pizza."

"Ah, yes. I knew of Mikey Pizza. You gotta be careful around those fucking guineas, you know."

"Knew? Past tense? Is he dead?"

"I can say for certain that Mikey Pizza is not alive, but that's about all I can say on that."

Duff felt a surge of anger. He kicked a dumpster nearby. It made a loud, hollow thud. "Is he *dead* dead or *presumed* dead."

"To the authorities, he is presumed dead. From what I understand personally, he's quite dead dead."

"How dead dead?"

Meyer chuckled. "I shouldn't be telling you this, but you and Abe—you're good boys. You're never late with the rent. You don't make excuses. You do good work. Plus, I know you know how this all works, and you're

not going to do anything stupid." There was a bit of a pause and Himmelman came back with a lower voice. "I have heard Mikey is bottom-of-Lake-Michigan dead."

"Who did it?"

"That, I cannot tell you."

"You can't tell me because you don't know or…other?"

"That, I cannot tell you. My sources only know so much."

"Do you know if Mikey Pizza had a second-in-command? Maybe someone knows something about the gambling he ran out of Rockland."

"This would have been what, the early Nineties?"

"Correct." Duff could hear Meyer flipping paper pages, possibly in a journal or notebook.

"Nah. That's too long ago. Most of the guys who would have been in that racket are dead or retired. Anyone who is still alive is probably out of the game, probably down in Florida perfecting their golf game."

"Well, that doesn't help me." Duff, defeated, wanted to rest his head against the edge of the dumpster, but even he had limits.

"Was this about that girl of yours?"

"Her father's name is in one of Mikey Pizza's old record books. He used to place bets through Mikey's bar."

"Interesting. Duff, I'm going to hang up on you now. I'm going to make some inquiries on your behalf. Maybe I find something. Maybe I don't. No promises."

"Thank you, Meyer. I appreciate it. Sincerely."

"You're a good boy, Duff. Now go get that girl out of jail."

"That's Abe's department."

"Well, go help him. I worry about that boy."

The phone went dead. Meyer was gone. Duff slipped his phone back into his pocket. Mikey Pizza sleeps with the fishes. For how long? For how many years? And why? Was it connected to the Sigruds' deaths?

Duff's mind, so nimble and capable of putting together crazy puzzles from a few scraps of clues, was blank once again. The clues did not add up. The mystery was not solved. Duff's fists clenched involuntarily. He needed a hint. He needed a piece which remained out of his grasp. He felt close to the truth, but still light years away.

7

ABE AND BUDDY sat in the minivan waiting for Duff to reappear. It took a long time. When the big man eventually wandered back to where they parked, he was still clutching the record book. Duff opened the rear sliding door of the van and climbed into the center row of seats without a word.

Abe held up the Styrofoam container with Duff's lunch in it. "I brought your burger. It's still warm."

"I'm not hungry." Duff was sullen, his mind elsewhere.

"Who are you and what did you do with Duff?" Buddy said.

Duff didn't answer. He was staring out the window with a distant look in his eye. It was his *I'm-solving-a-puzzle* face. Abe knew he would be useless for a while. At least he would be quiet.

"Where to?" Buddy asked.

"I guess the campus. We need to see Sarah's room. We need to see the crime scene. We need to talk to people who knew Sarah and Nate."

"I guess that's as good a place as any."

Abe checked his watch. It was just after 1:00 p.m. He shifted the van into drive and pulled out into traffic.

Abe's phone started ringing. He fished it out of his right front pocket and answered it without looking at who was calling. "This is Abe."

Maggie Novak's voice came over the phone. She sounded panicked. It sounded as though she had been crying. "Abe, I just got a call from someone at the jail. Sarah got attacked today. Two women beat her badly."

Abe's stomach twisted in a knot. "What? Why?"

"I don't know! I don't know! They won't let me see her. I'm so scared.

Please help."

"I'll go to the jail immediately. I'll call you back when I know something." Abe canceled the call. "Change of plans." He signaled for a lane shift and pulled a hard U-turn at the first intersection they passed. Abe still was not one hundred percent in tune with the van, and its turn radius was just slightly larger than his old Volvo wagon, so he ended up bumping the curb just hard enough to bounce the van as it rode up the cement berm. Abe recovered from the jouncing and sped up. The Sienna responded gamely, as something with a halfway decent engine would. Abe was grateful for the power because the old Volvo would have been complaining and backfiring.

"Ease up on the gas, pardner, you ain't chasing anyone," said Buddy. "You get tagged in town here, and you're getting a ticket. The local PD makes a mint off college students not paying attention to the ol' speedometer."

Abe glanced down and saw that he was doing fifteen over the speed limit. He eased off the gas. It took them fifteen minutes to get from Rockland to Waukesha with Abe flirting with a traffic citation the whole way. Normally, Abe was the kind of guy who set his cruise control one mile per hour under the posted limit.

Abe and Buddy leapt out of the van at the courthouse. Duff stayed in the backseat, lost in thought. Abe wondered if Duff even knew where they were at that moment.

Inside the jailhouse there was a chunky young man working the reception desk. He was clad in the standard deputy sheriff's uniform. He recognized Buddy right away. "Hey, Sheriff. How you been?"

"Good, Duane. Real good. Listen, this is my friend Abe Allard. He's a big-shot lawyer from Chicago, up to represent Sarah Novak."

Duane Simmons's face darkened immediately. "Oh, then I guess he's here about—"

"That's precisely why he's here. He'd like to see his client now."

Duane looked back over his shoulder at the other deputies working in the county jail office. "She's in the infirmary. I don't know if—"

"Son, this is a lawyer looking to speak with his client. His client has been attacked. He has a right to know how she is and see her with his own eyes so he can verify."

Duane's face reddened. Once your boss, always your boss. "Sorry, Buddy. I'll get someone to take him back right away."

"Thank you, Duane." The sheriff changed his tone to ease any ruffled feathers as any practiced politician would. "How's your mom?"

"She's okay. Doctors are really optimistic after her last round of chemo."

"Real good. You send her my best. Tell her I expect to see her back the VFW for Bingo."

Duane hustled away to get someone to assist Abe.

"Are attacks in the county jail common?"

Buddy shrugged. "Yes and no. Little fights are common. A couple punches here and there. That's typical. Occasionally, we've seen full-on rumbles when there are enough gang members in lock-up, but usually we try to stave that off by separating the men into different areas. With the women, we've only got one area for them."

A sturdy-looking Latina deputy came up from the back. She was short but looked like she could go toe-to-toe with a T-Rex. Her hair was pulled into a tight bun on the back of her head. The nameplate on the left pocket of her uniform shirt said *Perez*. She gave Abe and Buddy visitor's passes. "C'mon back."

Abe and Buddy went through the first security door and waited for the deputy to open the second. She closed the second door behind them and led them down a corridor. Abe cleared his throat. "Can you tell me what happened?"

"We got it on security video if you want to see it. Two big gals jumped Inmate Novak and beat the holy crap outta her."

"Any idea why?"

Perez shrugged. "Who knows? Nobody's talking, like usual. Probably because they wanted money."

Abe looked to Buddy. Buddy gave Abe a short nod of his head. "Pretty common, unfortunately. Someone finds out that Sarah's family has money. They demand she calls her parents and have them put money into another inmate's commissary account under threat of violence. If that money doesn't show up, the inmate who made the threat has to make good on it or they look weak."

"Has anyone thought about maybe just not having commissary accounts?"

"Oh, many times. However, it's a good money-maker. These jails don't pay for themselves. We need every penny we can get."

Perez led the two men to the infirmary. It was a long, rectangular room with four hospital gurneys set up at the far end and a nurse's station near the door. There were a couple of large, metal cabinets with heavy padlocks on the doors, presumably where the drugs and supplies were kept. The infirmary had a large, locked door to keep people out, as well. When Perez knocked on the door, she had to wait for the nurse to leave her desk and open the door.

Perez introduced the nurse to Abe and Buddy. "This is Judy Nesheim.

She's the nurse." Perez jabbed a thumb toward Abe. "This is Novak's lawyer."

Abe held out hand. "Abe Allard."

Judy shook his hand. "Nice to meet you." She turned to Buddy and opened her arms for a hug. "Nice to see you again, you old slug. How are you?"

"I'm still above ground, so that's something." Buddy returned her hug.

"I'll be in the hallway." Perez shut the door behind them and took up a sentry position in the hallway on the wall opposite the infirmary.

"How's the patient?" asked Buddy.

"Not too bad considering how they brought her in here."

Abe and Buddy followed Judy back to the bed furthest from the door. In it was a blanket-draped body. Sarah lay on her back, arms covered by the gray wool blanket and low-grade sheets. Only her head was visible. She looked tiny in that hospital bed which was made to hold almost anyone. The side rails were taller than her thin frame, so she was almost blocked entirely from view, save for her face which had a large square of gauze taped to one cheek.

"She's been resting comfortably," said Judy.

"Injuries?" asked Abe.

"She'll be fine, eventually. She's got a few abrasions on her face including a really good one on her left cheek. She's got a cracked rib, but there's really nothing we can do about that except keep her isolated in protective custody until the judge decides if she'll get a bond."

"I will see about getting her out as soon as I can, but until then I think protective custody sounds best."

Abe moved to the side of the gurney. "Sarah, it's Abe Allard." He touched her shoulder gently. "Can you wake up?"

Sarah's eyes blinked slowly. Her left eye was black-and-blue, almost swollen shut. Her lower lip was split in the middle. There were bruises on her face and neck. She winced and tried to sit up in bed.

Abe pressed her shoulder with his hand. "Stay down. Relax. No reason to get up."

Sarah let her body relax. She seemed to merge with the mattress. She let out a long breath. "It hurts."

"It's going to for a while, I'm afraid," said Judy. "Not much we can do about it."

"How about an ice pack?" asked Buddy. "Surely we have room in the county budget for one of those."

Judy nodded and retreated to the locked cabinets, undoing the padlocks with a key from her keyring.

"What happened, Sarah? Why did those women attack you?"

Sarah blew out a long breath. "Those women, they somehow found out my dad was a contractor. They looked up his business, then found my address on the computer in the library. They used Google Maps to find our house and see it on Street View. They said that I must be loaded, so the two women who attacked me told me my parents had to put $5,000 into their accounts by lunchtime today."

"And you didn't?"

"I told them that it was my dad's house, not mine. I told them we weren't as rich as the house looked, and that my dad worked really hard." Sarah winced again. Her hand went to the ribs on her left side. She huffed out a slow breath through pursed lips. "Apparently it didn't matter much to them."

"They just attacked you out of the blue?"

"Rushed me during lunch. I was sitting alone at a table, and then suddenly I was on the ground and they were kicking me. That's all I remember."

Buddy said solemnly, "That's how they do it. If you don't have your head on a swivel they try to get you from behind, surprise you."

"Can I go home, yet?" Sarah's eyes welled with tears. "I hate it here."

Abe shook his head sadly. "I'm sorry. I'm going to request a bail be set as soon as I can. Until the judge grants bail, you have to stay here."

"How long will it take to get bail?"

Abe and Buddy exchanged a glance. They both knew that a judge had the option of not granting bail. They both knew that in a high-profile case like this, it was often safer for the accused to stay inside a jail. If Sarah was granted free access to the community, who knows who might make a run at her for any reason. "The judge might decide to keep you in jail until the trial."

"How long will it take to get to a trial?"

"Three months. Maybe six," said Buddy. "It's going to depend on other factors."

Sarah's brave face broke into sob. She repeated, "I hate it here."

"We're going to try to get them to let you see your parents in a meeting room, no glass. That's the best I can do for now. I cannot make any promises, though." Abe hated to even suggest that he might get Sarah a face-to-face meeting with her parents. If he could not make it happen, it would be a crushing blow to her, but he also felt she needed a light in the distance to look to at the moment.

Sarah bit back her tears and nodded. She swallowed hard. "Thank you."

"They are going to put you in protective custody for the time being, as

well. You will be alone in a cell for most of the day, but you will be safe that way."

"I would rather be alone." Sarah's face became an emotionless mask. The tears still glittered on her cheek, but her cheeks and eyes were slack, dead to the world. "Thank you for coming to see me."

Judy came back with an instant cold pack and put it on Sarah's cheek. Sarah winced and gave a little moan, but she held it to her face despite the discomfort.

There was nothing else Abe could do. His client was in acceptable circumstances at the moment. The jail was going to protect her until she could receive a bond. Abe had done his duty.

Judy let Abe and Buddy out of the infirmary. Perez walked them back to the reception area, and they walked out of the Waukesha County Courthouse.

Henry and Maggie Novak were in the parking lot, waiting in Henry's truck. The moment Maggie saw Abe, she leapt out of the truck and ran to him. "Mr. Allard, please tell me. Is she okay? Is my baby okay?"

Abe calmed her down. "She's fine for now. It will be alright." Henry walked up to join them. Abe explained the attack and the injuries Sarah suffered. He explained how the jail was going to protect her.

Maggie was a wreck. Her eyes were red rimmed from crying. "When can I see her?"

"Soon, I hope. She is still in the infirmary, and probably will be for another day or two. Once they move her to protective custody, I will appeal for a personal meeting."

"Who is the judge on this case?" asked Buddy. "I never saw a name in the papers."

"Balmer. Judge John Balmer." Henry put a hand on Maggie's shoulder.

Abe saw Maggie shift slightly. It was not an overt move, but at the same time it spoke volumes to Abe. She did not want Henry to touch her at that moment. She was not comforted by his touch.

"I know John well. He's a stand-up guy. I might be able to get us a meeting with him," said Buddy.

"Please do." Maggie dipped her shoulder out from under her husband's hand. It did not look like an awkward move, but only people who were paying attention would have noticed it as a deliberate move. Abe wondered if it was just the stress of the moment, of if there was more to it.

"We will see about arranging a bond as soon as we can. If we can get her a bond, will you be able to raise the cash necessary to get her out?"

"How does that work?" asked Henry. "Is it still ten-percent?"

Abe nodded. "As far as I know, yes. A million-dollar bond is going to

require a hundred-thousand cash."

"I can get it," said Henry. "Even if I have to sell a few things."

"We will get it," said Maggie.

A plain, black SUV pulled up in front of the courthouse. A grim-faced Pam Jahnke got out from behind the wheel. She was dressed in an unflattering gray pants suit over a light blue blouse. Her badge was on her belt near the Glock 22 on her hip. She strode around the front of the SUV. "Hey, you—lawyer."

Abe looked up with raised eyebrows. "Can I help you, detective?"

Jahnke walked up and stepped to Abe's face, her jaw squared in barely contained rage. "I hear you're trying to blow up my investigation."

Abe took a step backward. "I wouldn't say we're blowing it up. We're just conducting our own investigation into the murder. We might end up proving your theory on it. We don't know."

"Oh, is this the cop who locked up my little girl?" Henry Novak stepped toward Jahnke. "Maybe you should just be quiet, *detective*." He made the word sound like a slur. His lips were pressed thin in anger.

"Ease up, now." Buddy tried to put a hand on Henry's chest, but Novak strode through it. He got right into Jahnke's face.

"My little girl isn't a killer."

"Back up, sir. I will not hesitate to take you down." Jahnke's hand went to the butt of her gun on her hip.

"Do it! I dare you." Novak squared his shoulders and used his size to try to intimidate Jahnke. The detective was unimpressed. She threw a hand to the man's chest and shoved him backwards.

"Henry!" Maggie threw her arms around Henry's waist and tried to prevent him from retaliating.

Abe attempted to help, but Henry shoved him aside like he was made of balsa. Abe was launched sideways. He barely kept himself upright.

Buddy stepped between Jahnke and Novak. "You know, Pammy— best detective I ever had was a guy named Cecil Montrose. You know what made him the best detective? In almost twenty-five years as a detective, he never once drew his gun."

"Sheriff, with all due respect, get out of my line of fire."

Buddy reached out and put his own hand on Jahnke's hand. "Pulling that thing ain't going to help you or Mr. Novak right now. Cooler heads need to prevail."

A couple of Waukesha deputies, having seen the disturbance from the courthouse windows, came streaming out of the doors to separate the parties. Jahnke let her hand fall off the handle of her service piece.

"The evidence points to your daughter, Mr. Novak. I can't help that. I

would be remiss in my duty if I didn't arrest her, based on the evidence." One of the deputies led Jahnke away from the Novaks in a wide arc. "Even good kids do stupid things sometimes."

"My daughter is innocent, you stupid bitch!" Henry Novak's face was bright red. Fury radiated from him. Abe felt certain that Novak would have tried something stupid if there had not been people there to stop him.

Maggie Novak was crying again. Her fists were balled and held to her mouth. "Just stop it, Henry. Stop it!"

Buddy patted one of the deputies on the back. "Get Pammy out of here, Dave. Take her inside. I'll get the Novaks out of here."

There were several seconds of confusion as different people tried to gently lead different members of the group in different directions. Henry Novak flipped a strong middle finger at Jahnke. Jahnke spat on the ground in frustration. Abe was able to read her lips as the detective said under her breath, *"Fucking hicks."*

Buddy and Abe were able to corral the Novaks and get them to their truck. Abe convinced them to return to the hotel reminding them he was on the job, and he would take care of everything.

It was only once the Novaks' truck was heading out of the parking lot did Abe turn toward his own vehicle. The maroon Sienna was where he left it. The fat man who had been daydreaming in the backseat was not. The van was empty.

"Buddy, where did Duff go?"

DUFF HAD BEEN sitting quietly in the back of the van. His high-precision eidetic memory had been going over every detail of the Sigrud crime scene except the bodies. He could not rid his subconscious brain of the murdered corpses, but he sure as hell could block them out of his conscious brain when he needed to through an act of brute mental force. In his reconstructed memory palace of the crime, the bodies were black outlines, dull and flat against the living color and clarity of the rest of the scene.

Duff's memory was a blessing and curse. His memory and superb recall made him an excellent detective. However, it also meant that he could replay with painstakingly precise detail any lapse of judgment from his own life, any moment where he put his foot in his mouth, any embarrassing scene, and any argument he had ever had with his parents. He could remember the sting of every punch he ever took from every bully he encountered in his youth. He could remember the smells of the horrific bathrooms at Bensonhurst. He remembered the humiliation and shame of the communal

showers in the asylum. He could remember the smell of blood and vomit and shit from crime scenes. He could taste the rank foulness of death anytime he desired simply by giving a passing thought to any crime scene in which he had ever set foot. They all could rush into his mind on command.

Whether or not he wanted to admit it, his memory was responsible for his addiction to video games. While he was immersed in a rich, deeply inventive adventuring world like *Grand Theft Auto* or *Red Dead Redemption,* his brain could go into autopilot taking in enough data through the screen to force his memory into a sleeping subroutine while his eyes and fingers had to coordinate with the on-screen avatar. For those hours he was playing games he could simply forget to remember, and that was a blessing. Sherlock Holmes might have injected cocaine to stimulate his brain in periods of idleness, but Duff used *Assassin's Creed* or *Call of Duty* to negate his brain's obsessive recall when it was not needed. It was arguable whether the drugs or the video games did more damage.

Duff's father's idol, the author and theologian C.S. Lewis, the man whom Duff was named after, was said to possess an eidetic memory. Duff's father used to love to point that fact out as if his son was Lewis reborn. It was said that Lewis had memorized the entirety of Milton's epic poem *Paradise Lost*, and a student could select any book from Lewis's shelves, begin reading the page aloud, and Lewis could summarize the rest of the page. Duff's own memory did not work in quite the same fashion. He could not quote pieces of literature from memory. His mind worked more for physical spaces than recall of words. His ability to remember a moment in time was as complete as Lewis's memory of his own library. Because of this ability, Duff spent many, many hours in the Sigrud household on that terrible day in 1989. The completeness of the memory was permanent. It would never leave him.

Now, while he was mentally in the reconstruction of the scene, Duff found himself searching through every detail in the room. He was looking for betting slips. As a fourteen-year-old, betting had never occurred to him as a motive for the crime. Fourteen-year-olds were not known for being big gamblers as it was rare for a fourteen-year-old to have that sort of expendable cash. As an adult, Duff knew the gambling world well. Betting on sports had cost him a few bucks here and there, but nowhere near the sort of thing where it was problematic. It was $20 on the Superbowl or putting $50 on the Brewers to win the N.L. Central. It was harmless betting. He never bet on credit. No one ever came to the office looking to break his thumbs.

In the Sigrud house he could only search the first floor. While he had been on the second floor many times in his youth playing games or reading

comic books with Becky, he had not gone up to the second floor the day he found the three members of the Sigurd family dead in their living room. Because of that lapse, the stairs ended in a fuzzy, black static void in his mind. No matter how hard he tried to push past that void, it was blocked to him. He only had access to the living room, kitchen, and whatever he could see through the open door to Hal Sigrud's study. He did not enter the study that day, so much of it was blocked to him. Thirty-one years later, he still cursed himself for not spending more time going through the house before he called the police. He would have had the memories of that house. Maybe the key to solving their murder was on the desk in the study. He would never know.

Instead, he continually replayed every inch of the house he did see that day. He went through the kitchen and looked at the magazines on the counter next to the stylish crocks that held flour and sugar. He looked to see if there were any betting slips used as bookmarks he might not have remembered. He looked through the picture books on the coffee table in front of the blood-spattered couch. He could even see under the couch because he had dropped to his knees on that fateful morning crying out in agony when he saw Becky. He remembered there was a cat toy under the couch, a little neon-green mouse Becky's cat, Roly-poly Ole, used to love to bat around.

Whatever happened to Ole the cat? Probably got taken to the pound and adopted to another family who would never know anything about the cat's former life and why he ended up at the pound. Like so many other things in Duff's childhood, the cat's fate was forever lost to him. Ole was certainly deceased by now. He had been at least eight or nine the year of the murder. For a fleeting second, Duff tried to bury his atheistic inclinations for a happy, imagined thought of Becky and Ole meeting in some form of an afterlife.

Still in his memory palace, Duff heard a phone ringing. That was strange. And new. The phone never once rang while he had been in the house that day. It was forceful, too. Stronger than a standard phone ringing. In his mental reconstruction of the scene, Duff walked to the phone and looked at it. It was one of those old rotary-dial phones made from bright-red plastic. A sticker was on the back of the handset with the number of a once-popular pizza place that no longer existed. The phone rang again.

Duff reached out and answered it. *Hello?* On the other end of the line was silence.

Duff hung the handset back on the two metal hooks on the top of the housing. The phone immediately rang again. Duff answered again, and only heard silence. He went on the defensive. Something was wrong. Something

in his brain was misfiring for some reason.

The phone rang again. Duff picked up the handset and slammed it back on the receiver with force. The phone broke and fell off the wall, clattering to the floor. There were no wires coming from the back. The spot on the wall where it had been was blank and smooth. The phone continued to ring.

The memory palace in his mind suddenly stripped away, and Duff was yanked from it, thrust back into the present moment where he was still sitting in the back seat of Abe's Toyota Sienna.

Duff blinked twice. His brain was trying to tell him something he had not yet considered.

With a burst of energy, Duff grabbed the files from the murder investigation. He started flipping through pages like crazy, scanning the details. Page after page, he did not see the one thing he wanted to see. When he came to the final page, he was still left with one question.

Duff left the minivan slamming the sliding door behind him. He limped his gimp ankle across the parking lot, up the stairs at the courthouse, and into the sheriff's department.

A civilian worker at the desk smiled and started to greet him. Duff cut her off. "I need to see Detective Jahnke."

"The detective should be back shortly if you'd like to wait." The woman at the desk indicated some wooden benches by the wall. Duff sat and waited. He took in the little details of the office, burning them into his brain without really wanting them to be there, another downside to his strangely thorough memory. He remembered everything whether he wanted to or not, whether the details were important or not.

At one point, several deputies fled from the office and ran outside. Duff did not take notice. It was not his concern.

When Jahnke did appear, she was flustered and angry, flanked by a pair of sheriff's deputies. All three were talking rapidly and flinging a lot of curses. The two deputies and the detective turned to enter the office area of the sheriff's department.

Duff stood. "Detective Jahnke?"

Jahnke stopped. She turned to face Duff. Recognizing him, her eyes narrowed. "Now's not a good time, Mr. Duffy. Get out of here."

"Just Duff is fine. I need to talk to you about the Riegert investigation. Something's missing."

"Nothing is missing, Mr. Duff."

"No mister, just Duff. And something is missing. Something so obvious I didn't even think about it myself."

Jahnke sighed. She rested a hand on her hip just above her weapon. "Fine. What's missing, then?"

"Where is Nate Riegert's phone?"

Jahnke's eyes narrowed. "What?"

"His phone. He has a cell phone. Everyone has a cell phone, especially college kids. Kids today— they don't go anywhere without them. They're like pacifiers to toddlers. They run people's lives. Where is Nate Riegert's phone? It wasn't in his apartment; we searched there this morning. It wasn't recovered at the crime scene, and it wasn't in his locker at the gym; that was all covered in your reports. Nowhere in your reports does it mention one of your people at the crime scene recovering his phone. You never searched for his phone. It just disappeared."

Jahnke's nostrils flared slightly. She looked like she was going to say something flippant for a moment, but she bit her lip. She turned on her heel and strode into the office. Without being asked, Duff followed.

Jahnke went to her desk and typed in her password to unlock her laptop. She brought up the case files and started searching. Duff stood behind her and watched her do it. She brought up reports and did Control-F searches for the words cell and phone, and then did it for cellphone, just in case. All the references to the cell phones were of the one that was recovered at the scene, the one that belonged to Sarah Novak.

Resigned, Jahnke sank back in her chair. The hinge underneath it gave a mournful squeak. "Maybe he didn't have one?"

"Most popular guy on campus just didn't have a device that told him of all the latest parties? He didn't have a device that let him get dirty messages from horny girls? He didn't have a device that allowed him to speak to college recruiters who wanted to give him full rides at Division One schools? C'mon, Detective. Do better."

Jahnke's face grew tight. Her lips pursed. She threw up her hands. "What does it matter?"

"Because whoever killed Nate Riegert took his phone."

8

DUFF AND JAHNKE walked out of the Waukesha County Sheriff's Department together. They were quickly spotted by Abe and Buddy. Abe had been trying to call Duff on his cell phone, but Duff had the phone on silent, so it had been going straight to voice mail which Duff never bothered to check anyhow.

Abe heaved a small sigh of relief when he spotted Duff. Sometimes when Duff was in the Otherworlds of his mind he did not think about all the reality around him. Abe had seen Duff walk into moving traffic in Chicago without a second thought when he had been trying to solve a case.

Duff and Jahnke met Abe and Buddy at the sidewalk in front of the building. "The cell phone. We need to find Nate's cell phone." Duff explained his revelation to Abe and Buddy.

Jahnke looked contrite. "I should have thought about that. I didn't. Never even occurred to me."

"Doesn't matter. We need to find it now," said Buddy. "Can you contact the carrier company and get a search? We can get a ping on it if you act fast."

"Battery is dead by now," said Abe.

"Unless someone has been keeping it plugged in for some reason." Duff gestured to *Rose*, the Toyota Sienna. "We need to go search Sarah Novak's room."

"We already searched it," said Jahnke. "There wasn't anything there."

"Clearly you didn't search it well enough if you didn't find a cell phone, and she's still your main suspect."

"Her phone was at the scene of the crime!" Jahnke's face grew tight

with barely simmering rage. "What do you expect me to do? Dismiss it as a coincidence?"

Duff never backed down from someone like Jahnke, even with her gun on her hip. He squared up, chin out. "I would have done another half-hour's worth of work. Her motive was weak. Crimes of passion happen in the moment. They don't happen hours after the fact where the suspect has to track down the victim."

"This isn't helping us find that cell phone," said Buddy.

Abe positioned himself between Duff and Jahnke. He took Duff's elbow. "Someone might know if she did something with it."

"C'mon, princess." Buddy grabbed Jahnke's elbow and steered her away from Duff. "I'll help you with the paperwork to get a carrier search. You guys go see what you can find at Sarah's dorm."

"I think it's called a residence hall now." Abe's need to be pedantic could not be helped.

"Whatever it's called, go." Buddy was already to the stairs.

UW-ROCKLAND BENEFITED FROM having the second most beautiful campus in the UW System, a public school with an expensive private school feel. For a relatively newer addition to the University of Wisconsin school system, it had a charm usually found at older schools. Rockland had originally been called the Rockland Normal School, a Christian academy of teacher training until the UW swallowed the little, private institution by offering cheaper degrees and more activities. Rockland Normal shuttered its doors in 1964. For a while, the school languished empty before being purchased and assimilated by the UW System in the early 1970s and transformed into the hallowed halls of learning it was now. The main buildings on Rockland's campus were the original normal school structures, all built in the early part of the 1900s. The original Milwaukee Cream-colored brick of the buildings had been stained dark by years of weathering, and the windows were all tall and narrow, as it was the popular style of the time. The main buildings look like they came straight out of the historical record. Black-and-white photos of the buildings matched almost perfectly with ones taken a hundred years ago.

The campus was blessed with an ocean of trees, many of the oaks and maples were well over a century old. They rose high into the sky and their limbs stretched over sidewalks to create a shady, tunnel-like feel. The newer buildings surrounded the four original buildings, and each one reflected the particular architectural stylistics of the decade in which it was built.

The residence halls were plain. They were long, narrow buildings four

stories high. Each room was cramped, barely big enough for two twin beds, two small desks, a dresser, and two small closets. They were holdovers from the normal school era when comfort and convenience was an afterthought or dismissed as unnecessary. Living in such crowding was a good catalyst to get students to graduate as soon as possible, after all.

Duff and Abe found the hall where Sarah had been living, Joyman Hall, named for one of the original heads of the old normal school, Edward Joyman. The hall was designated by a large plaque in front of it bearing the name of the hall and its designation as a co-ed building. The women lived on the south side of the hall, the men on the north side. Obviously, having so many young men and women experiencing their first tastes of adult freedom in a claustrophobic house of hormones led to many puns on the name of Joyman. At Northwestern, where Abe got his undergrad education, he remembered the women's residential college, Hobart House, having all kinds of puns revolving around the prefix "Ho."

Duff and Abe walked to the south entrance. Back in the days when Abe had been an undergrad, they probably would have been able to walk into the lobby, walk past the bored young woman working the front desk, and walk straight to Sarah's room. School safety concerns in recent years forced major changes, and now all the halls were constantly locked and monitored. Entry was only available by scanning badges which all students carried, or by being rung through by the person working the front desk.

Duff and Abe were able to enter the first door of the building, but they were quickly rodeoed in the small, rectangular foyer. A young woman was sitting at the front desk beyond the foyer, perched in a little service window of the office of the hall. A young man was leaning against the counter of the service window. They appeared to be in conversation. The woman did not notice the two detectives until Abe rapped his knuckles against the glass.

Startled, the woman sprang into action. She appeared to be fumbling with something on the desk in front of her.

A moment later, an intercom box on the wall of the foyer crackled to life and the woman's voice was broadcast through it. "Can I help you?"

Abe produced his Illinois private detective's license from his wallet. He never flipped it out in its plastic sheath like detectives did in the movies. Duff did when he would actually deign to show it to someone, but Abe always carefully pulled it from its spot in his wallet and held it clearly between his fingers and thumb. He held it near the glass where she could see it. It was too small for her to make out any details at that distance. He might as well have been holding up a Starbucks gift card. "My name is Abe Allard. I'm a private detective investigating the Nate Riegert murder. Can my partner and I speak with you?" The girl and guy at the desk exchanged

looks. The guy shrugged as if to say, *It's up to you.* After a pause, a strong buzzing sound erupted from the electric lock.

The girl behind the counter stood as Abe and Duff walked to the desk. Abe continued to hold out his license for her and slipped her one of his business cards. She squinted at both proffered items. The girl was dressed in jeans and a black t-shirt that advertised a band Abe had never heard of, and she wore her straight brown hair simply with a single clip near her ear to keep her tresses out of her face. The young man standing at the window was in shorts and unlaced cross-trainers. He was clean-shaven with shaggy reddish hair that hung around his face. His blue t-shirt had a white, screen-printed logo emblazoned across the chest in a 1970s-style font.

Duff glanced at the logo. He cocked an eyebrow. "Should I even ask about the Yogurt Slingers?"

The kid chuckled, a little embarrassed. He drew a line under the logo with his finger. "It's the name of my Ultimate team."

Abe cocked his head to the side. "Ultimate what?"

"Ultimate Frisbee," said Duff.

Abe adjusted his glasses and leaned closer to the kid to look at the logo. "What's Ultimate Frisbee? Is that a video game?"

"It's a sport, sort of like football with Frisbees," said Duff.

"Not exactly." The kid tugged the bottom of his shirt down. "More like handball with Frisbees with a touch of hockey thrown in, really."

"I've never met a private detective before," said the girl at the desk. "Is it as cool a job as TV makes it out to be?"

Duff snorted. "Oh, fuck no. It's mind-numbingly boring most days."

"It's not that bad," said Abe. "Some days are boring. Some days are kind of exciting."

"If you can call talking to a guy with a euphemism for ejaculation on his shirt exciting, that is." Duff took a seat in one of the plush chairs in the lobby. "Look, we're in the backwoods of southern Wisconsin at a tiny college talking to you. How exciting could this gig be?"

"Ignore him," said Abe. "Could I get your names?" He pulled his notebook and pen from his pocket.

The girl perked up. "I'm Jessica. Jessica Thurow. That's my friend, Aiden Vogel."

"Do either of you know Sarah Novak and Nate Riegert?"

Jessica nodded. "Oh, yeah, of course. This is a pretty small school. Everyone knows everyone, sort of. Sarah and I live on the same floor." She paused, and then corrected herself. "Lived on the same floor, I guess."

"What about Nate?"

Jessica looked down at the desk. Abe saw a flash of discomfort cross

her face. She looked to Aiden. He shrugged. "We saw him. We never really talked to him much."

"He came by the residence hall to see Sarah sometimes, of course. Usually when her roommate was home for the weekend so they could have sex." Jessica exchanged a glance with Aiden. Abe recognized the look immediately. She was looking for guidance. She wanted to know if she should say more.

Abe decided to lend her that guidance. "I heard they fought a lot." Jessica's shoulders relaxed. Abe opened the gate for her to keep speaking.

"They fought almost every time they saw each other. In only a few weeks of dating, they had several blow-ups. It was like they lived for each other's drama."

Aiden backed up that statement. "They were like two toxic moons orbiting each other. They were bad for each other, but they could not break away."

"Did either of you see Sarah the night of the murder?"

"Oh, yes." Jessica gestured in front of her at the desk. "I was working that night."

"What did you see?"

Jessica was quiet for a moment. She lowered her eyes. "I already told the police all this."

"Please, tell me again. I haven't read their report," said Abe.

Jessica and Aiden exchanged another glance. She swallowed hard and closed her eyes. "I was working the desk. I know Sarah had a fight with Nate earlier that day. At some point, she came through the lobby. She was stumbling drunk. I called out to her, but she ignored me. About an hour later, she came back and went to her room without saying a word."

"Were you working the desk when the police arrived?"

Jessica shook her head. "No. I was already asleep by then. I didn't find out about the arrest until Saturday morning."

Abe and Duff exchanged a glance. Neither had to speak to know what they were both thinking: Jessica's story confirmed Sarah left the residence hall. Would an hour have been enough time for her to get to the gym, hit Nate with the weight plate, and get back? Judging by the size of the small campus, it probably would have been more than enough.

"Do you know how Sarah got the vodka she was drinking?" said Abe. "She was underage."

Jessica gave Abe a look that suggested he was a moron. Abe had a teenage daughter; he was more than familiar with that particular expression. "It's vodka. It's all over the place here."

"It's practically on tap at the water fountains," said Aiden.

"I thought beer was the drink of choice for poor college students," said Duff.

"It is, usually. However, getting drunk on beer takes too long if your goal is to get blind-stupid shit-faced. That's when you turn to hard alcohol. Vodka tends to be the favorite choice for that around here. Mixes well with everything." Aiden sounded like he was speaking from experience.

"Why didn't anyone try to stop Sarah when she left the dorm drunk?" asked Abe.

Jessica squinted at him. "Seeing drunkies doing stupid things on a Friday night is nothing new. This isn't a dry campus, Mr. Allard."

"What do you do here, Jessica?" Duff gestured to the office area in which Jessica sat.

"I'm security. I make sure people don't get in this building if they're not supposed to be in here, and I help students with things like getting their mail or checking out vacuums if they want to clean their rooms."

"So, a security person didn't want to help a drunk student?"

"We're all adults. If she had fallen and gotten hurt, I would have helped her. Drunk people going out on Taco Bell runs is pretty commonplace."

Duff got a dreamy, faraway look in his eye. "Ah, yes. The magical siren song of cheap burritos and Baja Blast has lured me from my slumber many a time."

Abe jabbed a thumb toward the door to the residence area beyond the lobby. "Can my partner and I go down to Sarah's room?"

Jessica gave her desk a furtive look, as if she were reading the hall's rules from a card hidden below the lip of the service window, but then she shrugged. "I'm not supposed to let people go into this hall, but you're kind of here on official business, aren't you?"

"We were hired by Sarah's parents. They gave us permission to search her room for anything that might help prove her innocence."

Jessica chewed on this for a moment before giving a permissive shrug. "I guess it's okay. Her room is 202. One flight up, to the left. Her roommate is probably in there. If she's not, come back, and I can probably get you in."

"Thanks so much." Abe gave Jessica as genuine a smile as he could muster. His smiles were always awkward, like an AI structure attempting to mimic real humanity. It could not be helped.

Duff pushed himself from his chair and limped through the lobby door to the hall. The ceilings were low, barely eight feet. The hall smelled of a strange mixture of cleaning agents, incense, and age. It was a dull, flat smell that was not exactly offensive, but it was not pleasant, either. Abe, who had lived in residence halls in his undergrad years, knew the smell well. No matter what college he was in, all the residence halls smelled exactly alike.

"This place smells like Bensonhurst." Duff's nose was wrinkled in horror. "This smells almost exactly like the asylum."

"Almost?"

"Needs a more pervasive smell of shit to be completely correct. A couple of the real wackos at Bensonhurst used to like finger-painting on the walls of their rooms with feces. Some real Picassos, let me tell you."

Abe gulped and shuddered. Duff never really opened up about his time at Bensonhurst all at once. He trickled little bits of information over the years in candid moments of conversation. Abe mentally stored all those hints. He had a good image of the horrors Duff suffered, but even with all the stories of abuse and dealing with clinically insane juveniles in the home, Abe believed the totality of Duff's experiences there were worse than he was willing to divulge.

They climbed the small flights of stairs to the second floor. At the end of the hall, the stretch of dark brown, well-used, wooden doors and faded gray industrial carpet called to mind a scene from The Shining. It was a true liminal space, stretching the length of the hall. The second door down from the stairs had a plain, sans serif set of fading numbers painted on the middle of the door: 202. On either side of the numbers were cute, construction paper hearts with the names Sarah and Grace. A notebook-sized whiteboard was below the numbers. Someone had written *We love you Grace* on the board with a green marker. Duff pointed out the missing comma. "Probably failed their English classes."

Abe knocked gently. Any hard rap would have sounded like a shotgun in the quiet din of the hallway. A faint voice from inside the room called out, "It's open."

Abe opened the door. A young woman was sitting on the bed on the left side of the room. She was petite, almost elfin, and dressed in a bulky, over-sized sweatshirt tented out over her knees. Bare feet poked out from under the shirt. A large young man was sitting in the desk chair on the left side of the room. He wore jeans, unlaced high-top sneakers, and a t-shirt that read "God's Gym" featuring a rather ripped image of the Messiah, complete with stigmata and a crown of thorns, doing a push-up with a massive, oppressive cross on his back. The young man also had a dark blue cap with *IVCF* written on it in bright orange thread. The girl's eyes widened. She pulled the shirt from around her knees and tried to smooth it out by tenting it at an angle jutting away from her body. "Can I help you?"

Abe produced his detective's license, holding it out for the young woman to see. "I'm Abe Allard. This is Duff. We're private detectives hired by Sarah's parents. If you have a few minutes, we would like to talk to you about Sarah."

Grace swallowed hard, eyes darting to the young man in the chair. He stood up, drawing himself to his full height. It was not exactly a threatening move, but it was meant to intimidate. He was at least an inch or two taller than Abe and outweighed him by a hundred pounds, easy. He also had slab o' beef arms that showed a dedication to heavy lifting neither Abe nor Duff had ever been able to acquire. Grace's face plainly showed worry. She spoke in a small voice. "I don't know much. I wasn't here that night."

Abe sensed the tension rise in the room. "It's okay. We're not the police. We're not here to offend you or make you uncomfortable. If you want, you can just ask us to leave, and we'll go."

Duff was already opening dresser drawers on Sarah's side of the tiny room. "Yeah, just ignore us."

"What are you doing?" Grace looked concerned, but she did not move to stop Duff.

"Looking for evidence."

"Don't you need a warrant?" asked the big kid.

"Why? I'm not the police." Duff continued going through the dresses without a second thought.

Abe took a seat on the edge of Sarah's bed. He extended a hand toward the large man standing near him. "I'm Abe."

"Thomas Mueller. Tommy." The young man shook Abe's hand. His hand engulfed Abe's like a catcher's mitt.

"You play football?"

"Offensive line. Left guard. Sometimes I play center."

Abe tried to smile. "You must know Oliver Coleman, then."

"Of course. Ollie's a good guy. One of my best friends." Mueller returned to sitting in the chair. The tension in the room eased.

"We met Ollie this morning. He seems like a good guy." Abe leaned backward slightly. Subconsciously, Tommy mimicked Abe's posture. The room tension eased another few degrees. It was an old psychological trick, but it worked. Sit. Be calm. Distract. Find common ground. Lean back. Diffuse. Everyone is friends again.

"One of the best."

Abe turned to the young woman on the bed. "And you're Grace, right? What was your last name?"

"Boylan. Grace Boylan."

"That's a fine Irish name. It's nice to meet you, Grace."

From the dresser, Duff held up an obscenely small pair of women's underwear, all lace and string with almost zero coverage area. "Who can wear something like this?"

Abe felt his ears go red with embarrassment. "Duff, put the underwear

down."

"I'm just saying, I don't think I could get this past my thigh."

"Why would you want to try?"

Duff considered this. "Good point. Who am I supposed to look fancy for?"

Thomas huffed a hard breath through his nose but did not say anything.

Abe saw a flash of crimson in the kid's cheeks. He was embarrassed by seeing the underwear, a clear sign of serious repression.

"I take it you object on religious grounds, Tommy?" said Duff.

Thomas held up his hands defensively. "Hey, I try not to judge."

"Your religion would say otherwise, friend."

Tommy shrugged off Duff's cheap jab. "Live and let live, right? Turn the other cheek."

Abe interjected before Duff started on a rant. He coughed lightly to get Grace's attention. "You said you weren't here last Friday night?"

"I already told the police everything I know."

"Please, one more time for me. I'm not the police. I need to compile my own notes. You were not here, then?"

Grace shook her head. "I go home to work most weekends. Usually leave right after class on Friday morning."

"That's nice. You have a job back home? What do you do?"

"I work in a nursing home. I help clean rooms, make beds, and sometimes do activities with the residents."

"That's nice. I imagine the pay is low, though." Abe had a method to his line of questioning. By asking low impact, no harm questions, he was not only making Grace more comfortable, but he was gaining a baseline of behavior so that if she did attempt to lie on a future question, Abe would be much more likely to catch it.

"It is, but my grandmother is a resident in the home where I work. I like to see her."

"That's nice." Abe let the silence hang for a few seconds. He pointed a finger from Grace, to Tommy, and back to Grace. "Are you two involved? Dating?"

Tommy nodded. "Been going out for three years now. We went to the same high school. I'm a year ahead of Grace, though."

Grace stared down at Abe's feet. All of Abe's warning bells went off simultaneously. There was a problem between them. Abe glanced at Grace's side of the room. No crosses. No Bible. No crucifix around her neck. No religious symbols anywhere. Was Grace not as involved in Tommy's religion? Did Tommy find Jesus recently? That could drive a big wedge between two people. Either way, Abe noted heavy emotional distance between them.

Duff switched sides of the room. He was staring at the make-up containers and assorted things on the top of Grace's dresser. All the bottles were lined up in order from largest to smallest, labels facing front like a store display. "This is all Sephora stuff."

Grace raised her face to look at Duff. "I like their make-up."

"Expensive, isn't it?"

"I don't buy much, and I use it sparingly."

"Wise."

Tommy smiled proudly. "Grace is a natural beauty. She doesn't need to get tramped-up like some girls."

"Grace, Duff and I are looking for a cell phone. Did you see one after you got back to this room?"

Grace looked around at Sarah's side of the room. "No. Not at all. Whose cell phone?"

"Not important," said Abe.

Duff held up a bottle from Grace's dresser. "Hey, you got Flintstones chewable vitamins? Do they still make those?" There was no sarcasm in his voice, only genuine excitement for some reason.

"Oh, yeah. You can get them at Walmart. I take the ones with calcium because my mom worries about my bone density."

"I always wanted to get these when I was a kid." Duff turned the bottle in his hands. He looked wistful and sad. "My mom said I needed to learn to swallow real pills because not everything was chewable and tasted good." Duff put the bottle down. He picked up another bottle, a purple plastic jar with no label. "What's in here?"

"Oh, just a muscle supplement," said Grace.

Duff twisted off the cap and looked inside the bottle. After a moment, he put the cap back on and put it back. He pulled out his cell phone and started typing something.

"Grace, do you think Sarah could have killed Nate?"

Grace looked mortified at the suggestion. "Goodness, no."

"Care to elaborate?"

Grace hesitated. Abe saw a little tinge of red creeping into the tips of Grace's ears. Her fair skin could never hide any blush. "Sarah is a little wild and reckless, but she's a good person. She's a good friend."

Duff pocketed his cell phone and moved back over to Sarah's side of the room. He slowly dropped to his knees, every move deliberate and painful, and he flipped the comforter on the bed up to look beneath it. There were plastic containers filled with all kinds of college staples. The first one was a couple of half-empty bottles of booze, at least twenty packages of dry instant ramen, and two sleeves of Chips Ahoy cookies. The next held

a Costco-sized bottle of ibuprofen, a selection of cold medicines worthy of anyone wishing to reshoot some scenes from Breaking Bad, and two bottles of Pepto Bismol. Another container held supplies of a more delicate nature: tampons, pads, cotton balls, and condoms. Duff held up the string of unused condoms. "Man, I'm glad I didn't go to college."

"Duff, put those away." Abe's neck was red now. No matter what else was going on, Duff had a knack for embarrassing Abe.

"Dude, Tilda is going to be in college in two years."

"I know," said Abe.

Duff put the condoms back. "Is it too late to send her to a nunnery?"

Tommy looked distinctly uncomfortable. He pushed himself out of the chair. "You know what? I've got class in twenty minutes. I might as well start heading over." He leaned down and kissed Grace. It was a close-mouthed, chaste, quick peck. Abe wondered if that was their standard kiss, or if it was just a possessive display for Abe and Duff's benefit, the male turkey puffing up his chest and beating his wings. Tommy excused himself, nodding toward Abe and Duff. "Nice meeting you both." He left the room, leaving the door wide open as he did. That was on purpose. He was not about to leave Grace in a closed room with two strangers. Abe and Duff heard Tommy knock on another door and speak to someone in a low voice. A moment later, a couple of curious young women passed the door and glanced in, sent by Tommy to check on his girl. Grace gave them a thumbs-up sign to let them know she was alright. The two girls stood in the hall, just in case.

Duff continued his search through Sarah's things, while Abe continued to talk to Grace. "Did you know Sarah was arrested before you came back?"

Grace nodded. "Oh, yes. My cell phone blew up at four in the morning." Grace was purposely not making eye contact. She looked at the floor. Her shoulders were hunched. She looked like she was being held captive.

Abe gestured to the door. "You look uncomfortable. Should I take this big idiot and leave?"

Grace shook her head. "Oh, no. I'm fine. It's just…it's been a lot to deal with. Sarah was a really good friend, and she and I weren't really on speaking terms because of a stupid argument when I left last weekend, and now…"

"I understand. I really do. You're under no obligation to answer any of our questions—"

Something whizzed between Abe and Grace. It slammed into the heating register under the windows on the far side of the little room with a tremendous boom of metal and a dull thud a split-second later. Both Abe and Grace jumped. Grace gave a yelp of fright.

"What in the world was that?" Abe looked down at the ground by the

register. A thick tome of a textbook was laying there. Abe turned and looked at Duff. He had taken the textbook from the top shelf of Sarah's closet where the rest of her books were and thrown it.

"It slipped." Duff's tone was unapologetic. "My bad." He retrieved the book and put it back on the shelf. "I don't think there's a cell phone in Sarah's stuff."

Abe stood. He apologized to Grace. "I'm sorry about that. I'll take my lumbering oaf of a companion and leave you alone now." He held out a business card. "If you think of anything you can tell us that will help prove Sarah innocent, or if you find a cell phone you cannot explain, please let us know right away."

Grace accepted the card with her slim fingers. She placed it on her desk. "I will. I promise."

"Thank you." Abe gave Grace a small bow. He grabbed Duff by the shoulder and walked him into the hallway.

"Hey, you're stretching my sweatshirt." Duff jerked out of Abe's grasp.

"How will anyone ever be able to tell?"

The moribund duo clattered down the steps to the first floor. Jessica and Aiden were still at the front desk. Abe thanked Jessica for allowing them upstairs.

"I was just about to head up and check on you," Jessica said. "When Tommy left, he asked me to make sure Grace was alright."

"She's fine." Abe pushed Duff through the door. "You have our business card. If you think of anything that can help us prove Sarah's innocence or understand why she might have done this, please don't hesitate to call."

Abe pushed Duff through the foyer to the sidewalk outside of the hall. "What in the name of all that's good and holy is wrong with you?"

"What's wrong with you?" Duff was nonplussed. He was used to Abe being annoyed at him.

"That girl was clearly traumatized by this whole situation, and you go tramping around like a drunken circus elephant—"

"Zero-seven-nine-six."

Abe stopped short. "Say what?"

"Those numbers mean anything to you?"

"Not really."

"They didn't mean anything to me, either. That's why I looked them up on my phone."

"And?"

Duff handed his phone to Abe. There was a search page from a Physician's Desk Reference website. It was open to a page with a search bar

for the National Drug Code imprinted on over-the-counter pills. The digits 0796 was the signifier for CitraNatal Harmony Prenatal Multivitamins.

"That purple bottle wasn't a muscle supplement. It was a fetal supplement. All her other bottles had labels, she was fanatical about keeping the labels facing outward. This one did not have a label and stood out as weird. I noticed a slight scrape on the bottle where she'd used a scissor blade or an X-Acto knife to cut off the label. Why would someone who needed labels to be a certain way cut off a label? Didn't make sense. That's why I looked inside. She cut the label off because she did not want people glancing at the bottle to know what she was taking."

"Grace is pregnant?" Abe was stunned. Grace was all of eighteen. It made him think of Matilda, who was not that far behind her. The thought of Matilda being pregnant made him get weak in the knees. He was by no means ready to be a grandfather.

"I threw the book because I wanted to see her reaction. You jumped like anyone would— arms up, defensive, shocked. Your arms immediately went up to protect your head and neck, which is normal. Grace jumped, but her arms went to her stomach. Did you notice?"

"No, I was too busy being surprised."

"Grace is pregnant." Duff's tone was flat and mellow, like diagnosing pregnancies was something he did every day. "You want to bet money Tommy's not the father?"

Abe knew Tommy wasn't before Duff suggested it. The body posture. The disconnect. It now made sense Grace was guarded.

"Good Christian boy like Tommy, with all his Jesus apparel and InterVarsity Christian Fellowship hats, I'm betting there ain't no way he's sexually active."

Abe knew who the father was. It was in Grace's posture, her micro-expressions, her worry. "It's Nate Riegert's baby, isn't it?"

"I don't know for sure, and I certainly don't have proof of it, but I'd be willing to drop a large stack of bills at Larry Panner's bookmaking bar on that kid's parentage."

It made perfect sense. Nate was the proverbial Big Man on Campus. Grace was in a long-term relationship with a good Christian boy who probably did not want to take things to the next level. Nate and Grace probably spent a lot of time around each other at parties and while Nate was hanging out in their room with Sarah. Things happen.

"I hope I'm wrong," said Duff. "But I'm never wrong."

"You're wrong all the time."

Duff patted Abe on the back condescendingly. "That's where you're wrong."

"I'm wrong about a lot of things, but I'm not wrong about you being wrong."

"Wrong again, friend."

Abe knew that arguing with Duff any further would give him a migraine. "What does this all mean?"

Duff began to walk back toward the Toyota. "It means if I'm Tommy, I've got a reason for wanting to kill Nate Riegert. It also means Grace probably has a reason for wanting to kill Nate Riegert."

"We have two new suspects."

"Both of whom have a far better motive than Sarah's drunken relationship rage."

"How many more suspects could there be?"

"I count at least one more: the backup quarterback." Duff began walking away from Joyman Hall. In the distance, the monolithic UW-Rockland athletic complex loomed. "Let's go see if we can get in to look at the crime scene."

"I thought you said you didn't need to look at the crime scene?"

"I do now."

"So, you were wrong about needing to look at the crime scene."

Duff flipped a fist above his shoulder and extended his middle finger at Abe as he walked away.

9

THE CLAY UPSHAW Memorial Athletic Complex of UW-Rockland was a $4,000,000 gift to the university from the Upshaw family. The Upshaw family was the wealthiest family in Rockland, Wisconsin. The principal reason the family was able to amass their wealth was three generations of Upshaws owning almost all the rental properties around the UW-Rockland campus. Students had long accused the Upshaws of being monopolistic slumlords, and the condition of most of the rental units around campus would support that assessment, but it never bothered the Upshaws. They owned more than thirty apartment buildings around the campus ranging from a couple converted houses with only eight rooms, to some more traditional fifty or sixty-unit complexes, and if students did not want to battle for the painfully few parking spaces on campus every morning, living within walking distance was the only alternative. They had no choice but to grossly overpay for the oft abused and poorly kept Upshaw Properties apartments.

The Upshaw complex was the newest building on campus, and it stuck out like a sore thumb. It was nestled at the farthest reaches of the campus property and housed a beautiful natatorium, a massive indoor track-and-field area, a 50-yard indoor football and baseball practice facility, basketball courts, and the UW-Rockland field house where the basketball, volleyball, gymnastics, and wrestling teams competed. In addition, it held locker rooms, multiple weight rooms, an athlete spa, a dozen classrooms, a couple of conference rooms, one meeting hall, and two dozen assorted offices for the various sports coaches and staff members whose time on campus was great

enough to necessitate an office. There was even a small dining area for athletes and a coffee bar and concessions for fans coming to events.

The Upshaw Complex was given the name Uppie's House by the student body, and it was easily the busiest building on campus. Even in the late afternoon, as Abe and Duff made their way toward it, a steady stream of students headed to and from the building. When the facilities were not being used for sports teams, the various spaces were open to the student body for their own activity and workout needs. The indoor track and basketball practice courts were under constant use for pickup games or intramural sports.

When the detectives entered the lobby, the first thing they noticed was the noise. The building had a constant echo. There was a ton of sound. Basketballs bounced. Music played at loud volumes. Various metallic sounds creaked. There was a low din of noise from voices, be they shouting or whispered. There was a constant cacophony of shoe-squeaks from the parquet floors of the basketball courts. The high ceilings and great open spaces of the athletic sections only made the noise worse.

The tumult got to Abe immediately. So much for avoiding a migraine. He preferred quiet. He liked silence. Duff, who spent most of his free time away from the office at a bar belonging to his friend Wheels was not fazed by the noise. He sniffed the air and rocked back on his heels, stretching his back. "You could have an argument and then murder someone in here, and no one would hear it."

They walked to the front counter. A pair of students, male and female, in UW-Rockland Athletics t-shirts were manning the front desk. They each wore a name tag. The man's tag read "Eli" and the woman's, "Natalee." Abe produced his detective license and business card, and he launched into his standard introductory speech, yet again, this time concluding it with, "We need to see the crime scene, please."

Natalee and Eli looked at each other, neither certain of how to handle that request. They were told that the general public could not access the scene, but licensed private detectives hired by the family of the woman accused of the crime were not exactly "general public."

"I guess I can take them." Eli was a broad-shouldered, square-jawed young man with bulging biceps and a narrow waist. The only thing keeping him from being a perfect physical specimen was a smattering of acne across his cheeks and chin, a reminder that he was still young, a boy evolving a man's body. Eli grabbed a set of keys off the desk and stepped around the edge. "Follow me."

"Did you know Sarah Novak?" Abe asked Eli as they walked.

"Not really. I might have seen her if she worked out a lot, but I don't

know what she looks like offhand."

Abe and Duff followed him down a hall. Duff noticed a round bulb of smoked glass on the ceiling. "Did you get the closed-circuit cameras fixed?"

Eli looked confused for a moment. His eyes followed Duff's gaze to the ceiling. "Oh, the video. Yeah, it's fixed now. It was down for a couple days. No one really knows why."

"Strange that it was down the night the murder happened."

"Very strange. It went down a day or two before the murder. It took the IT kids a while to get it up again."

"IT kids?" Abe cocked his head to the side. "Children?"

"Students. Adults, technically. But, I wonder sometimes." Eli pointed at a WiFi router on the wall. "Rockland has a really good computer program. The students majoring in IT are in charge of fixing our computer issues around here. They are overseen by their instructors, but they're the ones who make stuff happen. It's good experience for them." Eli turned a corner and led them down another hall. The signs on the walls said they were heading toward the football practice area.

"How come no one else was in the weight room when Nate Riegert was murdered?"

Eli snorted and shot Abe a look that suggested Abe had a negative IQ. Abe was getting tired of seeing those looks. Eli said, "It was Friday night." He said it in a tone that made it sound like that statement explained everything.

"No one works out on Friday nights?"

"Not usually. Thursday, Friday, and Saturday nights are a ghost town around here unless there is a home sporting event." Eli led them to a door marked *Football Players & Coaches Only*. He used a key from the ring he carried to get them past the door. "There wasn't that night. Football team was home on Saturday morning, but that Friday was dead." Eli reconsidered his phrasing. "I guess that's not really a good term to use, given what happened. *Dead. Ghost town.* Stupid, Eli."

"Nate Riegert was working out, though?"

Eli shrugged. "Nate was looking to play Division One ball next year. I think he felt he had to keep pace. I know he got a few letters about workout protocols for the big schools. Division Three is not nearly that strict. He was really turning it on, trying to get shredded."

"That doesn't sound good," said Abe.

"Shredded means muscular," said Duff. "The opposite of what we are."

Eli stopped at the football team's personal weight room. They were the only sport on the Rockland campus with their own weight room. The other sports had to use the two main general rooms. Title IX proponents had

launched a war against this, but it was defeated because a judge decided the football weight room was a private gift from Clay Upshaw's family and not subject to the fair distribution of funds. The jocks got to keep their jockery femme-free.

The weight room was cordoned off with yellow crime scene tape, still. Eli stopped the detectives at the door. "I don't think I can let you cross the tape."

"Don't worry. I don't think we were going to." Abe pointed to a corner. "Is that where the body was?"

Eli looked where Abe was pointing. His shoulders bobbed. "I don't know. I wasn't here that day. They didn't draw a chalk outline, I guess."

"That's a film trope that almost never happens in real police work," said Duff. "It contaminates the crime scene."

"Well, this crime scene is already contaminated. Tons of guys used this room every day."

"Did anyone happen to turn in a cell phone to the lost-and-found?" asked Abe.

Eli laughed. "If someone found a cell phone, they'd either sell it for cash or wipe it and use it themselves. You don't *find* phones anymore. If you lose one, they're gone."

"Did you know Nate?"

Eli turned to Abe. "No. Not really. I mean, I saw him a lot, of course. But we weren't friends."

"You don't play football? You look like you play."

"I did in high school, not here. Here, I'm a wrestler, and I dabble in track. I was faster when I was a first-year, but now I'm a little too slow for sprints, so I mainly just work third-leg in the relays and do some middle-distance stuff."

Abe smiled and pretended to know what he was talking about. "What did people say about Nate?"

Eli squinted. "How do you mean?"

"Just…in a general sense, what did they say about him. What did you hear about him?"

Eli paused, weighing out his answer for a moment. Eventually, he spoke flatly. "Total horn-dog. He'd sleep with just about anyone with a vagina. He's probably been with thirty or forty girls on this campus, maybe more."

"Did he have any enemies?" Abe leaned toward Eli slightly. There was no surprise in his face. His posture did not change. Eli knew that Nate Riegert burned a few bridges.

"Yes, and no. He got along with the guys on his team really well, and no other dude on campus would dare step to the football team. I know there

were a lot of girls who weren't his biggest fans, but that's not a surprise for someone with his record."

Abe slipped in the next question quickly. "What about Robbie Conroy?"

"What about him?" Eli was confused by the new assertion.

"Could Robbie have killed Nate?"

"I have no idea. You can ask him yourself." Eli jabbed a thumb down the hall. There was a small meeting room with a large glass panel in the door. Above the glass panel was a sign that said *Film Room*. A young man sat in one of the chairs surrounding a brown, polished wood conference table. He was watching game film on a large projection monitor on the wall. "That's Robbie, there."

Robbie Conroy was about as nondescript as a human could get. He looked like the default character mannequin in a video game. His hair was short and brown. His body was average, not fat, not thin. His face was as Irish as a potato, but it was without notable features outside of a thin smattering of freckles. He was as plain as vanilla yogurt.

Abe knocked on the door to the film room. Robbie turned to look at the door, and then beckoned him into the room. Robbie stood to greet Abe. "Are you the guy from the Milwaukee paper?"

"No. Not a reporter." Abe produced the card and license yet again. He introduced Duff. "We just want to ask you about Nate Riegert, if you have a few seconds."

Robbie immediately went into a defensive posture. He leaned back in his chair and looked at Abe and Duff with a critical eye. "You cops or something?"

Abe rattled off his introductory spiel for what felt like the hundredth time that day.

Robbie took the card and squinted at it. He offered the card back to Abe, but Abe waved it away. "I didn't do it, if that's what you're here for."

"No?" Abe was watching Robbie's eyes, his face. He was looking for a tic or a microexpression that would betray his story. There were none. "Where were you last Friday?"

"Here." Robbie gestured to the room around them. "In this very room. Watching film. Like usual."

"How late?"

"Midnight."

Duff looked toward the weight room down the hall. "And you didn't see anything or hear anything?"

"Not a thing." Robbie's voice was flat and casual. There was no stress in his tone. "I had the window shade above the door pulled, so I couldn't even see into the hallway. I stopped watching film just before midnight, and I left.

Went out the field doors at the end of the hall."

Abe looked over his shoulder at Duff. Duff shrugged. "You know why people would suspect you, right?"

Robbie ran a hand through his hair and rolled his eyes. "Anyone who would think that doesn't know how little I care about playing football. I did this for my dad. He went to Rockland in the late Eighties. He played quarterback, was a real BMOC. Told me it was the best time of his life. I'm not as good an athlete as he was, and I'm certainly not the athlete that Nate was. I'm only here busting my balls in the film room to help the team because I like these guys, and I want them to do well. Frankly, if I hadn't played a down all season, I would have been fine with it."

Duff leaned forward, arms on his knees. "Why, though? Most athletes are competitors. They want to be out there."

Nate gestured to the computer he was using to study film. "I've gotten an education in the game. I'm using that to get a modest scholarship to UW-Madison as a graduate assistant next year. If all goes well, I'll get a Master's degree and maybe a chance to coach at the college or pro level. If that doesn't work, I might get a chance to go overseas and help teach the game to others or coach in Canada, Mexico, or Japan. Did you know they have football in Europe? It's not popular, but it's there. Read John Grisham's *Playing for Pizza*. My life is going to be fine, regardless. I didn't need to play. I'm happy, and more importantly, I'm healthy. I've got two good knees and no concussions."

Abe watched Robbie's face. No deception. No sarcasm. No hint of exaggeration. He was completely honest and upfront. Abe felt confident he was not the murderer. However, his gut feelings based on his years of reading people's faces would never hold up in court. Robbie Conroy was still a suspect. He had a motive. He definitely had opportunity. And no one could back up his alibi.

"Do you think Sarah Novak killed Nate Riegert?" asked Abe.

Robbie sat back in his chair and considered his answer for several beats. "No. I only met her a couple times, but she is petite, tiny. Nate liked really thin, small girls like that. He liked to pick them up and make himself feel big. I don't think she had the physical strength to do it, to swing a weight plate."

"So, you think he was murdered by a man?" Duff's eyebrow arched.

"Aren't most murders committed by men?"

"Touché," said Duff.

"One last question," said Abe. "If you had to name a suspect, who do you think killed Nate Riegert."

Robbie's eyes darted upward and to the left. Abe caught it immediately. Old microexpression wisdom used to mean that eyes moving up and left

meant deception, a lie. However, to Abe it only meant that someone knew something. Possibly something important.

Abe cajoled the boy. "If you know something that could get an innocent person out of jail, don't you have a responsibility to tell us? How would you like it if Sarah Novak gets fifteen-to-life for murder and you might have known who the real culprit was?"

Robbie leaned forward and beckoned the detectives to move closer.

Duff's chair was on wheels. He spun backwards, propelled himself toward Robbie, and stopped short of hitting the boy before spinning back around to face him. "Lay it on me, brother."

Robbie glanced toward the door. "If you pinned me to the wall and told me to name someone, I'd guess it was Coach Martinez."

Duff slapped his thigh. "Of course! It makes perfect sense!" He paused and leaned closer to Robbie, dropping his voice. "Who's Coach Martinez?"

"Coach Jay Martinez," said Robbie. "He's our quarterbacks coach and the offensive coordinator on the team. He and Nate were tight, like brothers tight. Coach Martinez, he is the one who got Nate into football shape last year. He is the mind responsible for the play calls that let Nate rack up all those stats this year."

"Why would a quarterbacks' coach kill his star player, though?" Duff's face was wrinkled in confusion. "Doesn't make sense."

"If he did it, it wasn't premeditated. It was in the spur of the moment, you dig?"

"In our business, we'd call it a crime of passion," said Abe.

"They weren't gay."

"Passion just means anger." Duff flicked his index finger at Abe to silence him. "Go on, Robbie."

Robbie paused and picked up a bottle of water sitting on the desk next to his playbook. He took a swig and recapped it. "This doesn't leave this room, right?"

"We won't be broadcasting it unless it factors into the solving of this crime." Duff wheeled his finger in a circle in a *hurry-up* gesture.

"Coach Jay, he convinced the athletic coordinator at Michigan State that if he could get Nate to go play for the Spartans, MSU would hire him on as their quarterbacks coach."

"Seems smart," said Duff.

Robbie shook his head. "Problem is Nate decided to play for Wisconsin. Wisconsin wasn't going to hire Coach. That pissed Coach off big time. I heard them screaming at each other in Coach's office one day last week. Coach was telling Nate he wasn't going to be shit without him, and Nate was telling Coach the was going to the NFL. It was ugly."

"If Coach Martinez is as good as he thinks he is, wouldn't he have gotten a chance at the next level on his own, eventually?"

"He would. Probably. But it could take years, and more than likely he'd go off to some smaller school and coach the sacrificial lambs: Buffalo, Western Kentucky, Pitt, or maybe even a D-2 school. At Michigan, he would have made something like *two-and-a-half large* right off the bat. Those smaller schools, he'd be lucky to see low six figures."

Duff let out a low whistle. "Two-point-five million is definitely murder-worthy."

Robbie picked up his cell phone from the desk and tapped the screen. "Almost four, guys. I have to get to practice. We have a game this weekend."

"You starting?" asked Duff.

"I don't have much of a choice in the matter, now. I just hope I don't piss all over my shoes." Robbie shouldered a black backpack and moved toward the door. He pocketed his cell phone.

"Do you know where Nate kept his phone while he worked out?" asked Abe.

Robbie paused at the door. He thought for a second. "He carried it with him. Like we all do."

"Why? Why not keep it in a locker?"

Robbie's lip curled in a small smirk. "Because our phones have our music on them, and they have cameras so you can take pictures of the guns for the 'Gram." Robbie flexed his arms in a Schwarzeneggerian weightlifter's pose. "Ladies love the guns, man." Robbie walked out of the film room and the door closed. Abe and Duff were left in silence.

After a moment, the door opened again. Robbie stuck his head into the room. "I'm sorry, sirs. This is our meeting room, and I'm not supposed to let non-team members in here without supervision. Do you mind leaving?"

ABE AND DUFF regrouped outside the Upshaw Complex. The fresh air was welcome. The smell of sweat, chlorine, plastic, and rubber permeated the center. A chilly breeze blew in out of the northwest and carried a fresh, cold smell with it. It was a chance for snow. In the early fall, snow was usually trace amounts, and it would not last long, melting the next day when the sun rose. But, it was the harbinger of the coming winter.

Abe was starting to get tired. There were too many tidbits of information gleaned that day, too many pieces of the puzzle to organize properly. He wanted to go back to the hotel and lie down, but Abe did not dare mention that to his partner.

Duff was awake and alive, vibrant even. Well, as vibrant as a fat man

with severe misanthropy could be, at least. The puzzles kept him moving. The puzzles kept him alive. Without something to solve, he would retreat to the dark depths of his bedroom, bury himself in whatever looked interesting on his PlayStation, and cease interacting with the world.

"Well, compadre?" Duff leaned his frame against a metal railing outside the complex. The sun was setting. The campus was slowly getting dark. "Thoughts? General feelings? Did you figure out whodunit?"

Abe was at a loss. He rubbed at his temples and squeezed his eyes shut. "I don't know anything anymore. How many different suspects did we turn up in a day of work on this?"

"Well, let's see." Duff held out a fist and started counting off suspects on his fingers. "We got the Coach, the back-up quarterback, the pregnant girl, the pregnant girl's boyfriend, big school boosters, and whoever might be involved with Nate Riegert's gambling problem."

"And Sarah."

Duff nodded. "True. Sarah is still a viable suspect."

"I really don't think Sarah did it, though."

Duff inhaled hard through his nose. "Right now, she's leading the list solely because of her cell phone being at the scene."

"Grace or Tommy could have had access to Sarah's cell phone. Also, maybe Sarah went to the gym, fought with Nate, and then left, leaving her phone in a drunken haze. Then, it's possible someone else killed him. The phone could just be a horrible, unfortunate coincidence."

Duff hated to concur with Abe. He wanted the puzzle to play by the rules. He wanted the puzzle neat and clean with definite edges. "Everything hangs on the whereabouts of Nate's cell phone, doesn't it?"

"Most likely." Abe pinched the bridge of his nose. His headache was not going away. He used to carry a little pocket case with some Tylenol in it, but he stopped after his divorce. His headaches got better after that. It eliminated a large portion of strain and stress from his daily life. He wished it had it again at that moment. "Remind me to stop at a Walgreens and get some aspirin."

Duff's phone rang. He pulled it out of his pocket, glanced at the screen, and answered on speakerphone holding it between him and Abe. "Hey, Buddy. Abe's listening, so don't talk about how much you like his legs."

"You boys find anything?" The old sheriff's voice sounded tinny and hollow over the speaker.

"A few things," said Duff. "Nothing definite, though. How about you?"

"Pam and I got the warrant for the cell phone ping and delivered it to the carrier. They should get us a result by tomorrow. I also talked to Judge Balmer. He said he's willing to meet with Sarah Novak's new lawyer

tomorrow. The district attorney will be in his office at nine tomorrow, and they're willing to listen to your spiel about getting bail set for Sarah, especially after what happened to her this morning."

Abe's knees went out from under him, and he fell heavily against the railing. *Oh Lord, I have to meet with a judge*. He broke out in flop sweat.

"It's a good thing she's a pretty little white girl, I guess. Legal system loves pretty white girls." Duff sniffed. "You okay, Aberforth?"

Abe tried to smile, but it was a grimace, a wince. He struggled to stand. "I'm fine."

"What's wrong with Abe?" asked Buddy. "He sounds like someone punched him in the dick."

"Life did that to him a long time ago. He still hasn't recovered."

"Tell him to rub some dirt on it and walk it off."

"He heard you."

"You boys want to get some dinner?"

"I do," said Duff. "I don't think the solicitor general over here will. He looks green."

Abe's normal pallor, which was fish-belly pale to begin with, had taken a step toward aquamarine. Abe tried to wave Duff off. "I'm fine. No worries. You go ahead."

"Where are you at? I'll come get you."

"We're at the athletic complex on campus."

"Be there in fifteen," said Buddy. "Over and out." The phone went silent in Duff's hand. He slipped it into his pocket.

Abe had no desire to eat the moment. However, he was strongly considering buying whiskey. Abe was not a drinker. He tried booze once in high school, it burned his throat and he didn't like it, and he never touched it again. Abe preferred water or chocolate milk. "I think I'm going back to the hotel to lie down."

"Sounds good. I'll have Buddy drop me off when we're done."

Abe's throat felt like it was closing. He made the OK sign with his thumb and forefinger.

Duff watched his partner stand on wobbly knees. "You want me to give you a piggyback ride to the van?"

"We both know you'd never make it on your ankle."

"Or my knees. I'm all talk, no ability. Still, feels like it would be impolite not to offer."

Abe sucked in a deep, cleansing breath of air. "I'm good. I'm fine."

"Tell yourself it's not a court appearance. It's a closed-door meeting. That will make it better, right?"

Abe grimaced and nodded. "Yeah, thanks, pal." Abe pushed himself

away from the railing and began to beeline for the van. He tried to mind-over-matter himself past his fear of legalese and judges. He tried not to remember his time working for a law firm as an intern, or his first job after he graduated. The worry. The terror. The panic. In college, in practice sessions and mock trials, Abe was exactly who he wanted to be. He was whip-smart and quick. He could recall just about anything with nary a pause. He destroyed opponents in the classroom. The first time he set foot in a real courtroom, with a real judge, with a real case, and real consequences if he failed— he folded like an origami accordion. If Abe failed to perform under pressure, his client went to jail for ten years. If he really blew it, maybe twelve. The man had a wife and a child who would be without their sole support system. The unyielding weight of the moment crushed him, and Abe resigned from the case and his legal career. He was a smart man; he was not a tough man.

Abe used sheer force of will to propel himself to the van. Then, he permitted himself a solid ten minutes for a panic attack. He huffed breath through his teeth. He wiped rivulets of sweat from his forehead with the back of his wrist. He clenched and unclenched his hands until he felt a wave of calm. It was a small wave, but it was enough. His heart rate decelerated. He stopped sweating. He was still panicking, but he was used to having a small level of panic in his daily life, so it felt normal.

Whenever Abe was at the edge of the cliff, Katherine was usually the one who talked him off it as she had so many times throughout college, law school, and twenty years-and-change with having one of the most selfish and least empathetic human beings ever put on the Earth as a business partner. He had not needed to talk to her since their divorce, at least not in the way he used to need her to talk him off the ledge. He had suffered their divorce largely silently. Duff was sympathetic to a small degree, but when it came to understanding the great ebb and flow of two people joined in a martial union, Duff did not have the patience for it or the willingness to learn. When Abe and Katherine's marriage was heading down the drain of divorce, Duff would listen to Abe complain about things, and then bring up something completely and utterly unrelated. *I think we should get a pinball machine for the office; it would take your mind off things.*

This would, of course, lead Abe to counter with a long-winded rant about how he really needed Duff to listen to him and help him through this crisis because he was losing his sanity.

Duff would listen quietly until Abe finished. Then he would blink twice and say, *Maybe the Addams Family pinball game. That was a good one.*

Abe wanted someone to tell him he would do well, everything would be alright. He wanted to have someone offer him a hug, but he was not likely to

get that from Duff unless Duff somehow spooned him while they were in bed asleep.

Abe held his phone at arm's length. His thumb found the contacts app, scrolled to Katherine's name, and paused over it. One touch on the smart phone's screen and it would instantly dial her number. In less than five seconds— ten if she could not get to the phone quickly— he could be looking at her face, asking her advice, seeing the sympathy in her eyes, hearing the caring tone of her voice. Abe knew Katherine would listen to him. He knew she would help him.

But, he also knew he was on his own now. They had divorced. The papers were signed. The lawyer was paid. He had his own apartment. They divested all their accounts. They split property. Sure, they had been more amicable than most divorcing couples, but it was still a divorce. They no longer talked every night like they used to. They no longer called each other during the day to check in, to see how they were each doing. There were fewer and fewer text messages between them. The gap in their lives was widening. Only Matilda really kept them in contact. She would be their mutual touchstone for the remainder of their lives, but Abe wondered how much contact they would have once Tilda graduated from high school. Or college. Once she was on her own, married with kids, they might see each other at special occasions, but would they ever talk like they used to?

Probably not.

Abe's thumb dropped to the cancel button, and the phone jumped to its home screen. Abe tossed the phone onto the passenger side of the car. He would suffer this panic attack alone.

It was time to get used to being alone for such things.

ROSE, THE RED minivan, pulled into the parking lot of the Super 8 in Waukesha. Abe guided her into a parking spot, slipped the gear shift into park, and killed the engine. He let his damp forehead drop against the steering wheel. It was quiet in the car. No radio. No outside noise. He could listen to his heartbeat. There was a steady pulse in his head that felt like a blood vessel was coursing over his eardrum. Eventually, Abe forced himself to open the door, step out of the car, and walk into the hotel on unsteady legs.

The lobby of the hotel had a window allowing the front desk workers to look into the unsupervised pool area. Being it was just after 5:30 p.m., the pool was free of families with small children at that moment. They were off getting supper somewhere. An elderly man sipped a coffee and read a book by the windows, and a large man was swimming laps. Abe recognized the

man in the pool as Henry Novak.

Who can swim when their daughter is up on murder charges? Abe thought. If it had been Matilda, the last thing he ever would have thought of doing was getting into some trunks and doing a few hundred meters of the butterfly or Australian crawl. He would not have even thought to pack a swimming suit. *To each his own, I guess.*

Abe went to his room. He was about to pull out his wallet to get the key card but stopped. He moved one door over to the Novaks' room. He raised a hand to knock on the door. He wanted to see if Maggie Novak was doing well. He wanted to see if she was okay with her husband swimming. He wanted to see how she was holding up after that confrontation at the courthouse. From behind the door, Abe could hear the light sound of sobs. She was crying.

Perhaps, Abe he was a better man, he would have knocked. Perhaps, if he was a more confident, he could have said something that might have helped her. But, standing in the hallway, he suddenly felt awkward and afraid. As Duff would have told him, he pussed out. Abe pulled his own key card out of his wallet, entered his room, undressed, and climbed into the shower.

Abe had stayed in his fair share of hotels over the years. Every year while they were married, he and Katherine tried to take Matilda somewhere fun once a year in the summer during her school vacation. Usually, they tried to make it someplace cultural like the Grand Canyon or Gettysburg, but once they went to Walt Disney World in Florida. All Abe really remembered from that trip was he wore the wrong shorts to the park and after a full day of walking in the living sauna of central Florida, his inner thighs chafed all to hell and he walked like a cowboy the rest of his time in the Magic Kingdom. All the hotels in which he had ever stayed on those vacations were similar. They were all cheap, chain-quality places like Super 8, Motel 6, or Days Inn. The towels were like sandpaper, the toilet paper was like thin sandpaper, the drinking water tasted faintly chemical, and the showers were hard, mineral-laden water that stripped the dead skin off the body and refused to allow soap to lather.

At least the showers were always hot.

Most hotels had a water setting that felt like it was hot enough to cook a packet of instant ramen. Abe stood under the water and let the shower turn his skin bright pink. Every time he started to become accustomed to the temperature, he reached down and cranked it another millimeter to the left.

Abe was angry at himself. He was angry at his father, whom he never knew. Abe was raised by a single mother who worked two jobs. He spent all his time watching television and reading books. Nowhere in those books did he find a methodology for confidence. He saw men on television acting

confident, and sometimes he wished he could have the flippant behavior of Hawkeye on *M*A*S*H* or the macho suaveness of Tom Selleck in *Magnum, P.I.,* but he never quite figured out how to do it. In his mind, he could see it, but he could not make the images of himself in his mind translate to the real world. He could never put on the mask.

Where would he be if he could have figured out how to be a good trial attorney? Would he have a nice house in Oak Park? Maybe he could have afforded to send Tilda to a private school for a better education. Maybe he would not have been too embarrassed to attend any of his law school reunions in Madison.

When his skin felt like it was peeling off his back, Abe finally shut off the water. He toweled off with a 60-grit bath towel and wrapped it around his waist. He shaved, scraping a full day's worth of bristles from his face with a cheap Gillette disposable. He tossed some Brüt aftershave on his face and slapped his cheeks lightly until the burn went away. Abe left the bathroom and put on his pajamas. It was only 7:00 p.m., but he was not planing to go anywhere for the rest of the night. He had no appetite. He turned on the TV and flipped through the dozen channels offered to him endlessly. He did not actually process anything he saw on the screen. It was just something to do.

10

GO AHEAD AND drop me off here." Duff pointed at the Kwik Trip down the street from the Super 8. Buddy did as he was told, angling his pickup truck into a spot on the side of the gas station. Duff got out and shut the door. He walked around to the driver's side.

Buddy leaned an elbow out the open window. "You think your boy is going to be okay tomorrow?"

Duff shook his head. "No. He'll probably piss himself. I'd also put even money on him passing loud gas in front of the judge. He gets nervous guts."

"Does he know that he's not on trial?"

"Wouldn't matter." Duff patted the pick-up truck as he started to walk to the convenience store. "He'll overthink it, regardless."

Duff loved Kwik Trip. When he was a kid, Kwik Trip was where he could get candy, soda, and comic books— all forbidden pleasures his parents denied him. He would steal a five-dollar bill from his father's stash atop the dresser in his parents' bedroom, and he would walk to the Kwik Trip down the road from his parents' home to indulge in the three C's: Coke, Carbs, and Captain America.

Kwik Trip was a Wisconsin staple, as bred into the Badger State's DNA as the Green Bay Packers, deer hunting, and dangerously cold winters. Kwik Trip was a gas station/convenience store combo that was slowly becoming a

monopoly in the state offering its own brand of water, donuts, and grab-and-go sandwiches. And Duff reveled in it. When he was young, Kwik Trip was really just a standard gas station shop with a candy rack and coolers for sodas. Now, it was practically its own one-stop entity, bigger than your standard gas station and smaller than any grocery store. Kwik Trip was trying to be all things to everyone, and they were nearly succeeding.

Duff's particular Kwik Trip addiction was the chocolate milk. There was something about premade chocolate milk that pleased his palate to no end. Like so many things in his extremely restrictive upbringing, chocolate milk had been *verboten* in his house, so Kwik Trip became his dealer of all things sugary. When he was ten, a quart of Kwik Trip chocolate milk had been less than a dollar. With that pilfered $5, it left him with enough money for two comic books off the magazine rack. He would take that month's Captain America, and whatever caught his eye that day, and he would steal off to a nearby park gazebo.

In the shade of the pavilion shelter he would drink his milk and read his comics. Then, he would take the comics to Becky Sigrud's house for her to read and keep. If Duff's mother found them, they would just end up feeding the fire, and even though it was just newsprint and ink, the comics actually meant something to Duff. They represented someone he once aspired to be. Steve Rogers, the brainy little nerd with a big heart who somehow, against all odds, became a Super Soldier thanks to a scientist's serum. It was didn't take a PhD in behavioral psychology to see why someone like Duff, his school's perpetual punching bag, would gravitate toward Steve Rogers.

Duff bought a quart of chocolate milk from a disinterested older woman at the counter. He took it outside and stood in the pale, yellow light of the Kwik Trip's parking lot and took steady pulls from the bottle. Thirty-five years ago, the chocolate milk was decadent. He was breaking rules to get it. Now, it was just milk, and he drank it even though it would probably give him diarrhea later. He did not even taste it. It was just something to put into his face.

A vibration in his pocket startled Duff. He put his phone on silent during dinner at Arby's with Buddy. He pulled it out and glanced at the screen. It was a number he did not recognize, someone not stored in his phone contacts. Typically, he dealt with those sorts of calls by letting them ring to voice mail. If someone felt the need to leave a message, it was probably important. If they did not, it probably wasn't. The number had a Chicago area code, and the first three digits were common enough for cell phones in northern Illinois. Duff decided to take a chance. It wasn't like he had anything better to do at that moment. He thumbed the green accept icon and answered.

"This that guy who was looking for Mikey Pizza?" The voice was thick, brusque, male. He had a heavy Chicago accent to the point where it sounded like he said, *Disdat guy whoowuz lookinfer Mikey Pizza?*

"This is that guy. Who are you?"

The voice on the other end of the line ignored Duff's question. "I heard you were looking for information. Friend to friend, I'd advise you to stop."

"I don't give a shit who killed Mikey."

"Regardless. Some things are best left in the past."

"I need to know who killed Hal Sigrud."

"Don't know that guy."

"Mikey Pizza took bets off him in the Nineties."

"That's not my lookout. I'm only calling to—"

"Yeah, yeah, yeah." Duff was losing patience. "No more with Mikey Pizza. I got it. Can you tell me who carried his business after Mikey left Waukesha?"

"No. Let it lie, friend."

"I'm not after anything to do with Mikey's death. I'm looking into Hal Sigrud's death. If you can't tell me something useful, I will have no choice to keep looking. If you don't want me poking around things you think we should let lie, then tell me something that'll take me in a different direction."

There was a long, poignant pause. Duff could hear a faint mumbling and the sound of something scraping, like the caller had put his hand over the microphone to talk to someone else in the room. After a moment, the caller returned. "Mikey had a guy, Kenny Hansen. He was at the bar in the Nineties, and he's still in Waukesha. He might know something about your guy. Now, you don't go poking after Mikey no more, you got it?"

"Mikey who?"

"That's right." The line went dead.

Abe spent a minute looking at his phone. That was not a call one gets every day. He copy-and-pasted the number from his contacts list to Google. When that did not turn up anything useful, he used a search app on his phone, one he and Abe paid a lot of money for each year. It, too, came up snake-eyes. *Burner phone,* Duff thought. Probably a really cheap one, the kind you snap in half when you finish the call you have to make and then chuck into the Chicago River. Untraceable.

Duff typed *Kenny Hansen* into Google. There were two hits in Waukesha. One was a guy his own age, the other was a guy in his seventies. A father and son, perhaps? The younger one was not the guy he wanted. The older one had to be the right guy. Using the criminal locator app on his phone, another one that cost him and Abe a small fortune to access, he typed

Kenny Hansen's name with his thumbs and uncovered a long history on the elder Hansen. The guy had a modest rap sheet with crimes including petty theft, DUI, and aggravated assault. No crime in the last thirty years, though. An old mug shot loaded up on Abe's phone. He saw a large, square-jawed, thick-skull type. A big, shaggy, Viking-looking fellow with a piercing stare and a casual smirk. He was broad-shouldered in the mug shot and wore a sleeveless denim vest that looked suspiciously like a biker gang's kutte, although Duff could not make out any of the insignias in the mug shot. In his prime, Kenny Hansen would have been a man to be reckoned with.

The locator app provided an address for Hansen. He was residing at Lot 131 in the American Dream Mobile Home Park. Duff checked Google Maps. It was a little over two miles from his current location. Walkable, easily. Duff did not have his cane with him, but he would not let that stop him.

Duff chucked the empty milk bottle into the plastic recycling bin, wrapped his jacket tightly around himself, and started walking.

TO SAY ALL mobile home parks are full of low-rent, trailer-trash failures of humanity would be a heinous stereotype and wrong. To say the residents of the American Dream Mobile Home Park in Waukesha, Wisconsin were low-rent, trailer-trash failures of humanity would be a dead-balls-on accurate summation of the place. The American Dream Mobile Home Park was as close to Hell's waiting room as you would care to get.

Duff saw every stereotypical trailer-park convention within seconds of crossing the threshold of the park. He saw broken-down trailers with expensive muscle cars parked in front of them. He saw one trailer proudly displaying a Confederate flag in the window. He saw a rusted-out Mustang with a small swastika insignia next to the license plate. Almost every trailer had a satellite dish mounted on it, regardless of the condition of the trailer itself. There were beer cans scattered in the small, ill-kept yards of most of the homes. Bits of litter were bogged down in the mud alongside the main, poorly paved road. There were lights on in most of the homes. A few loud arguments could be heard in some of them. There were more cheap, broken-down cars than Duff would have cared to see that day. Telltale grass growth around the wheels of a few of the cars indicated that they had not moved in months, maybe years. The whole park looked and felt grimy, and there was a general sense that the place was just a holding tank for people who were just waiting for a rogue tornado to end their collective misery.

The trailer park was arranged in a small, square shape. The homes were angled to the main loop around the park at thirty-degree angles with a small

grass area that served as a home's lawn, and a single, gravel-covered parking space in front of each home. The homes with more than one car either sacrificed their lawns as a parking space, or they parked them on the other side of the road, tires wearing deep mud bogs in the dirt. In the center of the park was an anemic-looking playground with all the items on it heavily tagged with gang graffiti and badly drawn neo-Nazi logos. The park was lit by two dim halogen streetlights, both humming with a low, buzzy static. Duff could not imagine any parents allowing their children to play there, but two small children sat on the swings, neither actively swinging. They just sat, their legs hanging limply, and they stared at the sand beneath their feet while murmuring lowly to each other.

Duff walked the single road around the square until he arrived at Lot 131. The trailer was a twelve-by-twenty, single-wide. It dated somewhere between the late Sixties and early Seventies. Most of the trailers in the park were well-aged, at best, but 131 was definitely one of the oldest. It showed every year of its age, too. The place was falling apart. More than fifty years of harsh, Midwestern winters and cruel Midwestern summers had beaten the vinyl and warped the wood. The eaves were separated. The siding was hanging on with a few nails, spit, and hope. The place was caked in dust, mold, and dirt which clung thickly to the sides. When Mr. Hansen moved on from that residence, the trailer would never be sold to a new buyer. It would be condemned, dragged away, dismantled, and left to rot, an ignoble end for a tiny home which had given its all.

Duff stepped up the decomposing wooden steps and knocked on the storm door. In his head, Duff wanted to call it a screen door, but it was missing its screen. The interior door was sun-beaten and peeling its false-wood façade. After a moment, the interior door opened, and a grizzled elderly man filled the frame squinting at Duff. Even though years had passed, Duff could still make out the bone structure that gave the biker in the old mug shot his features. The man in the door was a shell of the man in the mug shot, but it was still him. He was well-wrinkled from years of hard living, booze, and cigarettes. Craggy lines crisscrossed his face. When he opened the door, a small mist of old Kools and Parliaments had hit Duff in the face. There was a half-empty bottle of a generic Tennessee whiskey on the kitchen counter, the cheapest kind, and a few empty, crushed beer cans keeping the bottle company.

"Who the fuck are you?" Hansen had a voice that sounded like six miles of gravel road. He was breathing heavy, a thick Emphysema wheeze. He stood at the door, right shoulder purposely pressed to the jamb, right arm hidden from view.

Duff's spider-senses started to tingle. Hidden arm meant gun. "Mr.

Hansen? I'm Duff. Can I ask you a few questions?"

Hansen's eyes narrowed. "You a fucking pig?"

"I've been known to do some heavy damage at a pizza buffet, but I'm not a cop."

"Lawyer?"

"Not even if someone offered to pay me. I'm a private detective." Unlike Abe, Duff never carried business cards and only produced his license if Abe told him to, or someone demanded to see it. Most people did not even know private detectives had to be licensed by the state.

"Detective? Really?" Hansen hocked phlegm in his throat and spat it through the gaping hole in the missing screen to the deck near Duff's feet. "Ain't that like cop-light?"

"Not really. I'm just as big a sleezeball as anyone else."

Hansen did not relax, nor did he seem to notice Duff's joke. "What the fuck you want, then?"

"I wanted to ask you about working for Michael Pizzarelli in the late Eighties, early Nineties. You knew him, right?"

Hansen's right arm popped into view. He was holding a large revolver, a long-barreled Smith and Wesson .44 Magnum worthy of Harry Callahan. It was an old-school gun. At the range between Hansen and himself, the gun had more than enough power to blow Duff clear off the porch and leave a smoking, vast nothingness where his heart used to be. In the grand scheme of things it wasn't the worst way to die; at least it was fast. Hansen did not point the weapon at Duff. He let it dangle at the end of his arm, pointing at the floor. He just wanted Duff to know it was there.

"Nice gun," said Duff. "I bet it would hurt if you shot me. What can you tell me about Hal Sigrud and his family?"

"Who the fuck is Hal Sigrud?"

"Hal, his wife, Connie, and their daughter Becky were murdered in the spring of 1989. Remember the story?"

Hansen's face slackened a bit. He was searching his memory. "I might… I mean, I don't know. It sounds sort of familiar, but my mind is shit lately. Had prostate cancer last year. Fucking chemo fucked me all up. Can't remember shit anymore."

"Must have sucked. You remember Michael Pizzarelli, at least?"

"Mikey Pizza? Sure. Hell, yeah. He and I were good friends."

"Can I come in to talk to you about him, at least?"

Hansen looked down at the handgun, and then back to Duff. Duff saw a look pass over the man's face. If Abe had been there, he probably could have told Duff what the look meant. To Duff, it was just a look, a change in his attitude, perhaps. Hansen waved Duff into the trailer. "Sure. C'mon in. I

might have a few things to say. You want a beer?"

Hansen did not open the storm door for Duff. He just left the interior door open, limping back to a recliner that was beaten nearly to death by years of use, cigarette burns, and spills. The seat was shot, and a couple of old, folded blankets just as stained as the chair were put in its place to help keep Hansen propped up. The older man fell heavily into the chair with a long, extended wheeze. He put the handgun on a TV table next to the chair amidst used tissues, an ash-laden ashtray, a few beer cans, and a small collection of TV remote controls.

Duff stepped into the room gingerly. The walls practically dripped with nicotine. A fine, wavy yellow stain encircled the room at the ceiling line. The carpet was so worn that it was threadbare along the main passage arteries, dirty plywood showing through the gaps. What little art there was on the walls were all somehow related to Harley-Davidson, bald eagles, or the American flag, and often all three simultaneously.

"Have a seat." Hansen gestured to a newspaper-covered couch.

"Not without a tetanus shot." Duff moved toward the center of room. "I don't want to take up too much time, Mr. Hansen—"

"Call me Kenny. Everyone else does."

"Kenny, I'm looking into the death of the Sigruds, and I have a feeling Mikey Pizza might have been involved."

Hansen lit a Parliament with a BIC lighter. He inhaled deeply, held it for a second, and huffed the mist through his nose like a dragon. "Mikey was a good guy. He did some lousy shit, but he was a good guy."

"Lousy shit? Like murder?"

"Nah. He might have ordered a hit or two in his time, but he never dirtied his hands. You know who he was affiliated with?"

"Not off the top of my head."

"Vince Martelli. He was the bookmaker outta Chicago Mikey answered to."

It felt like Kenny Hansen had just handed Duff a piece of the Sigruds' murder puzzle. Vincenzo Martelli had been a heavyweight in the Chicago mob for a long time. Abe and Duff never crossed paths with him, but they knew of him, and they knew he knew of them. Duff was familiar with Martelli's group, and he knew a little bit about how they worked. They were not big hitters. They did not like killing. Dead men don't pay debts, after all. They liked to run hard on the vig and bleed guys dry for years, sort of like getting someone indebted to the company store. It worked, too. Private student loan companies *wished* they had Martelli's numbers.

"Vince isn't really someone to kill someone's family for running a debt over a couple bad bets, though."

Hansen drew another puff on the cigarette. "No. Not really."

"What did you do for Mikey back in the day?"

Hansen reached down to a stack of books and magazines next to his chair. He pulled out a photo album, an old, cheap one that looked like a three-ring binder with a few dozen pages of sticky cardboard for mounting pictures. He flipped pages until he found the picture he was looking for, and then held it out for Duff to see. It was a picture of the shaggy Viking from the mug shot standing with a shorter man, both in front of a Harley-Davidson motorcycle laden with saddlebags and gear. "I was a biker. Real one-percenter shit. Ran with a group called the Savages, sometimes called the Greasy Savages. Did some light drug trafficking— weed, meth, a little coke. Did some pimping. Did a little protection. That's about it, though. Nothing too heavy."

Duff's mind ran through the list of outlaw motorcycle clubs he knew. The name Hansen gave did not ring a bell. "Never heard of them."

"That's 'cause they ain't around no more." Hansen sniffed. "I had a kid, and money got tight. Chicago guys were nosing in on the meth business. Cops were getting smarter. In 1990, I saw the writing on the wall. I went nomad from the group, settled down, got a regular job working construction. Tried to keep my nose clean. Somewhere in the mid-Nineties, the Savs got involved with heroin. Half of them got addicted, a lot OD'd and died. The rest went to jail. That was it for the Greasy Savages." Hansen took the photo album back and looked wistfully at the picture of the young behemoth in the photo. He closed the book. "Don't get old, kid. It ain't great."

"I take it the Savages did favors for Mikey Pizza?"

"We did some stuff. If a guy was late with payments, we might roll up and rough him up a little. Maybe we threaten him some. But we never killed anyone over bets, and we never really hurt anyone. Broken bones don't work, you know. Guy had to keep working to keep the money coming."

Duff never remembered Hal Sigrud with any bruises on his face. "You never roughed up Hal Sigrud, though."

Hansen shrugged. "Honestly, I don't remember no Hal Sigrud. Maybe we roughed him up. Maybe we didn't. I don't know."

"But you didn't kill him?"

Hansen blew a cone of smoke out. "I'm dying."

"We're all dying."

"Not as fast as I'm doing it. I'm a fuckin' black-belt in dying." Hansen picked up a half-empty pack of smokes from the end table and shook them. "Coffin nails. Ain't that the truth? I got Emphysema, got lung cancer, had prostate cancer. I probably got the rockin' pneumonia and the boogie-woogie flu, too."

Duff never knew how to respond when people unburdened themselves of heavy facts about their own mortality around him. He must have a face that made people think he would be a good listener. He wished he could change that about himself if that was the case.

"I'm not going to make it much past Christmas, doctor says. Should be good and dead before St. Patrick's Day next year."

Duff did not know how to respond to that. "Lucky you. Green beer is shit, anyhow."

"I'm only telling you this in case you start to think it's worth getting the pigs involved."

"Cops?"

"Cops are pigs. Always. If you call them, I ain't telling them shit. If they show up here, I'm gonna start shooting. Might as well go out in a blaze of glory. Be faster and hurt less than the cancer, you better believe that. You keep this shit to yourself, got me? Ain't gonna do either of us any good if you start shootin' off your mouth 'bout this."

Duff had been around enough degenerates over the years to know where Hansen was heading. The man was going to check out of the world and wanted someone to hear his final confession. He was looking to unburden himself of guilt to someone, anyone. Duff just happened to be in the right place at the wrong time."You killed people."

Hansen nodded slowly. "Only two. And they both deserved it."

"Why tell me?"

Hansen leaned back in his chair. He took in a deep, raspy breath and immediately started coughing. He hacked and wheezed for a moment until he expectorated a sizable chunk of something brown-green and unholy-looking into an empty peanut can on the side table. "I'm telling you because I could die in my sleep tonight, and I lately I've been feeling like I got to tell someone. I should tell a priest, but I ain't religious. I was thinking about telling my son, but he's a good boy. I managed to keep him from being a scumbag. He's got a good job. Good family. We don't talk much, and I don't see them grandkids of mine, but that's because I want it that way. He don't need to know my shames."

Duff leaned against the wall near the door. He crossed his arms across his chest. "I'll stay quiet. Scout's honor."

"You don't look like no scout."

"I was for a week. They tried to make me go camping. I quit then and there. Who did you kill?"

"Doesn't matter; they're dead. But, given you're here looking for someone who killed three people, I can tell you honestly and openly that it wasn't me."

"Mikey Pizza order you to kill the two you did kill?"

"One of them. And that was after I'd gone nomad. Mikey never asked the Savs to do any hitting for him. This one was between him and me, alone. The other one was for me. It was personal." Hansen got a faraway look in his eye. He was replaying the moment in his head. "I don't remember a lot of shit nowadays, but I remember every fucking second of that day. Some piece of shit wetback raped my buddy's daughter, so I paid him a little visit. I enjoyed that one. Enjoyed every second of it."

"What about the one for Mikey Pizza?" Duff was not wholly insensitive to the fact that Hansen was admitting to committing a murder, but it was not the murder he was there about, and he did not want to open up that bag of worms at the moment.

"What?" Hansen snapped back to reality. "Mikey?"

"You killed two people. One for yourself, and one for Mikey."

"Ah. Right. Mikey called me into the back room one day. Says some Russian guy in Wauwatosa is nosing in on his territory, and he wants him eliminated."

"What year was this?"

"1990. Maybe October."

Duff's parents put him in Bensonhurst in the late fall of 1989. He would not have seen anything about this murder in the newspapers in Canada. "How did it go down?"

"Mikey, he says he wants the guy dealt with. He gives me a gun, brand new .357. He says, go over there in the early morning, like 4:00 a.m., kick open the door, put two in the guy, and disappear. He pays me extra to take a vacation. Tells me to head up to Duluth for a week or two and chuck the gun into a backwoods creek on the way."

"And you did what he said?"

"I did. Kicked open the door, met the guy on the stairs. One in the chest, one in the forehead. Quick, clean, painless." Then, I was out the door. I ran between houses a few blocks to where my old lady was waiting in the car. We left and went up north for a week. Tossed the gun in a lake where we rented a cabin. Easy-peasy."

The back of Duff's neck tingled. Hansen's story was suspiciously similar to how the Sigruds were murdered. They were killed at some point after Duff had left their home for the evening, and before he returned to the house the next morning. It had been gunshots, but it had been a single shot for each of them. Was this a puzzle piece or not?

"Did Mikey have other people doing jobs for him? Similar in nature? Maybe murder?"

"He did. But I couldn't tell you nothing about them. He kept business low-key if you get me. If you did a job for him, that was it. You didn't talk

about it. Talking about it was a good way to find someone doing a job on you, if you know what I'm saying."

"But you know that hits were infrequent, right?"

Hansen rocked back in his recliner and snagged the bottle of whiskey off the counter. He twisted the cap off, took a slug from the bottle, and offered it to Duff, who declined with the wave of a hand. Hansen set the bottle on the table next to him. The glass banged into the metal of the gun. "Very. If the mob was knocking off a lot of people, it would have raised too much suspicion. It's like, the cops were willing to let the murders of a few low-lifes lie, simply because they knew it kept the business running smooth, but if it started to get crazy, we all would have gotten taken down, I'm sure of it."

"You think Mikey might have had Hal Sigrud and his family murdered?"

Hansen shook his head. "That ain't the way it works, normally. Guys like Mikey, guys who are connected— they don't kill families. They're not cruel; they're businessmen. It's not murder, it's just the way of the world. People gotta know their boundaries, you know?" A low rumble started in Hansen's chest. It built to a loud, wet, guttural coughing fit. The old man had tears in his eyes by the time he finished. He spat up more foulness from deep within his lungs, spitting the glob of phlegm into the empty peanut tin.

Hansen put a hand on the gun. "You know, if I was more of a man, I'd probably just end this shit right here, right now."

"Why don't you?"

Hansen was silent for a long moment. When he spoke, it was with a tired, withered voice. The big, tough, Viking warrior biker was missing completely. There was only a frail old man scared of whatever came after this life. "I don't do it because I've gone coward in my old age. If I knew it wouldn't hurt, if I knew what came next, I'd pull that trigger in an instant. Fact is, I don't know what comes next, and no one can tell me that it doesn't hurt, so I can't do it. I've tried. Oh, man— have I tried. I just can't bring myself to do it."

Duff did not even bother trying to respond. He moved toward the door. "Thank you for your time, Mr. Hansen."

Hansen waved him off. "Glad to have some company, I guess. No one comes to see an old, broken man except the lady from Meals on Wheels and my weekly grocery delivery."

Duff paused at the door. "I hope you die quickly and painlessly." It was the most comforting thing he could think to say.

"From your lips to God's ears, son. Thanks for listening to my confession."

Duff walked onto the porch.

Hansen called out to Duff with a final thought. "Let me tell you one last thing, though: the mob didn't take hits lightly; if somebody got knocked off by gangsters, then that fella truly *deserved* it."

Duff shut the interior door to the trailer behind him. He waited for a moment, half-expecting to hear a gunshot ring out, perhaps Hansen finally finding the strength to finish himself. There was only the sound of a TV being turned on and some inane game show playing. The old man went back to the torture of just waiting for the sand to run out of his hourglass.

Duff tromped down the rickety staircase and started heading out of the American Dream Mobile Home Park. It was full dark, and the sickly yellow glow of the two streetlights in the center of the park were the only illumination save for what emanated out of the trailer windows from behind thick curtains.

Duff felt like he had come to another dead end in the case of the Sigrud murderers. If what Kenny Hansen said was true, it was unlikely that a mob hitman would have killed Connie and Becky along with Hal. If Hal was only in trouble for a gambling debt, it was even less likely that they would have been killed.

However, that parting shot, the last thing Hansen said. It stuck in Duff's craw. *If somebody got knocked off, he deserved it.* That was what Duff was missing from the murder. The motive. Why? Why did the Sigruds deserve to get knocked off? Just before Duff was sent to Bensonhurst by his concerned parents, Buddy had told the obsessed, teen-aged Duff that sometimes murders were random. Sometimes, a guy just had a couple of screws loose, and some poor family had to suffer because of it. That explained why the Sigruds were killed, but no one was sexually assaulted, and nothing was taken from the house. At least, nothing obvious was taken. The money, the jewelry, the electronics— all that was still in the house. From what Duff and the Waukesha County detectives could tell, someone entered the house through an unlocked door, gathered the three members of the Sigrud family in the living room, shot them all in the head once, and left. No rhyme. No reason. No motive. No nothing.

Each time Duff butted his thick skull into another dead-end on the Sigruds' murder, he made himself consciously think about just accepting the fact their murders will never be solved. Duff knew that there were over a quarter-million unsolved murder cases open in the United States at that very moment. He knew, on average, another six-thousand murders went unsolved each year. Some might get solved down the line when DNA evidence catches up to the backlog of crime scene materials. Some cases— *most,* if he was being honest with himself— would never get solved. It was just the name of the game. Some murderers were just that good. Some were

just that lucky. And a handful were just that crazy. Maybe the person who murdered the Sigruds was some train-jumping wanderer who walked in, plugged all three of them, and left town. A murderer like that would be almost impossible to catch.

No. Not almost. It would be impossible to catch him. Full stop. End of story. You cannot match wits with crazy. That is what made the Joker such a formidable villain for Batman. Duff solved cases by seeing structure where there was none and finding pieces of a chaotic puzzle before fitting them into place. A true chaotic killer would have no motive. He would have no rationale. He would just kill. Typically, killers like that had to kill over and over again. That was the only way they got caught: the sheer volume of murders led to mistakes or evidence. However, there were probably people out there who killed just once, randomly, just to see what it felt like, and never killed again. Those people probably lived normal lives, had families, and never felt the need to do it again. They would never be caught. They would go to their graves innocent of the crime in the eyes of the Law, and their victims would never find justice. Those sorts of killers scared the bejeezus out of Duff. They did not fit into his world view in which everything could be examined. Duff knew it was possible a true chaotic killer did in the Sigruds. However, he also knew that those sorts of people were as rare as a unicorn under a blue moon. They might exist, but it was highly unlikely. Even fabled chaos killers like Richard Ramirez and Isreal Keyes had to keep killing. They eventually made mistakes. One-and-done guys were improbable. They were more myth than man.

Duff was so deep in his own thoughts he barely had time to register the scuffle of soft-soled shoes hitting asphalt. When he did hear it, it was too late. Duff, with his hands shoved deep in the pockets of his jacket, took a shot to the back of the head full blast. Someone hit him so hard he had no choice but to fall. The blow jellied his legs and sent his mind spiraling. It might have been a fist. It might have been a bat. It was hard, fast, and did its damage. Duff did not remember the fall. He opened his eyes, and he was lying face-down on the road near the exit of the trailer park. He started to stir, trying to force his arms to push him up to face his attacker, but a foot flew out of the darkness and caught him full in the chin. The kick clacked his teeth together and everything went dark.

Contrary to movie and TV treated a knock-out shot like that, the victim rarely stayed unconscious for long. More often than not, the unlucky recipient sprang back to a groggy form of awareness in less than a minute. The body's fight-or-flight instinct was strong, and it always tried to get the body back to motion as fast as possible. Usually, a body knocked unconscious came back to life throwing random punches at whatever he

thought was attacking him or trying to run away. Duff awoke with a rough, snore-snort that hurt the back of his throat. He was face-down on the ground with a mouthful of slick, coppery blood. He pushed himself to his knees. He ran his tongue around his teeth. They were still intact. Felt like he bit the ever-loving hell out of his tongue, though. He spat a gob of blood the size of a golf ball onto the cracked asphalt.

He felt his pockets. Wallet gone. Cell phone gone. Where was his Milwaukee Brewers hat? He felt around on the ground. It was also gone. Simple assault and robbery. His attackers weren't out to get him personally. It was not connected to the fact that he had just been visiting an ex-biker who once killed for a mobster. It had nothing to do with Nate Riegert's murder. He just happened to be walking alone at night in a place where that sort of transgression called for payment, and he had paid.

Luckily for him, he was used to living in Chicago, and this was by no means the first time he had been mugged, and it sure as hell was not the first time he'd been blindsided. Duff kept a few bucks in his wallet, but he never carried a credit card if he could help it. He had one, but it lived in his sock drawer back in Chicago. It was used for paying for PS4 games in PlayStation's online store and that was about it. His cell phone was cheap, easily replaceable. He just had to text it a numerical code from another phone, and it would automatically wipe it. He did not keep any information worth having on the phone, certainly nothing financial, and he had a lock screen with a good password. They would not be able to get into it, and they would not be able to sell it for much. His driver's license, PI license, $30 cash, and a card for a free foot-long from Subway were all that he really lost. Replacing his license was a simple process, but he would be angry about losing out on that sub for a while. He still had his emergency $50 in his shoe. If his muggers had simply asked him, Duff probably would have handed all that stuff over rather than take the second shot to the chops.

Duff dragged himself to his feet, staggering on wobbly legs. He could not call for an Uber. He could not call 911. He thought about asking someone in one of the trailers to call Abe for him, but he decided not to call. The cold night air felt good. Inhaling through his nose helped clear his head. The cuts on his tongue were already starting to stop bleeding. He would be alright, he told himself. He would be fine.

Duff resumed walking. Each step felt tentative, but he refused to let himself think about it. He touched the back of his head gingerly. There was blood, but it was sticky and matted. It was not freely flowing. He thought of the parallel between the shot he just took and the blow that killed Nate Riegert. Duff could not help but wonder why Riegert died from a blow to the back of the head, but he only got knocked unconscious. He made a

mental note to look at the coroner's report when he got back to the hotel, and then he hoped the concussion would let him keep that mental note.

Two miles was not a long way, and Duff had certainly walked two miles many, many times before, but trying to do it on wobbly legs was a new challenge, and it slowed him even more than having a gimp ankle did.

11

DUFF SPENT WELL over an hour limping two miles back to the Kwik Trip. When he got there he saw Henry Novak standing in the pale, yellow lights of the store's overhanging eaves smoking a cigarette. Duff remembered Henry used to smoke a lot at Bensonhurst. Most of the older boys did. It was Canada, and cigarettes were abundant at that time. The staff at the home discouraged smoking, but they did not ban it. As long as it was done outside in the rec yard, no one told them to stop. Usually, Duff knew a smoker by smell. It was impossible to hide the heavy scent of tobacco and ash that wormed into clothes and hair. When Duff was near Henry before, he had not smelled cigarettes, only cheap aftershave. Duff assumed the man quit smoking, but perhaps the stress of having his daughter in jail had compelled him to start again. Duff's personal vices were sugar and caffeine, and he was powerless to quit either.

Duff saw Henry watching him. There was no place for him to hide or act as though they had not seen each other. Duff limped to the store and bought a bottle of Sprite. He was feeling sick to his stomach from the concussion and felt the soda might calm his stomach enough to keep him from throwing up again. He tossed everything he had inside of him three times, fertilizing some people's yards on his hike from the trailer park. Bile still stung the back of his nose and coated his tongue. Duff hated throwing up more than just about anything.

Duff walked out of the shop and took a position near Henry. He sipped his drink. Neither man said anything. Duff wondered about the differences between who he was thirty years ago and who he was now. Was he people or not? He wasn't sure.

Henry finished his cigarette, stubbed it out on the red brick half-wall in front of the store, and lit another. He broke the silence between them. "I haven't smoked in more than twenty years."

"I figured." The Sprite was not exactly settling Duff's stomach, but the taste killed the bile-burn in the back of his throat, and that wasn't nothing.

"When I first met Maggie, she said she would never kiss a smoker. I figured I wanted to kiss her more than I wanted to smoke, so I quit."

"I take it that is no longer holding true, then?"

Henry looked at the lit cigarette between his fingers with a sheepish grin. "It's been a rough week."

"I've had my share of those."

They lapsed into silence. There was no doubt as to who made Duff's weeks rough. Henry took a long drag from his cigarette and blew out a cone of smoke. Henry turned slightly to better see Duff. The new injuries were brought into clear focus. "Jesus. You look like you got fucked up."

"Got mugged." Duff rubbed a hand over the low scrub of what little hair he had on his head. He felt utterly naked without a cap. "They took my hat."

"You got a goose egg on the back of your head."

Duff reached back and touched the wound gingerly. "Yeah. I think they hit me with a Little League bat."

"How do you know it was Little League?"

"Major League would have left a bigger lump."

Novak chuckled. "You know, Clive—"

"Duff."

"Sorry. Duff. You know, we used to be scared of you."

"Who? You?"

"All of us back at the nut house. Me, especially."

Duff's could not believe that. "You? Scared of me? Did you not remember all the times you beat my ass like a rented mule? How did I scare anyone?"

"You were different. Scary different. You weren't like the rest of us."

That was an elementary observation. Of course he wasn't. Duff prided himself on being unlike anyone else, but it seemed odd to hear someone else voice that opinion. "How do you mean?"

Henry took a big drag from his cigarette, speaking with his breath held. "Remember when you first got to Benny's?" He woofed out a big cloud of smoke.

Duff winced at the nickname. The other kids called the place Benny's, Benst, or Uncle Ben's House of Hurt. He never called it that. He had no wish to humanize that house of depression in any way. "Of course I

remember. I arrived on a Thursday morning after driving overnight thirteen hours from Waukesha. I was fourteen. My parents actually sedated me to get me into the car."

Henry's eyebrows raised in surprise. "Really?"

"Really. Ground up pills in a milkshake at McDonald's. By the time I woke up, we were over the Canadian border."

Henry let out a low whistle. "That's rough. I got taken there by a police van."

"I would have preferred that. Less dehumanizing."

"Well, that's beside the point. When you first arrived you looked super intense, like you were burning holes in people with your eyes."

Duff did not tell Henry he was precisely trying to do that exact thing, however he was unable to summon mutant powers and lay waste to his surroundings.

"Two days after you arrived Jeff Maxwell arrived. You remember?"

Duff had tried not to think of Jeff Maxwell since he left Bensonhurst. He tried but failed miserably. Jeff was one of the students who was stuck in Bensonhurst at the behest of the Ontario Provincial Government because Jeff had poor impulse control combined with obsessive sexual fetishes. He was a chronic onanist. "I remember Jeff."

"Captain Grabby." Henry spoke the nickname everyone ended up calling him.

"Captain Grabby." Duff echoed the sobriquet. The female staff nurses and therapists had to be sure where Maxwell was at all times, otherwise they would quickly find a stray hand on their breasts or buttocks.

"Well, you remember how Captain Grabby stepped to you his first day? I don't even remember what it was for."

"He thought I took his spot in line for dinner. I was not even in line at the time."

"That's right! You sat there and listened to him yell at you about nothing for like five minutes, and then you stepped back and absolutely *wrecked* that fool. You diagnosed his issues. You somehow knew where he came from, what he did, how he ended up there— it was crazy. Then, you walked out of the room like you hadn't just dropped a bomb. Everyone up there was always trying to hide their faults, hide their weaknesses, but you always knew what they were. It was like you could read our minds."

Duff remembered the day in question with perfect clarity. He had made simple inductions based on what little he had happened to see of Maxwell. He had glimpsed Maxwell's parents' home address on a clipboard at the nurses' station. He walked past the kid's room while he was unpacking and saw enough items in the suitcase to get an idea of his character. He

observed how Maxwell's right arm was always close to his groin. He had an involuntary flexion of the wrist that belied his particular chronic habit. The rest was plain as day to anyone with eyes. It was the way he gawked at the female staff members, the leer, the smirk. Duff did not think it was any sort of big reveal. The rest of them would have found out rather quickly, especially the next day when Maxwell unzipped his jeans and let his flag fly in front of everyone.

"You were always two steps ahead of us, man." Henry took another drag on his cigarette. He almost sounded wistful. "That's why I marked you as an enemy right away. You were too smart. You were too mean."

"*I* was mean?" Duff could not keep the incredulity out of his voice. "Fuck off. You were mean. You were a fucking savage animal." He tapped his brow. "Broken fucking orbital bone, remember."

"I know I was. And I apologized for it, right? I was a class-A bastard without excuse. If it is any consolation, I truly do feel badly about it. I figured it would only be a matter of time before you tried that spooky shit on me, and I wanted to stop it before it started."

"You realize if you had just left me alone, nothing ever would have happened."

"I realize that now. I was sixteen, remember; all my bingo balls weren't in the tank, yet." Novak tapped a finger against his temple.

They lapsed into silence again. There was still a wall of awkwardness between them, an intangible defensive barrier. Duff doubted it would ever go away completely.

Henry broke the silence when he finished his cigarette. He tossed the butt on the asphalt and ground it down with the heel of his work boot. "You really handled yourself so well at Benny's. You were like, not even there, you know?"

"No. I have no idea what you're saying. I was terrified every day."

"You never looked it, man. All the staff, the orderlies— no one really wanted to mess with you. You drifted around that place like you weren't even there, like your brain was always somewhere else."

That was a true statement. Duff spent almost all his time in his memory palace reconstruction of the Sigruds' living room trying to piece together their murders. It helped keep him from confronting the reality of his surroundings. It also allowed other patients to jump him without having to set up elaborate ambushes. They'd just start swinging and be three or four punches into the beating before Duff could come back to reality to try to defend himself.

Another prolonged silence fell. It still felt like an uneasy alliance between them. Duff could not push past his childhood distrust. It was likely Henry

was carrying some sort of guilt for his teenage behaviors, but Duff did not care about that. If the behemoth felt some guilt, good. Fuck him. Carry that guilt.

"You know, you're about the only guy in the world I can talk to about Bensonhurst."

Duff remained silent.

Henry elaborated, "I try to tell Maggie about it, but I think she thinks some of it is lies. I don't think she can fathom a mental hospital staff treating teenage boys so cruelly. At least, not in the Nineties."

"Northern Canada is hardly a bastion of progressive influence and open-arm caring."

Henry snorted a laugh. "That's pretty true. I'm surprised they had indoor plumbing."

"Those toilet seats—" Duff began.

Henry cut him off. "Holy shit, those were fucking freezing all the time. The bathrooms were not insulated well."

"I think they did it on purpose to keep our showers short." The water in the communal showers was never hot. At best, it was lukewarm. At worst, it was a mountain stream in winter. "At least the cold kept Maxwell's ween from standing at attention."

Henry barked out a short laugh. "Did you just make a joke?"

"Nope. Dead serious. I saw enough of that poor dude's erections to last me a lifetime."

Henry broke out laughing. Hard. He doubled over and put his hands on his knees. "See, these are the things I can't get Maggie to believe." He straightened up and wiped a tear from the corner of his eye. "Goddamn. That dude loved his wang, didn't he?"

"Constantly."

There was a pause. Duff and Henry made eye contact, and then they both burst out laughing. It was cathartic.

When the laughter faded, Henry asked Duff, "You think we'll stay in contact after this is over? I might like to call and check up on you on occasion. Or maybe just talk through some of the baggage I'm still carrying from Benny's. I imagine you might have a few things to get off your chest about that place, too."

Duff did not want to extend Henry an olive branch, but his niece-by-proxy's voice popped into his mind. In most things, when he had the proverbial angel and devil fighting on his shoulder, Matilda was the angel. Tilda was always trying to enhance Duff's social circles, to get him to be more gregarious in situations where the only expectation was conversation and company. Duff hated those situations. *Friends can be found everywhere, Duff.*

No matter how much she cajoled him, Duff remained content with Abe as his only friend. Well, not *only*. He had Katherine, Matilda, Wheels, and a couple of the regulars at Wheels's bar, but he really was fine with the lack of social contact. He thought about telling Henry to stick it, go fuck himself, eat a bag of pox-ridden capybara dicks, and a dozen other clever ways to say no, but he acquiesced to the angel this time. "If you email me, I'll probably reply."

Henry smiled warmly. It was an honest smile. "That's good to hear. Thank you. I might just do that, then." Henry's phone beeped in his pocket. He pulled it out and used a thick, calloused forefinger to navigate the touchscreen. Duff glanced at the phone. The overhead light glinted off the screen at an angle revealing myriad fingerprints, smudges, and grease trails on the screen protector.

Duff's brain sounded its puzzle piece alert. He froze. His eyes darted back and forth as he mentally went through the case notes. His memory, while not recalling every word of the case report, recalled enough to find a gaping hole in the detective's case.

"We have to go to sleep now." Duff's voice was flat and monotone. He began walking back to the Super 8.

"What? Why?" Henry was confused.

"Because that's the fastest way to get to morning."

"Why do we have to get to morning?"

"Because I'm going to get your daughter released from jail tomorrow."

"What? How?"

Duff did not answer. He continued to limp toward the hotel.

Henry pulled the pack of Camels from his pocket, crushed them in his fist, and threw them into the trash. He started jogging after Duff. "Do you really think you ought to sleep, though? You look like you probably got a concussion. Maybe I should take you to the emergency room?"

"I'll be fine." Duff continued walking forward like an automaton. "I need the sleep."

"I've heard if you go to sleep with a concussion, you might not wake up."

Duff would not stop. "Wouldn't that be nice?"

12

ABE WAS NOT asleep when Duff walked into the room. How could he sleep? He was going to face a judge in the morning and likely screw over a young woman's life. Who needed sleep when he had a full, rich morning like that to look forward to?

"Lucy, I'm home." Duff staggered into the room. For a moment, he was backlit by the bright lights in the hallway. Abe only saw Duff's face in shadow. When he moved into the ring of light cast by the bedside end table lamp, Abe temporarily forgot about the courtroom.

"What happened?" Abe propelled himself out of bed. "You look like six miles of bad road."

"Only six? Then I'm fine." Duff kicked off his shoes and dropped his pants. He stepped out of his jeans and crawled into bed, faceplanting the pillow.

"Wow. The back of your head looks even worse."

Duff did not move. He spoke into the pillow, voice muffled. "There goes my modeling career."

"I think we need to go to the ER."

Duff rolled to his side. "I'll be fine. It's been over an hour and my headache has gone from a ten to a nine-point-five, so that means it's improving."

"Let me go get you an ice pack, at least." Abe started pulling on a sweatshirt and track pants. "There's an ice machine in the hallway."

"Wisconsin is an ice machine."

"Not in late October." Abe grabbed the plastic liner from the empty

trashcan and his room card. He hustled barefoot down the hall trying not to think about the worrisome levels of bacteria and filth on hotel carpeting.

Maggie Novak emerged from her room, a look of concern on her face. She was in sweats and flip-flops. "Henry said Duff was hurt, said he got mugged."

Abe flipped the cover of the ice machine and scooped a hefty amount of cubed ice into the trash can liner, tying off the bag to make it leak-proof. "Wouldn't be the first time. Probably won't be the last."

Abe and Duff's partnership was full of discrepancies. Abe was thin; Duff was fat. Abe was a family man; Duff was an isolated loner. Duff liked sports; Abe could barely tell the difference between a baseball and a hockey puck. However, the one major discrepancy tended to be about who got hurt. If someone was going to fall, get hit in the mouth by some thug, or attacked by an ornery raccoon it was going to be Duff. He was a trouble magnet. Abe had managed to survive more than twenty years in Chicago without being mugged once. Duff had been mugged at least a half-dozen times. Abe had yet to break a bone. Duff had broken several. Abe had never fallen down a gala staircase in front of a group of strangers while trying to make a point about a murder investigation. Duff had done it twice. Abe was used to being Duff's nursemaid in such events. He felt an odd sense of loyalty to him in those moments. Duff always took the hit so Abe did not.

Maggie waited at Abe and Duff's door for Abe to return. She fast-walked to the bed and looked at the back of Duff's head. "Oh my. That's pretty bad. I'm going to go get my first aid kit."

"Hey, we should get one of those," said Duff.

"We have one."

"We do? Where is it?"

"In the office in Chicago."

"Perfect. It's doing us plenty of good there."

There was a light knock at the door, and Abe let Maggie into the room. Henry Novak followed her. Maggie carried a small, canvas satchel with a first-aid kit inside it. She set it on the bedside table and began tending to Duff's wound. She worked quickly with a practiced hand.

Abe was impressed. "You look like you know what you're doing."

"I was a nurse for a few years. At least, I was until our kids were born. Then, daycare would have cost more than I was making at the hospital, and Henry's company was doing well enough for me to step back from nursing to be a mom and run Henry's books for him." Maggie used Steri-strips to seal the wound in the back of Duff's head. "It's not that bad once the blood was cleaned up."

"It's not that good, either." Henry stood back by the bathroom. He

blocked most of the light from the hallway with his presence.

Maggie took the makeshift ice pack from Abe's hand. "Get me one of those hand towels from the bathroom, please." Henry retrieved one and threw it to her. She spread the towel over Duff's head and put the ice pack on the swelling lump. "Does that hurt?"

Voice still muffled in the pillow, Duff responded, "Nope."

Maggie moved from the edge of the bed to the wing chair at the little table in the room. "That's about all I can do. He should probably go to the hospital."

"Duff hates hospitals. He needs to have bone sticking out of his skin to even think about going." Abe sat in the other wing chair.

Maggie took a deep breath. She said in a quiet voice, "Henry, I can smell the cigarettes."

Henry shrugged. "I had a weak moment. I'll shower and brush my teeth. Don't worry."

Maggie wrinkled her nose. "It's in your clothes, too."

"I get it." There was a sharpness to Henry's voice. Abe recognized it immediately. The couple might have been playing the loving relationship card, but the stress of the week was starting to push them apart, exacerbating underlying issues which existed before Sarah's arrest. Abe knew because it was the same tone of voice Katherine used to use on him before she came out. Abe saw Maggie's cheeks redden, but she said nothing. Abe realized what was drawing him toward her: they were the same.

Henry took a breath and adjusted his attitude. "Duff said he might have a way to get Sarah out of jail."

Duff, from the bed, gave a thumbs-up.

Maggie's eyes widened. "What is it?"

Abe had no idea. "Usually when Duff says things like this, he has not told me how. I just trust he will be able to do it."

Duff suddenly sat up and the bag of ice flopped off his head onto the bed. "Need to call Buddy. Have him meet us at the courthouse tomorrow morning." After a moment, another thought occurred to him. "Crap. I forgot to blank my phone." He walrused across the bed and grabbed Abe's phone. He sent his phone the text that would lock it.

Abe asked, "How are you going to get Sarah out of jail tomorrow?"

Duff gave him a half-smile and licked his dry lips. "Let's… let's let it be a secret, eh? I'm not certain it will work."

Abe's stomach tightened into a knot. The meeting with the judge loomed like a pressing weight on his chest.

DUFF SOMEHOW SLEPT. Abe did not. Abe sat in the wing chair at the table watching his partner-in-crime-solving sleep all night after Maggie raised concerns Duff's concussion was probably worse than he said it was. If he stopped breathing in the middle of the night, Abe would have to call 911. This coupled with the appointment with the judge resulted in a long, sleepless night filled with worry and fret.

At 7:00 a.m., Abe figured Duff was not going to die, and he let himself take a shower despite not really needing one. He shaved. He applied deodorant and aftershave. He made himself look as presentable as possible. He dressed in his suit, tying a cardinal-red tie with small paisley icons dotting it. It was the tie he bought for his graduation from law school. It felt fitting. He once told Katherine it was the tie he wanted to be buried in if he predeceased her.

At 8:00 a.m., Abe woke Duff. Duff was never what one would refer to as a morning glory, and his glory was particularly loathsome the night after he suffered a concussion. Duff showered, but grudgingly. He dressed in his standard uniform: hooded sweatshirt, jeans, and a pair of black Asics sneakers.

"You're not going to dress up for court?"

Duff yawned and straightened the bottom of his sweatshirt. "I'm not a lawyer."

By 8:30 a.m., Duff and Abe were in the lobby of the hotel. They met the Novaks, both dressed in formal business attire. Abe and Duff drove over in *Rose*. The Novaks took their truck.

Abe drove to the courthouse carefully. It was only a couple miles, and they arrived with twenty minutes to kill before the meeting that hung over Abe like a guillotine blade. Abe breathed in through his nose, out through his mouth, and pretended he was a competent legal mind. He tried to project strength, but it was not working.

The Novaks picked up on his fear immediately. As they walked to the judge's office, Maggie touched his arm. "Are you alright, Mr. Allard?"

"Just fine. Fine. Fine, fine, fine." Abe's mouth was dry. He felt like he was vibrating.

"Could I get you a water or some coffee?"

"No. That's fine. Fine, fine, fine." Abe knew he was jabbering, but he could not stop. He turned to look for Duff, but he had stayed at the entrance to wait for Buddy. Abe was all alone, and he knew it.

Abe and the Novaks took seats in the waiting room at the end of the judicial chambers hall. A middle-aged secretary took Abe's name and business card and confirmed his appointment with Judge Balmer. "The judge should be in any minute now."

Abe thanked the secretary. He concentrated on not wetting himself. His left leg bounced involuntarily.

Maggie leaned toward Abe's shoulder. "Mr. Allard, if you don't mind, I know that you are technically a lawyer, but may I ask how many legal cases you have represented?"

"Represented? One."

"Did you win?"

"No. I resigned halfway through my first day in court."

"Oh." Maggie was silent for a long moment. "Well, I believe in you."

Abe wanted to thank her but hearing her vote of confidence made his stomach churn.

A thin, fit woman clacked down the hall in high heels and a pencil skirt. Abe knew from the way she moved she was a prosecutor. She walked into the judicial waiting room and sized Abe up immediately. "Mr. Allard? You're Sarah Novak's new attorney?"

Abe somehow found the strength to push himself to his feet. "I am." He stuck out his hand suddenly aware that his palms were damp as a Louisiana swamp.

The prosecutor shook Abe's hand. Her face flinched as she did. She pulled her hand back and subtly wiped it on her hip. "I am Janice Jackson. I'm overseeing the prosecution for the state. Please, no jokes about the name, and if you make any jokes about me being nasty, I'll punch you in the mouth."

"Fair enough."

"Aberforth is an interesting name, isn't it?"

Abe was used to questions about his name. "Old Gaelic."

"What does it mean?"

"From the river."

Jackson's eyebrows raised. "That's fascinating. How did you get that name?"

"My mother read a book when she was pregnant with me. One of the characters in it had a dog named Aberforth, and she thought it sounded unique because she had never seen the name before."

"So, you were named after a dog in a book?"

"It sounds really stupid if you say it out loud."

Footsteps slapping against the floor in the hall made Abe and the prosecutor look toward the sound. A large, balding man in khaki slacks and a blue Oxford shirt approached the waiting area. He carried a briefcase in one hand and casually dangled a dark blue sport coat in the other. "I take it you are my morning meeting?"

Judge John Balmer stepped into the waiting area. "Good morning, Stacey. Any messages?"

The secretary shook her head. "Just these two, your honor."

Balmer stepped to the prosecutor. "How are the kids, Janice?"

"Just fine, your honor."

"Good to hear, good to hear." He turned to Abe. "And you must be Mr. Allard from the Windy City."

Abe felt himself freeze. He forced his mouth to approximate a smile. "Good morning, your honor." The words were hard to force out of his mouth.

"I hear you're seeking bail for your client. You realize I don't like giving bail to first-degree murderers."

"The state will probably only seek second-degree, your honor," said Jackson. "It was a crime of passion, after all."

Abe opened his mouth, but no sound came out.

Balmer did not notice. He turned to the Novaks. "I assume you are the parents of Mr. Allard's client?"

Maggie came to Abe's rescue. She positioned herself at Abe's side and laid a hand on his forearm. "Yes, your honor. I'm Maggie. This is my husband, Henry."

"Hello. It's a bit odd to have the parents of a suspect in chambers."

"Oh, we're just here to support Abe. We'll be no trouble."

"Very well, then." Balmer turned back to Abe. "I also hear you are a detective of some note. I looked up your legal record and found there was none."

Abe knew he had to talk. He swallowed hard and forced the words to flow. "I am fully licensed to practice law; I choose not to. I have found detective work to be more rewarding."

Balmer chuckled, not buying Abe's line for a red second. "Sure it is. Tell you what— why don't you two give me five or ten minutes to check my email and get into the robe, and we'll knock this business out right quick."

"Uh, your honor— I'm waiting for my partner to arrive."

"Really, Counselor?"

Abe nodded. It was a little too frantic of a nod. "I believe he will be bringing evidence that will convince the DA to drop charges against my client, or at the very least grant her a favorable bond."

"Well, then!" Balmer walked away from the attorneys. "Your partner has five or ten minutes to get here."

JUDGING FROM HER face, Detective Pamela Jahnke was extremely unhappy. She was upright in her desk chair. Her arms were crossed high on her chest, her left knee was planted firmly over her right. Her lips were

curving into a permanent scowl. Her whole posture and bearing were of a creature on the defensive, pushed back against a wall, and preparing to fight. She glared hard at the two men in front of her. "You want me to do what?"

"I want to see the evidence box." Duff noticed the deepening lines in the detective's face. "You know, you seem tense. You should try to relax or you're going to end up prematurely wrinkled. Have you tried yoga? I hear good things."

"Fuck you, Mr. Duffy."

Buddy pushed Duff to the side with one hand. "What this gomer is trying to say is that he has a theory he wants to test out and was wondering if you would be so kind as to oblige him."

"Or, in simpler terms, just let me see the evidence."

Jahnke stuck out her lower jaw and huffed a breath that blew a few loose hairs out of her face. "How important is it?"

Duff shrugged. "Might be important. Might not be. Won't know until I see the evidence box."

"Why do you want to see it?"

"Because I saw your crime scene report, and it's unfinished."

Jahnke was out of her chair in an instant. She put her hands on her desk, clenched into fists, and leaned toward Duff. "I dot my I's and cross my T's."

Duff could not be intimidated. "If I were shitty at my job, I'd be defensive, too. Don't worry. Look at this as a personal growth opportunity."

Jahnke looked to Buddy, and the old sheriff nodded. "I trust this boy more than most of the cops I worked with over the years. If he wants to see something, let him see it. If he's wrong, no harm, no foul. But, if he's right you might learn something."

Jahnke threw up her hands. "Fine! Fine. Come with me."

The detective led the two men to the evidence room. She signed out the box, broke the red tape that sealed it, and put her initials on the form. "There was not a lot of evidence. It was pretty clear-cut." She opened the box. Inside was a couple items from the weight room, each wrapped in a sealed plastic bag, but Duff was only interested in one. He found Sarah Novak's cell phone and held it up.

"How did you know this was Sarah's phone?"

Jahnke rolled her eyes. "Because we turned it on and got the phone number, tracing it back to her. Although, the myriad of selfies on it would have served the same purpose."

"No screen lock?"

"No." Jahnke paused. "Why?"

"Just seems weird that someone in a college setting would leave their

phone unlocked. Lot of secret texts, maybe some dirty photos. I mean, I keep a screen lock on my phone. Do you?"

"Of course I do. Department policy."

"But the cell phone of an eighteen-year-old girl was unlocked?" Duff grabbed a pair of black nitrile gloves from a box and slipped them on his hands. Duff ripped open the bag. He expected resistance from Jahnke, but she stepped backward.

"You think I missed something on the phone?"

Duff pulled a small wooden box from his back pocket.

Jahnke leaned in slightly. "What's that?"

"Fingerprint kit. Powder and brush."

"That's a little old school, isn't it?"

Buddy shushed her with a finger to his lips. "Just let the boy work."

Duff dipped the fine hairs of the brush in the powder and quickly worked the brush on the two largest sides of the phone. He waited for a moment, turning the phone in the light to view it all angles. "Exactly what I thought."

Jahnke moved closer to the phone, squinting at it. "I'm not sure I'm seeing what you're seeing."

"That's because you're not seeing anything." Duff angled the phone more in the light. There was not a single fingerprint on the touchscreen or the pink, plastic exo-case. "Not a single fingerprint, Detective. That means someone wiped them all off before planting the phone at the crime scene. Now, Detective, please tell me what sort of criminal would wipe all of her own fingerprints from her own phone before leaving her phone at a murder scene in which she was the murderer."

Jahnke looked at the phone, looked again, and then grabbed a pair of gloves for herself. She took the phone from Duff and angled it at the light inspecting every millimeter of the phone. She dropped it back into the open evidence bag. Her shoulders sagged. "I got the wrong person, didn't I?"

Buddy patted her on the back. "You arrested the person the evidence pointed to at the time. Now, the evidence doesn't point to her anymore. You have to do what's right."

JUDGE JOHN BALMER slipped on a pair of half frame reading glasses and peered over the top of them at the two attorneys in his chambers. He nodded at his stenographer in the corner, a pleasant-looking woman with a broad, friendly face. She placed her hands over her machine and waited for someone to speak. "Mr. Allard, we're here for you, so make your case."

Abe could feel his heart in his throat. He sat in an uncomfortable chair across from the judge and tried to find a position where he felt like he was not being skewered by hot pokers. He tried telling himself it was just chambers, not a courtroom.

"Your honor—" Abe's voice cracked. He cleared his throat, coughing hard into his fist. "I'm sorry. Let me start that again. Your honor, I have reason to believe that Sarah Novak was arrested prematurely following the murder of Nathan Riegert. Her cell phone was found at the scene, but my partner has reason to believe her phone was planted as a red herring to fool police."

"Your proof, counselor?" Janice Jackson seemed pleasant enough in her question. There was no edge to her voice, no courtroom theatrics. Abe appreciated that.

"My partner should be here soon with the proof."

"No proof, no nothing, Counselor. You know that." Balmer rocked back in his chair and laced his fingers over his belly.

"Well, proof will be here soon. Until that time, my partner and I have uncovered several possible suspects with more likely motives to kill Mr. Riegert than Ms. Novak." Abe felt the flop sweat break out on his forehead. He resisted the urge to wipe it away with his sleeve for fear of drawing attention to it.

"Interesting," said Balmer. "And, I assume you have proof that makes these other suspects more likely?"

Abe's tongue turned to sawdust. "Not at this moment, your honor. We have only been on this case for two days. We have uncovered a number of other suspects that seem like more likely candidates."

"Seem, Counselor?" Balmer's voice leaned toward impatience.

"Your honor, I do not feel like we should be wasting your time with this triviality this morning." Jackson stood up from her chair. "If my colleague cannot produce proof, then I suggest we take this up at trial as scheduled in six weeks."

Abe knew he had to delay. Abe was not good at delay. He flipped through the file folder he brought in with the police case notes in it. He pretended to flip through the papers for a moment.

Balmer was a seasoned vet on the bench. He'd seen all the tricks. "While I'm young, Counselor."

Abe put down the folder. "Your honor, my colleague should be here. I mean, he's here in the building." Abe felt like Balmer's eyes were drilling holes in his forehead. "Duff is just conducting an experiment, and—"

"Experiments, your honor?" Jackson jumped all over Abe. "It feels like the good counselor is praying for a miracle."

Abe swallowed hard; his throat felt as though it was constricting. He choked, coughed once, and then spat forth a torrent of speech he had never once been able to summon in a courtroom. "Not a miracle, your honor. Just the dignity of a few minutes. My client was wrongly accused and was attacked and viciously beaten while in jail. Likely, this will end up being a lawsuit against the county from her parents. I think, given the circumstances, the court could grant us a few moments of leniency while my partner prepares the evidence for presentation." Abe was stunned at his own improvisation.

Across the desk Judge Balmer's eyebrows raised once, and his eyes shifted to the prosecutor. "Ms. Jackson, any counter?"

"Two minutes, your honor. No more."

"Your partner has two minutes, Mr. Allard." As if to emphasize the statement, Balmer took a small hourglass from his desk and set it on the table. Sand began to stream through the narrow port. "Two minutes."

Abe excused himself to check for Duff in the hallway. It was empty. Maggie Novak saw Abe's face pop out of the judge's chambers, and she gave him a double thumbs-up and a broad, toothy smile. The smile was forced. Her eyes and her forehead showed stress lines and the clench of her jaw showed her worry. Abe hissed to her, "Have you seen Duff?"

The smile disappeared, the thumbs-up, too. She shook her head and looked to Henry. Henry shook his head, as well.

"Find him. Fast. Tell him to run." Abe ducked back into the judge's chambers.

The judge was flipping the hourglass. "My one-minute hourglass has just been turned over, Counselor. Time, as you can plainly see, is running out."

"He'll be here." Abe sat back in the chair across from the judge. "I hope."

Jackson launched another volley at Abe. "You remember what they said in law school about cases built on hope, Mr. Allard."

A watched pot never boils, and a watched hourglass takes forever. Abe watched the little reservoir of sand slowly lower itself in the bulb. The cascading sand piling in a conical mound. He could feel sweat trickling down his back in a torrent.

"That's a nice little trinket." Abe was desperate to break the silence. "Where'd you get it?"

"One of my law school mentors gave it to me when I graduated thirty-some-odd years ago. He told me it would remind me of the value and the power of a single minute."

"It's nice. I should get one."

Jackson checked her watch. She glanced toward the door.

The hourglass continued to cascade. The level got lower. It was in its death throes, the final grains of sand speeding through the neck. Balmer looked expectantly at Abe.

"I don't suppose I could implore you for an extra minute, could I?"

"No."

There was a knock at the door. The breath Abe had been holding in his chest expelled with force. "Oh, thank God."

"Come," said Balmer in a raised voice.

The door opened. Crowded together in a group was a very winded Duff and Buddy, a less-winded Henry Novak, and Detective Pam Jahnke and Maggie Novak, neither of whom was winded in the least because they were both in shape. The judicial secretary, Stacey, was also there.

Stacey was red-faced. "Judge, I tried to stop them, but they just barreled through—"

"It's fine, Stacey." Balmer looked at the gathered mob at the door. "Hello, Buddy. You're looking well."

The sheriff gave him a nod. "How's the golf game, John?"

"Swinging like shit, as usual. But, I can't quit it."

"That's how they get you."

Balmer looked at Duff. "I take it you're Mr. Allard's partner?"

"I am." Duff stepped into the room. He was clutching the evidence bag with the phone in it.

"Nice of you to dress for the occasion."

"I'm not a lawyer," said Duff. "Besides, this is my good sweatshirt."

"I'd hate to see your bad sweatshirt," said Balmer. The judge noticed Abe's swollen and bruised face. "What happened to you?"

"I met some people who thought it would be a jolly good bit of fun to take my wallet."

"Fun for them," said Balmer.

"I was having a good time up until I lost consciousness." Duff looked at the judge, then glanced over at Abe and Jackson. "No one is wearing the little George Washington wigs. Disappointing."

"That's a British tradition," said Balmer.

"Oh, I know," said Duff. "They were originally put into use to cover hair loss caused by syphilis. I guess we no longer try to disguise our syphilis. Progress, am I right?"

Jackson looked shocked and disgusted at the same time. "Is that true?"

"Sadly, yes." Balmer ran a hand over his own balding pate. "Forgive my lack of sexually-transmitted diseases, Mr. Duffy. It's been a slow year for me."

"Hey, you and me, both."

"Detective Jahnke, you're the lead on this case?" The judge summoned her with a crooking finger. Jahnke stepped inside.

"Close the door, please, Stacey."

The secretary pushed the Novaks and Buddy Olson backward by stepping in front of them and shutting the door. Balmer looked expectantly at Duff. "Do you have evidence which will convince me to grant bail to Sarah Novak?"

"I dunno, Judge. What would you call evidence that would probably convince the ol' DA here to drop all charges?"

Balmer looked to Jackson. The prosecutor threw up her hands. "Give it to me, then. Let's hear it."

Duff handed her the evidence bag with the phone. "This is Sarah Novak's cell phone, recovered at the scene of the murder."

"Agreed." Jackson took the bag, turning it in her hands.

"Detective Jahnke was with me this morning when we dusted this phone for fingerprints."

"I was." Jahnke leaned back against the wall and crossed her arms. She looked angry with herself.

"We found—" Duff let the words hang in the air for emphasis, "—no fingerprints on it whatsoever."

There was silence. Balmer looked to Jackson. Jackson squinted at the phone, turning it faster in her hands, still wrapped in the evidence bag.

"Can you enlighten me on what this fact is supposed to mean, Mr. Allard?" Balmer leaned forward and rested his face on his hand. He looked suddenly tired.

Abe knew exactly what it meant. "It means the phone was cleaned by someone prior to being left at the scene, your honor. May I borrow your cell phone, sir?"

Balmer shrugged and pulled an expensive iPhone from his pocket. He slid it across the desk at Abe.

Abe picked up the phone by the edges. Duff was at his side in an instant, fingerprint kit in hand. Duff powdered the brush and dusted the phone. Dozens of fingerprints showed up on the glass immediately. It was covered in them. Abe offered the phone back to the judge. "You can plainly see cell phones are fingerprint magnets. This means someone cleaned off Sarah Novak's phone before leaving it at the scene of the murder."

In the chair beside Abe, Janice Jackson slouched backward. "Why would a murderer clean her own fingerprints off the phone if she was just going to leave it at the scene of the crime?"

Duff leaned toward her. "The logic says, she wouldn't. I submit this phone was planted. End of story. Sarah Novak is not the murderer."

"This does not definitively prove innocence," said Ballmer.

"Never said it did, your holy robeness. However, it makes it exceedingly *unlikely* she did it."

The judge looked at his own dusty, fingerprint-covered phone. He leaned forward and gestured for the evidence bag. He looked at the cell phone in the bag, turning it under the light from the banker's lamp on his desk. He looked at his own phone again. "Ms. Jackson, thoughts?"

Jackson stewed in silence for a moment. Abe knew what was going on in her head. Prosecutors go for convictions. Nothing else matters. Put 'em away at all costs and notch the W. That is what wins reelection campaigns. Now, Abe presented to her evidence which would cause any jury to start to wonder. It was no longer a guaranteed win. It got more complicated. Jackson finally leaned forward in her chair. "In light of this new evidence, your honor, I don't believe the State is completely giving up its case against Ms. Novak, but it is willing to entertain favorable bail conditions until further study can be given."

Balmer looked at the phone. He looked at Abe and Duff. "I hereby grant bail to Sarah Novak, signature bond. We'll send the order down to the jail immediately and get her out of there by this afternoon. If new evidence comes to light which implicates her further in the murder, I will issue an arrest warrant with all due prejudice and haste. Fair enough?"

Abe could not speak. He felt numb. Duff's hand clapped Abe on the shoulder to break him out of his stunned silence. Abe stood. "Fair enough, your honor."

"Detective Jahnke, I assume you have no complaints."

Jahnke was pink in the cheeks. "None at this time, Judge."

"Good. Everyone's happy. Get out of my office."

Abe and Duff were the first out the door. Henry and Maggie Novak were waiting by the secretary's desk. When Maggie saw the actual, genuine, human smile on Abe's face, she burst into tears and went limp in her husband's arms.

13

IN THE RELATIVE safety of *Rose*, Abe loosened his tie like a man clawing away a noose and unbuttoned the top two buttons of his shirt. He guzzled water from a bottle he purchased at a vending machine in the courthouse. "Never make me do that again."

In the passenger seat, Duff snorted. "I didn't make you do this in the first place. You're the one who made me do it. I would have been content to let ol' Hank's kid dangle."

Abe looked over to his partner. "You say that, but we both know you wouldn't have."

"I might have."

Abe said nothing. Duff liked to have the last word, so Abe was content to let him have it.

"What's next?" Duff flipped through the crime scene case file.

"Recap?"

"Recap," said Duff. There was a knock at the passenger window. Duff turned and saw Detective Jahnke and Buddy Olson outside the car. Jahnke was holding a sheet of paper with printing on it. Duff gestured for them to get in the back.

Jahnke opened the rear sliding door and clambered in with Buddy on her heels. "We got the trace from the phone carrier." She handed the sheet to Duff.

Duff scanned the printing. "Says the phone's last ping was from in or around the Upshaw Complex on Saturday morning."

"Which means it might be in a locker there," said Jahnke.

"Or, it was smashed and thrown in the garbage." Duff rubbed his temples with the tips of his index fingers. "Either way, I'm betting whoever has it pulled the SIM card to keep it from pinging any further."

"That means he knows his way around a cell phone," said Abe.

Duff continued to rub his temples. He squeezed his eyes shut and tried to piece together a cohesive vision of the puzzle. "I'm missing something."

"We're all missing something." Buddy was reading the case file over Duff's shoulder. "If we knew what we were missing, we wouldn't be missing it and everything would be solved."

"Gee, thanks, *sensei.* Real helpful." Duff looked at the clock on his cell phone. "Too early for lunch."

"Just the right time for brunch, though," said Buddy.

"I could go for some brunch." Duff opened his Yelp app.

"This is hardly time to eat. I fucked up the investigation, and I gotta make it right before I get my dumb ass fired." Jahnke was fuming, but the anger was directed inward for once. "Buddy said you'd help me make a proper arrest."

"We will," said Abe.

"Always good to hash things out over hash browns," said Buddy. "Back before I was dumb enough to run for sheriff, we would always go sit down, eat some chow, and talk through what we knew and what we didn't."

"We know I'm an idiot, and we don't know who killed Nate Riegert." Jahnke slumped back against the bench in the minivan and crossed her arms. "I really thought I was cut out for this job." Her tone was all dark clouds and foreboding.

"Pity parties are always a good place to start when you learn you fucked up, but they have a very limited guest list." Buddy patted the detective's knee in a paternal manner. "You take your lumps on this today, and tomorrow you're a better detective than you were yesterday. That's how it goes."

Duff found an old, throwback, Fifties-style diner on Yelp, the kind of place that offers a cup of hot lard as a side dish. Abe took the group there in the van.

Seated in the corner booth of the diner, the group ordered. Coffee for the three adults at the table, a diet cherry Coke for Duff. They pored over the menu before ordering. Everyone went with simple fare. Duff got the steak and eggs. Abe got the Heart Smart breakfast. Buddy and Jahnke went with the special of the day: a Belgian waffle with apple compote and bacon on the side.

Buddy fell back into his old role as a leader, as someone who took charge of situations. He poured French vanilla creamer into his coffee, swirled it twice around with a spoon, and tapped the spoon on the side of

the ceramic mug so it made a flat dinging sound. "So, tell me what we know for sure."

Abe pulled out a sheet of paper and started making a list of notes. "Grace Boylan is pregnant. We do not believe her boyfriend is the father. Going on a hunch, we think Nate Riegert is the father, and that gives both Grace and Tommy Mueller possible motives to kill Nate, but Tommy is only in the running if he knows about Grace's pregnancy."

Duff sipped his diet Coke and added the next possibility. "Robbie Conroy is the back-up quarterback of the Rockland Owls. He had his last year of eligibility yanked out from underneath him by Nate Riegert, so he has a motive, but he does not seem like the type who would kill. He suggested the quarterback coach, Jay Martinez, might have done it because, according to Conroy, Martinez was trying to work a backdoor deal to get Riegert to Michigan State, but Riegert was going to go to Wisconsin, instead. We have not had a chance to interview Martinez, yet."

"I don't like him as the killer, though," said Abe.

"Me neither," said Duff. "The cell phone. Someone who would have known to get Sarah's cell phone is likely a student with an intimate knowledge of the relationship between Sarah and Nate. To me, that points back to Grace or Tommy, someone who knows where Sarah sleeps."

Abe said, "Although, if what Conroy said about Martinez was true, not getting the job at Michigan State probably cost Martinez a ton of money and a chance to get into a big school."

"Power Five money is a big motivator," Duff added. "And Martinez and Riegert were close. Maybe Riegert confided in him about the problems he was having with Sarah. Campus directory would have given him her location and room number."

"So, is Martinez back in the running?" asked Jahnke.

"Maybe," said Duff with a shrug.

"Who else?" Buddy sipped his coffee and winced at the heat.

"Nate Riegert was getting a crap-ton of swag from athletic boosters from a bunch of Division One schools. One of them might have done it, but that's a ridiculous distant possibility. I doubt any of them would have known to go after Sarah's phone to cover their tracks," said Duff.

"There is also the question of who was giving Nate Riegert money to gamble with. Maybe someone was a little unhappy that he was spending their bribe money on betting." Abe sipped his coffee. Abe did not really like or enjoy coffee, but when other people were drinking it, he felt compelled to fit in with the crowd. It came out of a deep-seated desire to be liked by others. Abe scribbled down more notes.

"Sarah Novak is still technically a suspect, as well." Duff chewed on the

end of his straw while he thought. "I mean, I don't think she did it, but her cell phone was at the scene, and not having fingerprints on it is not concrete evidence. However, she's a dark horse at this point. I just don't see her cleaning her phone and then leaving it at the scene."

"That it?" Buddy looked to Jahnke.

The detective threw up her hands. "I don't know if I got anything interesting to add."

"Anything helps, Pam. If you got something itching in the back of your brain, you throw it on out here, and we'll see if it fits into the puzzle."

Jahnke looked around the table. She hesitated. Buddy gave her an encouraging nod. She tapped her nails on the table for a moment as she scanned through the case in her mind. "The cause of death always bugged me."

"Good. Why?" Buddy was interested. He leaned toward her. "Tell me."

"It just seemed like a one-in-a-million injury, to me."

Duff was now interested, as well. His eyes lit up. "How do you mean?"

"I mean, look at yourself. You took a shot to the noggin, right? Got a lump on the back of your head, right?"

Duff touched the swollen knot on the back of his skull. It was still painfully tender. "I do."

"Someone hit you with something, right? A rock. A bat. A crowbar. *Something*." Jahnke dropped her voice. "How come you're not dead?"

Duff had not thought about that. "You're saying it was a one-in-a-million shot because what normally would have knocked someone down or knocked them out resulted in a killing blow."

"That's what I'm saying." Jahnke slumped in her chair frustrated with her inability to explain what she had in her head. "Doris would explain it better than I can."

Duff's face lit up like Jahnke just told him they were going to Golden Corral for lunch. "Doris Parker?"

"Yeah," Jahnke looked confused.

Duff turned to Buddy and backhanded the old man in the shoulder. "Doris *freakin'* Parker is still the county ME?"

Buddy rubbed at the spot where Duff slapped him. "Ow, and yes, you pissant."

"Why didn't you tell me?"

"I didn't think you'd care."

Duff turned to Abe. "Dude, we have to go say hello to Doris. Like right away."

"Why?"

"Because she's the best. She taught me a ton about murder. Thirty years

ago, she was this angry, short, crass old broad. I can only imagine that time has only made her all that, but worse."

Buddy agreed. "You're not wrong. Doris could out-venom a rattlesnake."

"Doris will be able to tell you more about the killing shot, too," said Jahnke. "Buddy, you probably haven't seen Doris since you retired. You should stop in and say hello."

"Oh, I tried to keep away from Doris even when I was the sheriff. If you piss her off she might try to use a bone saw on you to teach you a lesson."

The waitress appeared with a tray of food. She set plates down in front of everyone and left as swiftly as she arrived.

Buddy roped them back to the task at hand. "What else do we need to know?"

Duff had already cut a plug of his steak and was chewing it. He stuffed it in his cheek so he could talk. "Nate's cell phone. Where is it?"

"And why did the killer take it?" added Abe. "That's what makes me think it has something to do with gambling. Everyone keeps all their important stuff on their phone. Maybe someone was working to fix a game or something?"

"Division Three football is small potatoes, Abe." Duff shook his head. He had placed enough bets to know there was not murder-worthy money to be made gambling on Division Three. "I don't think anyone was out fixing games, not at this level."

"The cell phone holds all the keys to this case, doesn't it?" Jahnke pulled a notebook from her jacket and started taking her own notes.

Duff shoved eggs in his face. "Every case comes down to one thing. When you find that keystone, all the other pieces fall into place."

DORIS PARKER ENTERED the US Navy straight out of high school. They trained her to be a nurse. When the Navy noticed how good she was at being an nurse, they sent her to college on Uncle Sam's dime to major in Nursing. Doris was good at college, too. After she earned her degree and her commission making her an officer, the Navy saw greater potential in her, and that ended up with Doris getting a Master's in Nursing (again, thanks to the generosity of the military and the American taxpayer). Doris kept taking classes while in the service and eventually became a Nurse Practitioner. When she got out of the Navy in the mid-Seventies, she finally earned an MD and a Ph.D in Pathology. In 1981, she became the first female medical examiner in southeast Wisconsin. She never married or had any interest in

men or women, preferring the solitary pursuit of her career. She definitely did not like children. She was barely five feet tall and never weighed more than a hundred and five pounds in her entire life. She was tough as a leather whip and ornery as a pit viper. Everyone, from Navy admirals, to cops, to politicians, was intimidated by Doris Parker.

But not Duff.

For whatever reason, Duff was charmed by her attitude and venomous tongue, and while he was pursuing the Sigruds' killer as a teen he spent a lot of time in the morgue with her, learning from her, and learning about crime.

Duff bounded into the morgue on the first sub-level of the Waukesha County Courthouse like a puppy running to greet its master returning home from work. The first door to the morgue opened to a dimly lit office the size of an average living room. There was a conference table in the near corner, shelves laden with books in the far corner. Opposite the door, there was an older woman seated at a large, military-issue tin-side office desk. She wore a simple gray blazer over a white sweater. No jewelry. No make-up. She wore her hair short in a no-nonsense cut. Not a single thing about the woman or her surroundings suggested she gladly suffered fools, but that never stopped Duff. He took up a hero pose in front of her desk, legs akimbo, fists on his hips. "Doris, you old peach! How the hell are you? Did you miss me?"

The old woman at the desk did not look up from her paperwork. She finished filling in the line she was working on, taking her sweet time to finish writing in her perfect, tedious script. Then, she set her pen down, took off the bifocals she wore on a librarian's chain around her neck, and looked up at the chubby man before her. Her face gave away no clues she recognized him, but Duff knew she did. She took in a deep breath through her nostrils, her lips pinched tightly. "Mr. Duffy, I presume?"

"Hi, lady. How's tricks?"

The ME took him in with a long stare. Her appraisal was frank and honest. "You got fat as fuck."

"Right? Who knew that living solely off of pizza, tacos, and depression would do this to a body?"

Doris looked over at the old sheriff with cold, piercing blue eyes. "Sheriff. You look like you've put on a few, as well."

"Can I blame pizza and depression, too?" Buddy touched two fingers to his brow in a salute. "You look good, Doris. We should get lunch sometime."

Doris looked at the other two people in the room. "I know Detective Jahnke. Who is this pale goon who dares disturb my work? What say you, Lurch?"

"That's my partner, Abe. I'm a detective now. We have our own firm."

Duff sounded as if he was fishing for a compliment from her, some sort of recognition.

Doris was unimpressed. "Are you a good detective?"

"Better than most."

"Then maybe I was able to teach you something when you were young and stupid." Doris leaned back in her chair, her fingers gripping the ends of her chair's armrests. "For what purpose are you gleefully disturbing my sanctum on this day?"

Duff looked over his shoulder at his compatriots. He was actually giddy. "See! I told you she talks like a comic book villain!"

Jahnke stepped forward. "Doris, could you tell this idiot what you told me about Nate Riegert's injury? I tried to explain how it was a one-in-a-million shot, but I couldn't do it justice."

As if she was speaking to a jury, Doris coolly rattled off the cause of death. "The victim was struck by a heavy object which crushed the top of his spine below the occipital bone of the skull. The resulting shock and damage to the spinal column and the nerves therein caused unconsciousness, paralysis, and an almost immediate spinal infarction that led to total respiratory failure." She paused. "Just as I wrote in the report which any of you could have read instead of bothering me."

"Infarction sounds like a dirty word," said Duff.

"What does that mean to simple detectives without medical degrees who usually do silly investigations for legal firms?" asked Abe.

The ME shot him a wicked stare. "It means someone hit him with something that crushed his spine below his occipital bone, and the damage to his spinal column made everything below his skull stop working, including his lungs."

"That sounds pretty awful," said Abe.

The ME shrugged. She was unfazed by the fickle nature and rigors of death. "Not the most pleasant way to go, but he was likely unconscious from the shot, and even if he wasn't, he could not feel any pain."

"What made it a one-in-a-million shot?" asked Jahnke. "Explain that part to them."

Doris did not try to hide a sigh or disguise boredom. If anything, she poured it on heavier to really drive home the point that she was annoyed by all of their very existences. "The occipital bone's job is to protect the spine from damage from the back. We have thick skulls for a reason, you know." She grabbed a plastic skull from the top of a file cabinet behind her. With a pencil from her desk as a pointer, she turned the skull sideways and pointed to the knobby protuberance at the back of the skull, down near where the skull would have joined the spine. "This is the occipital bone. It sticks out

over the cervical curvature of where the spine starts. This is so if someone or something hits you from the back, they are more likely to strike the skull than the spinal column."

"The skull can survive a hard shot. The spine is less likely to handle it." Duff rubbed the bump on the back of his head again. Still tender.

"Precisely. In this case, the shot appears it hit the victim on a slight upthrust." Doris moved to a plastic skeleton in the opposite corner of the office. She pointed at the vertebrae beneath the skull. "Here is the point of impact." She angled her hand on its edge and demonstrated the angle at which she believed the victim was stuck. "The killing blow came up at an angle like this, which is curious."

Abe picked up a textbook off a nearby table. "Detective Jahnke, pretend this book is the murder weapon. I'm Nate Riegert." Abe turned his back to her. "How do you kill me?"

"Probably like this." Jahnke lifted the book above her head with both hands and brought it down onto the top of Abe's head. "That's not the kill shot."

"Precisely." Abe moved to the skeleton in the corner. "How did someone, especially someone small like Sarah Novak or Grace Boylan thrust a weighted plate up and into the back of the victim's skull hard enough to crush his vertebrae and cause asphyxiation?" Abe looked to his partner. This was the sort of question to which Duff's weird brain could deduce the correct answer. "Does this eliminate the girls and make Tommy our suspect?"

Duff's eyes were darting left and right. He was not seeing anything in front of him. He was putting together the puzzle in his mind's eye.

Everyone became silent. They all looked to Duff. After what felt like an eternity, Duff's eyes stilled, and he stared into space. His voice was soft and very low. "I know who did it."

Abe, Buddy, and Jahnke heaved a collective sigh.

"I think." The portly detective's head jerked, and he came back to reality. "I need a new baseball cap. My fucking head is freezing."

14

DUFF LIVED FOR the endgame. He hated puzzles more than cardio or green vegetables. He liked order. He liked to see things make sense. He always got excited at the near closure of a case because it meant that something hidden was exposed and something wrong was set right. It was the single driving force behind his psyche.

"Buddy, take Pam and wait for us to call." Duff jabbed his thumb toward the minivan. "We're going to take *Rose* to campus."

"I should come with," said Jahnke. "I do have a badge, after all."

"No. Not right now." Duff shook his head, his face serious. "I am not certain I have the right person, so I just need to get evidence. No judge would write a warrant for this. If I get evidence, we will call you."

"At least tell me who it is," said Jahnke.

"Patience will be rewarded." Duff grabbed Abe by the arm and started walking him to the van. "If you care to be helpful, you could run out to a nearby mall and buy me a new Milwaukee Brewers cap. I like the kind with the cloth strap for sizing. Whatever their biggest size is, get that. And get the dark blue cap, with the wheat-M on it. I like that logo the best."

"I don't have a clue what you just said."

"Never mind, then. I'll get one myself."

Duff and Abe climbed into the van and shut the doors. Abe fumbled with the keys in the ignition. "Do you really know who did it?"

Duff nodded. "And so do you, if you think about it."

"I do?"

"Sure do."

"Is it Tommy Mueller?"

Duff's head see-sawed from side to side for a second. "I don't think so, but he's still an outside dark horse at the moment."

"Do I get a hint?" Abe was no dummy. He had a genius-level I.Q. and finished a Bachelor's degree with a double major and a Juris Doctorate in only six years. He could process large amounts of text quickly with superhuman retention of the material, and he possessed an expert's eye when it came to reading faces and postures, but he was used to Duff being a step ahead of him when it came to puzzles like this. Duff was almost forty-six. He had spent the last thirty years being obsessed with unsolved murders to a point that would put most people in a mental ward. He managed to get himself released from a mental ward by being declared competent without losing an ounce of the fire that drove him to solve mysteries. That's a special kind of crazy.

"It's not the quarterback coach."

"That's my hint?" Abe turned the van onto the highway toward Rockland and accelerated. His foot dropped a little heavier on the pedal that normal, fueled by the rising tension in the van.

"That's your hint."

"Do you know where Nate Riegert's cell phone is?"

Duff was slow to respond. "I…think so."

"Are we about to do something stupid?"

"Oh, yeah. Totally stupid."

"Like, we're-going-to-jail stupid?"

Duff held out a hand and rocked it from side to side. "Maybe."

Abe looked down at the suit he was still wearing. "I wish I'd dressed for prison."

THEY WERE BACK on the UW-Rockland campus in minutes, and they were parked at Joyman Hall shortly thereafter. By the time they arrived at the hall, Abe also knew whom Duff suspected. "You really think Aiden Vogel did this?"

"I do. One hundred percent. It makes sense, doesn't it? The angle of the impact and the damage inflicted would suggest a narrow gap of contact, a low angle, and since it had to come at an upward thrust, what makes more sense than someone Frisbeeing a circular object from waist-to-chest? And who do we know who plays Ultimate Frisbee?" While walking, Duff demonstrated a standard flying disc throw. "Kid got angry about something and threw the plate when Riegert had his back turned. And I'll tell you this, I think Jessica Thurow knew about it, too. That explains their glances at the

desk yesterday."

"But why?"

"That's what I don't know, and it bothers me. That's why we need to find that phone."

Jessica Thurow was not at the front desk when Abe and Duff arrived in the foyer of Joyman Hall. A sullen-looking Asian girl with thick glasses buzzed them into the lobby instead. She was alone at the desk. Her name tag read "Shelly." Abe handed her a card and showed his license. Duff, newly without license, stood with his hands in his sweatshirt pocket. Abe put on his best nice-guy voice. "We just need to speak to one of the students that lives in this building about Nate Riegert's murder. Would that be alright?"

The girl stared at him blankly. "Dude. I honestly don't give a shit. I'm tired of this whole mess already."

"Really? Not a football fan, then?"

She snorted. "Nate Riegert was gross. If someone hadn't killed him, I bet he would have died of herpes."

"You're not the first to suggest that."

"I dated him for a few weeks last year. I'm not glad he's dead, but I'm sure glad I don't have to see him anymore. He liked to prey on girls in this hall. He liked stupid freshman girls, of which I used to be one."

"You say *prey*. Do you think he was abusive?"

"He didn't need to be. With his face and body, he just got whatever he wanted. Girls were powerless around him. I was. I hate myself for that."

Duff nosed into the conversation. "And I take it he, what, cheated on you?"

"He cheated on everyone. That's how he functions. He was the dean of hookup culture."

"Well, can you tell us—"

Duff cut Abe off. "—Do you mind if we just go see if the person we need to interview is here?"

Shelly waved them to the door by the desk. "Go nuts. I hope you get whoever killed him. I just want to get back to studying."

Duff grabbed Abe's arm and dragged him to the door. Once they were in the hallway, Abe lowered his voice. "We don't know where Aiden lives."

"We didn't need to tell her. If we're wrong, we don't want to go screwing up Aiden's life like Jahnke screwed up Sarah's."

"How do we find Aiden's room, then?"

Duff gestured at the nearest door. There were two construction paper owls on the door with names on each, Christian and Doug. There were the same owls with different names on every door in the hall. "Aiden's not that

common of a name. What are the odds there's more than one?"

Abe had to admit Duff was right. When he was in college, his dorm room door was the only one with a decoration that said Aberforth on it.

They hustled down the south side of the hall scanning names on the doors. No Aiden on the first floor. They repeated this on the second floor, coming up snake-eyes again. On the third floor, they found Aiden's room, 306. The resident advisers were the people made all the cutesy nameplates for the door, and on the third floor, that particular adviser chose to make nameplates out of large, cut-paper letter R's. Aiden was written on one R. His roommate's name, Edward, was on the second. There was no doubt it was the right Aiden because a blue Yogurt-Slingers logo sticker was pinned to a corkboard at the top of the door.

Duff reached out and knocked on the door. No answer. Duff reached into his back pocket to get the lockpick kit he took out of the van before they entered Joyman Hall. "Watch my back, would you?"

Duff lowered himself to a knee using the doorknob for leverage. He groaned as his knee settled on the thin, industrial carpeting in the hallway. He inspected the lock in the door. The school was using key cards to access the main doors in the buildings because it was cheaper than issuing metal keys to every student. However, the old dormitories were still using metal keys because installing the electrics into every door would have been an astronomical cost. Duff selected an appropriate lock and hook. He figured it was a five-pin lock, no more. He jimmied the pick, moving the tumblers, and swept the hook through. In less than twenty seconds, Duff popped the well-worn lock.

The door swung open and they were rewarded with the first look into Aiden and Edward's room. The room was filled with an elaborate wooden structure elevating the beds almost five feet off the ground. Under one bed was a TV and game system, a mini-fridge, and a microwave. Under the other, a well-used couch. The desks in the far corners of the room were attached to the walls and unmovable. Duff and Abe surveyed the place. "Which side do you think is Aiden's?"

They walked into the room and looked at the desks. That gave them the answer they were looking for immediately. On one desk was a picture of Aiden and Jessica at the front desk. They were smiling and looked happy. Duff gave a low whistle. "Oh, yeah. She's totally in on this."

Abe looked closely at the picture. "She's not into him. They're just friends."

"You think?" Duff looked again.

Abe looked harder at the picture. Jessica was smiling, but she was angled back and away from Aiden, whereas he was leaning toward her, trying to get

closer. She might as well been pushing him away with a ten-foot pole. "She thinks they're just friends, at least. He doesn't."

Duff shook his head sadly. "I guarantee you she doesn't have any pictures of him on display in her room."

Duff closed the door to the dorm room and locked it behind them. "Where do we start?"

Abe glanced to the left. Aiden's dresser had been moved fully into the closet. "I'll take the closet," said Abe. "You get everything else."

"Work fast, hoss. I have no idea how much time we have."

They set to work quickly. Abe searched through all the drawers, even pulling out the one on the bottom to check to see if the phone was hidden in the gap space below the bottom drawer where a lot of his old schoolmates used to hide weed. He leaned the dresser forward to see if the phone was taped to the back and inspected all the clothes hanging in the closet in case it was hiding in the pocket of some item.

Duff rampaged through the desk. He paused when he got to the textbooks stacked neatly on the shelf. "Hey, check these out. He's a Computer Science major."

Abe's eyebrows went up. "You think he's one of those IT kids?"

"It would give him the ability to knock out the cameras, or at least know the cameras were not being used."

Duff continued ransacking all the food items on Aiden's side of the room. He was not nearly as neat about his search as Abe. Abe grimaced and pointed to the scattered items. "I think he's going to notice you're leaving a mess."

"And he'll blame his roommate."

As if invoking the roommate summoned him, at that moment there came the unmistakable sound of a key entering the lock on the door.

Edward Xiong opened the door to his dorm room after a long morning of sitting through lectures to find two middle-aged bald men sitting on his couch smiling awkwardly at him.

Duff held up a hand in a half-hearted wave. "Hey, Eddie. Can I call you Eddie?"

Abe held out his PI card. "We're detectives, Edward."

Edward entered the room. He had a backpack hanging off his left shoulder. He wore a black, leather jacket hanging open over a Sex Pistols t-shirt from Hot Topic. "Don't you need a warrant or something like that?"

"We would if we were the police, who we are not." Duff gestured to Edward's desk chair. "Please sit. Can we ask you a couple questions about Aiden?"

Edward crossed to his desk and sat. He set his backpack on the floor.

"What about Aiden?"

"Have you found a cell phone that you haven't seen before? Has Aiden been using a second cell phone in the past few days?" asked Abe.

Edward thought for a moment and shook his head. "Nope. Not that I've seen."

"Were you around this past weekend?" asked Abe.

Eddie opened his backpack and got out a laptop computer, opening it on his desk. "Nope. My parents only live like a half hour from here. I go home pretty much every weekend to work."

"Suitcase schools, man," said Duff. "What happened to the wild college parties on the weekends?"

"They take place on Thursday nights," said Edward.

"Has Aiden seemed different to you?" Abe took one last shot.

"Aiden is Aiden." Edward looked at his computer and pointed toward it. "Are you guys going to be here much longer? I have like two papers to write before I have to go to work tonight."

Abe and Duff stood. "Would you happen to know where Aiden is right now?"

Eddie glanced at his phone screen to check the time. "It's Friday. He's probably doing maintenance in the Upshaw building."

"Maintenance?" Abe knew what the kid was going to say before he said it.

"He's in the IT program. He fixes the servers and laptops over there as part of his coursework. Tech squad stuff." Eddie turned back to his computer, opened a file, and went to work as if finding two strange, older men in your dorm room was an everyday event in college.

Abe and Duff moved to the door of the room. "Thanks for your time, Eddie."

Eddie did not look up from his screen. "You know, the IT kids have lockers in the Upshaw building so they don't have to transport tools. If Aiden is hiding a phone you need to find, I'd think he probably hid it in his locker."

ABE AND DUFF hightailed it to the Upshaw Complex as fast as they could for two middle-aged men, factoring in Duff's gimp leg and general dislike of sweat and exercise. "If the kid doesn't have the phone in his locker, I'm going to kill him myself."

Abe, who had a naturally long stride, was able to keep pace with Duff easily. "It's a nice day, at least."

"Really? That's where your brain is going?"

Abe gestured at the few remaining leaves in the trees around campus. "Leaves are mostly fallen at this point. It's gotta be at least fifty degrees out. We've only got what— a week or two left of decent weather before Old Man Winter shows up."

"Sure. That's what I always think when I'm about to end some kid's life by making sure he gets charged with murder: How's the weather?"

At the front desk of the Upshaw Complex, Abe and Duff spotted a familiar face. Eli was working the counter again. He greeted them with a friendly smile. "Evening, gents. How can I help you today?"

Duff, winded from running, declined to speak. Abe took the lead. "Do you know Aiden Vogel?"

Eli scratched his head while he thought. "Sort of. He's one of the IT kids. He fixes computers here sometimes. I've never spoken to him. I just watch him when he signs the work logs we keep at the desk."

"Is he here today?"

Eli bent over to grab something under the desk. "I don't know. We can check, though." He pulled up a blue three-ring binder with a sheaf of papers in it and flipped to the most recent page. His finger traced down the list until he found Aiden Vogel's name written in Aiden's own hand. "He's here. Somewhere. I wouldn't know where, though. Could be anywhere in the building."

"Do you know where his locker is?"

"His gym locker, or the lockers for the IT stuff?"

"Probably the IT stuff."

"Oh, yeah. Those are in an unused classroom the IT department uses as their workspace." Eli inclined his head down the left hallway behind him. "End of that hall, last door on the left. If you have to turn a corner, you're going the wrong way."

"Is it locked?"

"Should be. Usually at least one person in there, though. They have to do office hours in case one of the faculty has a technical issue. If there's no one in there, you're shit outta luck. Only the IT department has keys for that room."

"Might as well go take a look." Abe patted the desk. "Thanks for the help."

The hall was long and well-lit. As it was early afternoon on a Friday at a suitcase school like Rockland, the classrooms were mostly empty, the doors open and rooms dark. There was still noise from the massive central complex, though. Basketballs bounced, shoes squeaked on the courts, and there was the occasional thud from someone throwing something or landing from a jump. They could hear the metallic clank of weights in one of the two main weight rooms. The football team's private facility was currently

off-limits due to the investigation, so the football team had to use the facilities alongside their schoolmates.

At the end of the long corridor, Abe and Duff found the IT office. It was a small classroom converted to a lab space for the tech kids. Half of the room was stuffed with audio-visual equipment for taping and editing games and practices for the sports teams, the other half had two square tables with various pieces and parts for fixing computers.

A bored-looking young woman was sitting on a metal stool at one of the tables surfing the Internet on a Macbook Pro. She was wearing jeans and a plain gray sweatshirt. One of her legs bounced involuntarily on a rung of the stool. She looked up from her computer when Abe and Duff entered the room. "Hi. What can I do for you?"

Abe held out his license and business card. "We're looking into something. Can you point us toward Aiden Vogel's equipment locker?"

The girl looked confused. "He doesn't have an equipment locker. We have equipment lockers and by that, I mean the IT department, but they're not for individual use or storage."

"Is Aiden here?"

The girl craned her neck to look around Abe and Duff down the hall. "Somewhere. I haven't seen him in a while. Figured he'd be back by now."

"Did he have a new cell phone, by chance?"

The girl's face was slack and impassive. "Look, I barely talk to Aiden. I certainly wouldn't know if he had a new cell phone or an old one."

"You seem fun," said Duff.

"If he was somewhere, where do you think he would be?"

"I honestly don't know." The girl pointed to the hall. "Look, stand in the corner of that hall and wait for him. He'll have to come back here at some point to get his backpack."

Abe and Duff scanned the room. There was a black Jansport backpack and a khaki canvas satchel in one corner. "Which one is his?" Duff was already moving toward them.

"The black one, but I don't think you should—"

Duff did not wait for the girl to tell him not to open it. It would not have mattered, either way. Duff unzipped the backpack and scanned through the contents quickly. Two notebooks. HP laptop. Bunch of pens. A couple flash drives. Lip balm. A cell phone.

Duff pulled the cell phone out of the bag. "We got something." He thumbed the power switch, and it sprang to life. There was a picture of an anime swordsman on the lock screen. "It's not Nate Riegert's."

The girl got off her stool to look over Duff's shoulder. "That's Aiden's phone. I've seen his lock screen before. That's a character from one of his

favorite cartoons."

"Anime," Abe corrected her. "Anime nerds get really touchy when you call their shows cartoons." Abe remembered the time he was harshly corrected by one of Tilda's friends a couple years ago.

Duff threw the phone back into the backpack. "Well, hell." He was getting impatient. "Was he working on a special project anywhere? Did he have to meet with anyone?"

The girl looked annoyed. "I came in for my shift in the lab. He was already here, sitting at that table. He said hello. Then, he stuck something in his pocket and left. I thought it was his cell phone." She paused and put two and two together. "Maybe he took a different cell phone with him."

"Where's the nearest bathroom?" Duff pointed back to the hallway they had just walked down, and then at the other hallway around the corner.

"Back up the hall." The girl pointed at the way they had come.

Duff was already on the move. "If you want some peace and quiet to try to crack a phone's lock screen, where would you go so no one could see what you're doing, Abe?"

"I guess the bathroom."

"Ah, the holy sanctity of the shitter. No better fortress for a college student. It's the only time you can be alone with your thoughts in a world where you have a roommate."

Abe, who had actually gone to college and still possessed a deeply entrenched hatred of communal bathrooms because of it, wrinkled his face at Duff. "I don't think you know what you're talking about."

"When I was at Bensonhurst, I used to lock myself in the bathroom stalls because it was the only place to get even the slightest modicum of privacy. Everywhere else, you were watched by staff, watched by other students. The bathroom was the best place to hide. I have a permanent ring on my ass from sitting on the crapper for hours just so I could read books and think without getting punched."

Abe and Duff found the men's room in the hallway. Duff held a finger to his lips. Abe repeated the gesture. They pushed open the door slowly and crept into the bathroom. The door opened into a short privacy wall and veered hard to the right. At the end of the little hall, the bathroom opened to the main space. There were three sinks on the right wall with three urinals along the wall past the sinks. A quartet of stalls were on the left, the largest was the ADA-Accessible stall at the far end of the room. Only one of the four stalls had its door closed. Duff crouched and looked beneath the closed door. He pointed at a pair of Nikes and blue-jeaned legs.

Duff pointed back at the hallway door. He and Abe crept back into the hall. "How do you want to do this?"

Abe had no clue. "What if he's actually using the facilities?"

Duff shook his head. "Jeans were pulled up. If he was pooping, then he's got bigger problems than seeing us right now."

"Should we call Jahnke?"

Duff contemplated this for a minute. "You think he did it?"

"Do you?"

"I'm pretty sure that cell phone he's trying to crack is probably the key to riddle." Duff snorted a quick breath through his nose. "Text Buddy. Tell him to get Jahnke and meet us here."

"Will do." Abe pulled his cell phone and set his thumbs flying. He sent the message and waited. A few seconds later, a reply arrived. "They're on their way."

Duff ran a hand over the short, stubbly hair on his head. "I miss my hat."

"We can buy you a UW-Rockland hat at the gift shop before we leave."

"Rockland Owls is so weak, though. Let's go to Whitewater and get a Warhawk hat. That at least sounds cool."

"Well, if we're going to go that direction before going home, we might as well swing past American Family Field and pick up a Brewers hat."

"Now you're talking." Duff blew out a quick huff of breath. He slapped himself in the face once. "Alright! Let's go ruin this idiot's life!"

15

AIDEN VOGEL WAS not prepared to see the broad, smiling face of C.S. Duffy peering over the top of the bathroom stall at him. He let out a short yelp and fumbled to cover the phone he was holding by jamming it under his arm. "What are you doing?"

"Me? I'm standing on a toilet. I understand why you'd want to know why. However, asking what you are doing is a better question."

"I'm…" The kid fumbled for words. "I'm using the bathroom."

"With your pants up?"

"Fuck off." Vogel jumped up from the toilet and yanked the door of the stall open.

Abe was standing next to the door. He waved. "Hey, kid."

Duff hopped off the toilet on which he was standing and strolled out of the stall. He casually leaned against the partition and crossed his arms. "Now, I know your first instinct will be to run, but don't do that. My partner was all-state in track, and he still runs a four-six forty. He is also a black belt in an obscure form of deadly jiu-jitsu called *wei zhou be*. If has to chase you, he will catch you, and then he'll hurt you."

"I will?"

Duff shot Abe an imploring look. "Yes. You will."

"That's right. I will." Abe drew himself to his full height and tried to look intimidating. He was at least two inches taller than the kid. "Why'd you kill Nate Riegert, Aiden?"

Any hint of color ran out of Aiden Vogel's face. To Abe, it was as good an admission of guilt as if he had simply declared he was a murderer. Aiden

was frozen in place. His mouth worked up and down, but he could not speak.

"Look, kid." Duff stepped forward and gently took the cell phone out of Aiden's hands. "Frankly, I don't give a shit if you go to prison for five years or fifty. I'm going to sleep well, either way. If you help us out, if you help out the detective who is waiting to arrest you, you can cut deals with prosecutors. My buddy here is a lawyer. He'd tell you to be honest, be upfront, explain everything, and maybe, if the situation fits, maybe you can plea-bargain down to manslaughter. Maybe it's only a seven-year sentence and you're back on the street in five years. This doesn't have to be the end of your life, you still have a lot of good years ahead of you."

Tears immediately began to flow down Aiden's face. His legs gave out and he sank to the floor. He began to sob hard, chest-wracking mournful wails of someone who had a lot of pent-up guilt suddenly freed. Through his wretched cries he rasped, "It was an accident."

Abe and Duff stood by and let the boy cry for several minutes. He cried so hard he could barely breathe. He kept repeating, "I didn't mean to do it," and, "It was an accident."

Abe finally crouched and put a hand on the kid's shoulder. "We all make mistakes. Telling us what happened goes a long way to putting mistakes right."

"What's on the cell phone that was worth killing Nate Riegert, Aiden?" Duff was less caring than Abe, but he had questions that needed answers.

Aiden's breath came in long, shuddering gulps. His face was blanched and tear streaked. He finally gasped a single word. "Pictures."

"Of Jessica?" Duff offered.

A nod.

"And you were trying to get Nate to delete them?"

Aiden took a deep breath. His voice was thin and distant. "She and Nate hooked up in August. He was here for football. She was doing RA training. Apparently, he came over one night, and they drank, and she got wild. He took a bunch of pictures of her on his phone. Bad ones."

"And then he moved on to the next girl," said Abe.

Aiden nodded his head. He looked defeated. "Jess was really sad. She wanted Nate to delete the pictures, but he wouldn't. Every so often, he would text her a picture of herself late at night to remind her that he had them. She was miserable."

"So, you figured what? You'd kill him and delete the photos for her?" Duff leaned back against the sinks and crossed his arms.

"No!" Aiden looked up at Duff, defiant. "I am not a killer!"

"Nate's corpse would beg to differ."

"You said it was an accident." Abe tried to reroute Aiden's attention.

The kid looked back at his lap. "I knew Nate worked out on Fridays because I saw him here a lot. I knew the football team's weight room was usually empty after 8:00 p.m., too. I worked a lot of Friday shifts here because it's quiet."

"So, you confronted Nate in the weight room?" said Duff.

"I wanted to steal his phone while he was working out; I thought I could steal it, delete the photos, and return it before he knew what was up, but he was using it as a music player. So, I went in and tried to ask him to delete them."

"And when he wouldn't, you got angry." Abe used his most sympathetic voice.

"He got angry. He punched me in the mouth and knocked me down. He called me names and told me Jessica would never love me. Called me a white knight and a simp. He spat on me and told me to leave, to get out of his weight room."

"Then you got angry," said Duff.

"Then I got angry." Aiden pressed the heels of his palms into his eyes for a moment. "Christ, it was an accident. I felt so fucking *powerless*. I stood up, and there was this weight just lying on a bench, and I grabbed it and threw it at him."

"Like a Frisbee," said Duff.

"I was so angry. I just wanted to hurt him. I wanted to hit him in the back and make him feel like I felt. But…" Aiden's voice trailed off. He started sobbing again.

"The plate hit him in the neck, he fell, and he died," said Duff.

"It was so scary. He just started seizing, and then he went still, and his eyes rolled back in his head. I couldn't do anything. I got scared." Aiden started rocking in place.

"So, you ran back to the dorm in a panic. Did Jessica tell you to get Sarah's phone?"

Aiden started to nod, but he suddenly stopped and looked up with fire in his eyes. "No. No. Jessica doesn't know anything about this." His tone was adamant. "I went to Sarah's door and tried it. It was unlocked. She was passed out. I took her phone, and…"

"You planted it at the scene." Abe finished the kid's thought. "What was up with you and Jessica making up the story about seeing Sarah walking out of the dorm?"

Aiden looked Abe square in the face. "I don't know what you're talking about."

Duff shook his head. "Kid, I don't know why you're protecting her.

She's definitely not going to love you if you're a felon."
There was a long pause before Aiden spoke again. His words were clipped. "Because only one of us made a mistake. Only one of us needs to be punished for this. I'm screwed no matter what, but she can still have a good life." Aiden swiped at his cheeks with his wrists. He rolled to standing. "I'm ready to go. I'll tell the police everything. I did it. But, honest to God, it was an *accident*."

A VERITABLE DISCO of red-and-blue lights illuminated the south doors of the Upshaw Complex when Abe and Duff walked Aiden Vogel into the fading late afternoon sun. Detective Pamela Jahnke put handcuffs on Vogel's wrists. He offered no resistance. She read him his Miranda Warning and slipped him into the back of a deputy sheriff's shop. When she closed the door, he rested his head against the cage and closed his eyes. He heaved a heavy, sad sigh.

Then, Jahnke turned her attentions to Abe and Duff. "So, he never got through the phone's lock screen?"

Duff held up the phone. It was an android model. Unlike the iPhones that would shut someone out permanently after so many missed attempts, this lock screen just kept resetting adding thirty seconds to the cooldown timer each time. "He snapped the SIM card so the phone couldn't be traced, basically turning it into a little hand-held computer. Then, he spent some time every day trying different combinations of numbers."

Abe was looking at the kid in the back of the patrol SUV. His heart went out to him. "He said he even got Riegert's Social Security number and tried that. It's only a four-digit combination. He thought he would get it eventually. Tried every combination of the kid's favorite athletes, important dates, and the usual stuff like four of the same numbers, or line patterns on the phone."

Jahnke looked skeptical. "Why didn't he just pull out the memory card and smash it?"

"Because the photos probably uploaded to a cloud," said Abe. "He wanted to get all of them."

Duff thumbed at the phone. "Kid didn't go with the most obvious numbers, though."

Jahnke's eyes narrowed. She moved closer to Abe. "What are the obvious numbers?"

"It's not the kid's fault. He didn't see Nate Riegert's closet, but I did." Duff's thumbs danced on the screen. "The Badgers were going to have Riegert wearing number seventeen next year. The Owls had him wearing number eleven." Duff typed in three ones and a seven. The phone screen unlocked immediately. Duff looked sad. "The kid was so close, but so far."

"How'd you know that?" said Jahnke.

"Riegert was a narcissist, at best. Of course the numbers were going to be about him." Duff rolled his head toward Vogel in the SUV. "Kid knew it, too. Tried Nate's football and baseball numbers. He found out Nate's high school numbers. Tried all the combinations, too. He just didn't know about the Badgers, didn't know about next year."

Abe, Jahnke, and Buddy gathered around the phone. Duff found the photos folder and opened it. Immediately dozens of thumbnails rolled up on the screen. The overwhelming majority of them were of women in various stages of undress or engaged in sexual acts. Sarah Novak was in a lot of them. There were more than a dozen of Jessica Thurow. Duff let out a low whistle. "Kid was busy, I'll give him that. When did he find the time to play football?"

Jahnke held out an evidence bag. Duff turned off the phone and dropped it into the bag. "Jessica Thurow was in on it, too. She might have even been the one who cajoled Aiden into trying to get the phone. Aiden didn't roll on her, though. I'm betting she probably gave Aiden a master key of the dorm that let him into Sarah's room so he could steal her phone to plant it at the scene."

"I'll bring Jessica to the station for questioning." Jahnke sealed the bag. She shook her head sadly. "These stupid kids. Such a waste."

"Accidents happen," said Abe.

"I will call Janice Jackson and let her know about this, immediately. I'm sure the State will drop all charges against Sarah Novak." Jahnke paused and rubbed her face with her hands. She looked ill. "I'm sorry I fucked up the investigation."

"You'll do better tomorrow." Buddy clapped her on the shoulder. "The right man will be in jail tonight, and that's all the matters in the end."

Duff did not look happy. His face was screwed up into a frown, his brow furrowed. "There are still a lot of pieces to this that haven't fit in, yet."

"Like what?" Jahnke was interested in seeing how Duff's mind worked. "We got the murderer."

"The money for gambling is the big one. And why were the cameras in the Upshaw Complex out? Was that Aiden's doing, or was it just coincidence?"

"You got the right guy." Buddy threw an arm over Duff's shoulder and began walking him away from the gaggle of cops. "At the end of the day, that's the only piece that matters."

16

HENRY AND MAGGIE Novak insisted Abe, Duff, and Buddy have dinner with them at a steakhouse in West Allis, Wisconsin before Abe and Duff headed back to Chicago. "It's the least we can do," Maggie said while hugging both Abe and Duff, her arms tight around their necks.

"Actually, paying us is the least you can do." Duff gingerly unthreaded himself from Maggie's grip and moved out of range of her arms.

A bruised and battered Sarah Novak stood nearby. She moved in to hug Abe and Duff just as soon as Maggie released them. "Thank you. Thank you both so much."

Duff, clearly uncomfortable, pulled away as quickly as he could without it being offensive. Abe gladly accepted the hug. It reminded him of Matilda. He could actually feel Sarah's relief in her arms. Abe took her by the shoulders and held her at arm's length. "I just hope you get back to living a normal life as soon as possible. Get back to college. Enjoy your life."

Sarah took a deep breath. "I think I'm going to leave Rockland. I went to get my things from my room after I got out today. The college was not keen to let me stay while I was still a murder suspect. They might let me back, but I think I'm just going to call this semester a wash and transfer to UW-Green Bay starting in January. I want to be closer to home."

"Go Phoenix," said Duff.

"Besides, my roommate told me she was pregnant today. I don't want to be around for that drama."

"You know who the father is?" asked Abe.

Sarah looked uncomfortable. "Not exactly. She didn't want to tell me, but I think I have a damn good guess. Poor Tommy's going to be so mad.

She's going to have to call Nate's family, too. I'm sure they will be shocked"

Henry Novak stepped up and shook Abe's hand, pumping it furiously. "Thank you, Mr. Allard. Thank you. If you had not agreed to help us—"

"It was my pleasure."

Novak moved to Duff. "And Clive— I mean, Duff. Thank you. Sincerely, thank you." He did not extend a hand toward Duff, and Duff seemed to appreciate the gesture.

"You're welcome." After a pause, Duff offered the closest thing he could think to offer as an olive branch. He invoked the name everyone called Henry at Bensonhurst. "You're welcome, Hammer." He extended his own hand, and Henry clasped it gratefully. They held each other's gaze for a knowing moment as years of past animosity were considerably lessened, even if it it was probably not possible to extinguish them entirely.

"Well, enough of this maudlin stuff." Buddy was walking toward Abe and Duff's van. "Let's go have some steak."

THE GROUP FEASTED. Sarah, still starving from having to endure nearly a week of prison chow, seemed to eat her own bodyweight in porterhouse and steak fries. Duff tried to match her, but even he had to tap out eventually. For a petite little girl, Sarah could put it away. Abe had a New York strip steak. Buddy had an eighteen-ounce T-bone. When the check came, Maggie and Henry would not even hear of Abe and Duff contributing. This was their treat, they said, a pale thank-you compared to what Abe and Duff had done for their daughter.

Abe noticed that Maggie and Henry seemed to be enjoying each other's company once again. All the stress of the previous week was gone, and they seemed practically giddy, lots of touches on each other's arms and shoulders, leaning toward each other during laughs. Abe hoped it was a permanent change for them, that they would remember how big problems could really get, and they remembered to truly appreciate each other.

When they walked out of the steakhouse, Buddy said his good nights, clambered into his truck, and left. Henry Novak reached into his coat and pulled out an envelope stuffed with cash. He handed it to Abe. "Paid in full, with all my gratitude."

Abe accepted the envelope and slipped it into his pocket. "Our pleasure."

There was one last round of hugs from Sarah and Maggie, and then Abe and Duff watched the Novaks climb into their truck. Sarah blew them a kiss from the window as the Novaks left the parking lot and merged into the traffic on the road.

Abe and Duff stood alone in the parking lot. Duff flipped the hood of his sweatshirt up over his bald head and shoved his hands into the pocket of his shirt. He looked like a chubby Sith lord. "I still don't have a Brewers hat."

Abe checked the clock on his phone. "Too late to get one today. We can go to the mall tomorrow."

"If we're going to the mall, I'm getting Sbarro."

"Sbarro and ball caps. Got it."

"Something's bugging me about this whole debacle, though: We got lucky. We never get lucky."

Abe looked at his partner. "Because Aiden was wearing the shirt at the counter, right?"

"Right. If he hadn't been wearing the Frisbee shirt I never would have linked him to being the one who threw the weight."

"Sometimes, detective work is luck. Look at how many serial killers got busted because the cops caught a lucky break."

"I don't like it, though. If Aiden hadn't been wearing the shirt, would I still have figured out the killer threw the weight plate like a Frisbee?"

"Probably," said Abe. "You're C.S. Duffy. That's what you do."

"We got lucky," Duff repeated. It bugged him. Luck had never been a companion of theirs.

They walked around the building. The parking lot of the steakhouse had been jammed, and Abe parked on the street. When they walked around the corner of the building, Abe noticed *Rose* was not exactly how he left her. Abe was an overly careful and precise parker. He never got too close to the curb. He never hung the end into traffic. Parking perfectly was one of his obsessions. Something had happened to the van while they were eating. The van's right front tire was jammed against the curb to the point that it looked like a burst can of biscuit dough overlapping the cement.

Abe ran in front of the car, cutting around the corner of the driver's side. He stopped short. His jaw gaped open. "Somebody hit us!"

Duff walked to Abe's side. The left rear panel of the van was smashed in. There was no doubt someone had hit them. Abe looked to the windows for a note under the wiper blade, but there was none. Whoever hit them had driven off into the night, probably because they were uninsured.

Duff was strangely optimistic. He squatted in the street to survey the damage. He ran his fingers over the smashed panel. "I like it!"

Abe was a patient man and not prone to anger, but he could feel fury building in his chest. "How can you like it? This van was in perfect condition three days ago, but then then side mirror…and now this!"

"It's really starting to look like the sort of hellscape shitbox we should be driving, isn't it? Unlock the doors. I'm cold."

Abe pressed the button on the key fob. Duff climbed in on the passenger side. Abe climbed into the driver's side. "We'll have to get a police report for the insurance company."

"Or we can just say fuck it and go home. This bad luck charm is really part of the team now." A sly smile crossed Duff's face. "Hey, I think this little minx just earned her true name!" He patted the dashboard lovingly. "I hereby christen thee *The Bad Luck Charm*."

Abe's head sank back against the seat. He closed his eyes. At least the interior was still in good shape and would be until Duff managed to spill a diet Coke or two. He blew out a long sigh. "I suppose it's better than the name you gave the old Volvo."

"It's fitting," said Duff. "If it weren't for bad luck, we wouldn't have any at all."

"Except for this case. Our luck was good."

"Aiden's wasn't, though. One-in-a-million shot. Bad luck follows us around, Abe. Sometimes, maybe it precedes us. We're carriers; we spread the virus." Duff patted the center console of the van. "Now, we'll get to drive bad luck around."

Abe decided Duff was right. It was a fitting name. At the very least, it was a better name than *The Fucking Embarrassment* or *The Pussy Wagon*. Abe shifted to drive and pulled away from the curb. The van was still drivable. The damage was only cosmetic.

Duff's face turned toward the passenger window. His eyes glazed over. Abe knew that look. Duff was already thinking about the Sigruds again, about Mikey Pizza, Kenny Hansen, and the possibility of the murders being connected to some branch of the Chicago mob.

Abe guided the van down the road, located the on-ramp to Highway 94, and accelerated. Home was less than three hours away. It was time to go back to Chicago.

About the Author

Sean Patrick Little lives in southern Wisconsin, somewhere in the City of Sun Prairie. He is patiently waiting for the state legislature to recognize his edict to be declared the rightful Archduke of Dane County. Most of the time, you can find him in a back booth of his local Culver's working on new books or staring blankly at the wall. By some unfortunate curse of location, he is a Wisconsin sports homer, a loyal Badger, Packer, and Brewers fan. It takes a special kind of person to be a Brewers fan, because it comes with such a healthy supply of constant disappointment.

Sean watches too much TV. He enjoys a liveley debate about the pros and cons of differing breeds of cats. He likes to pretend to play guitar, but possesses no natural gifts toward musicality and is only really good at making the switch between the G and D chords. When not writing, Sean tends to think he should be writing. When he is writing, he's often thinking he should be doing housework. He also thinks writing author bios is kind of a silly practice, so he refuses to take them seriously.

If you see him on the street, give him a Coke Zero, and tell him to go home before he hurts himself. He likes Coke Zero. And no, they're not paying him to say that. However, if the Coca-Cola Corp. wants to chuck a few shekels his way for being a soda shill, he is willing to listen to offers.

Connect with him online:
Twitter: @WiscoWriterGuy
Facebook: www.facebook.com/seanpatricklittlewriter

Other Books by Sean Patrick Little

The Centurion: The Balance of the Soul War
The Seven
*Longrider: Away From Home**
*Longrider: To the North**
*The Bride Price**
*Without Reason**
Family Ghosts: A Collection of True Tales of the Supernatural and Unexplained

The Survivor Journals
After Everyone Died
Long Empty Roads
All We Have
*The Survivor Journals Omnibus**

The TeslaCon Novels
Lord Bobbins and the Romanian Ruckus
Lord Bobbins and the Dome of Light
Lord Bobbins and the Clockwork Girl (printing TBD)

The Abe and Duff Mysteries
The Single Twin
Fourth and Wrong

All books are available as eBooks on your favorite online retailers. Hard copies can be ordered online or, preferably, through your favorite independent bookstore. Remember: local stores need your support more than major online retailers do.

**E-book only*

Publisher's Note

If you enjoyed this book, please help spread the word about it. Tell all your friends. If they buy copies and like it, ask them to tell their friends, and their friends' friends, and so on. Word of mouth is always the best sales tool.

If you are a creative type, doing things like posting fan art on social media, participating in message boards and plugging the book, doing cosplay and posting photos, or making models of things in the book is greatly appreciated. Use hashtags to make sure people know where the inspiration for the image originated and to what it relates. Anything that extends the reach and audience of the book is always a positive and always appreciated. Support the things you enjoy.

To further aid the cause, you can politely ask your local library to purchase a copy and ask your local bookstores to carry it, as well. Every little bit helps.

If you enjoyed this book, please leave a kind review on major websites like Amazon or Goodreads, or any of your other favorite book retailers. Link to the book on your Facebook pages or Twitter accounts. Good, honest reviews help more than you know, and we truly appreciate every review. The more positive reviews the book gets, the farther the reach of the book spreads. Reviews are any publisher's or writer's best friend.

If you have a bookstore or work in a library and want one of our authors to speak, or you would like to host a signing, please let us know. If we can make it happen, we will.

And if you really enjoyed this book, please let the author know. A kind word is sometimes the jolt a writer needs to keep working. That goes for any book you've enjoyed, ever. Most writers are on Twitter nowadays. Or they have email addresses or some other way to contact them. If you send them a message, they will see it. They might not reply, but they will be grateful.

You should probably also do the same things for anyone important in your life in general: your grandmother or grandfather, your parents, a favorite teacher, a friend that has been there for you—it really doesn't matter: If someone has done something that you have appreciated, please let them know.

Spread some positivity in this world. It will do you and others more good than you might know.

With sincere gratitude,
Spilled Inc. Press

Made in the USA
Middletown, DE
10 July 2021

43947461R00118

A NOTE ON THE TYPE

This book was set in Arno, a typeface designed by Adobe principal designer Robert Slimbach in 2007. Its namesake is the Arno River, which flows through Florence, the city at the heart of the Italian Renaissance. Inspired by the humanist letterforms of the fifteenth and sixteenth centuries, Slimbach designed Arno with the vitality and readability of Venetian and Aldine book typefaces in mind.

Composed by North Market Street Graphics,
Lancaster, Pennsylvania

Designed by Marisa Nakasone

A NOTE ABOUT THE AUTHOR

KEVIN YOUNG is the author of sixteen books of poetry and prose, including *Stones,* a finalist for the T. S. Eliot Prize. He is the poetry editor of *The New Yorker,* where he hosts the *Poetry Podcast,* and is the editor of eleven anthologies, including *African American Poetry: 250 Years of Struggle & Song* and *A Century of Poetry in* The New Yorker, *1925–2025.*